ALL
ABOUT
MORTGAGES

INSIDER TIPS TO FINANCE THE HOME

Julie Garton-Good

 **Real Estate
Education Company**
® a division of Dearborn Financial Publishing, Inc.

While a great deal of care has been taken to provide accurate and current information, the ideas, suggestions, general principles and conclusions presented in this text are subject to local, state and federal laws and regulations, court cases and any revisions of same. The reader is thus urged to consult legal counsel regarding any points of law—this publication should not be used as a substitute for competent legal advice.

Publisher: Kathleen A. Welton
Managing Editor: Jack L. Kiburz
Cover Design: Design Alliance, Inc.

Printed in the United States of America
94 95 96 10 9 8 7 6 5 4 3 2 1

Library of Congress Cataloging-in-Publication Data

Garton-Good, Julie.
   All about mortgages: insider tips to finance the home/Julie Garton-Good.
      p.   cm.
   Includes bibliographical references and index.
   ISBN 0-7931-0949-3 (paper)
   1. Real estate business—United States—Finance.   2. Mortgages—United States.   I. Title.
   HD1375.G378   1994
   332.7'2'0973—dc20   94-16467
                                                                   CIP

DEDICATION

To my parents, Cliff and Marion Martin, my mother-in-law, Anne Good, my daughter, Crystal, and my wonderful husband, Scott, who have always been there for me.

CONTENTS

PREFACE

"Just another mortgage information source?" Not at all. *All About Mortgages: Insider Tips to Finance the Home* pulls together all the little-known facts that make the difference between applying for a mortgage loan and actually *getting* one!

If you're looking for answers to tough questions about home mortgages, this book is for you. I'll share a gold mine of money-saving tips and financing traps, based on my 20 years as a real estate broker, international real estate educator, newspaper columnist and author. The time-saving question and answer format will help you find the information you need quickly and effortlessly.

This "ultimate" real estate finance handbook provides a behind-the-scenes look at such issues as:

- How the lender evaluates the borrower
- How to choose the most cost-effective loan (through the best lender)
- What to do if the lender says no
- How borrowers can check their credit and correct errors, if necessary
- How to negotiate with lenders
- Deciding on locking-in rates and discount points to pay
- In-depth coverage of conventional fixed-rate, adjustable rate, FHA, VA and home affordability loan programs.

Not all home purchases are alike. So there's an entire chapter devoted to financing creativity including win-win seller financing, buyers using sellers' debts as down payments and designing a lease purchase that does close!

All About Mortgages provides real-world solutions for buyers stretching to buy a home. You'll find tips for generating cash for down payments, alleviating long-term debt and working around qualifying roadblocks.

And once the home purchase is closed, this book will help answer the questions on refinancing a mortgage, prepaying the loan (without going bankrupt) and keeping the loan out of default!

Financing today's home sale is much more than just knowing the facts. It requires practical application and real-world experience. *All About Mortgages* guides you through the mortgage financing maze to sensible, cost-effective home ownership.

Enthusiastically,

Julie Garton-Good, DREI, GRI

CHAPTER 1

MORTGAGE MARKET OVERVIEW:
Players and Process

This chapter provides an overview of the mortgage process: an introduction to the network of institutions that make money available to consumers, the basics of the mortgage application and ways lenders review a loan application. Some of these topics may be covered in greater depth in chapters that apply to a particular loan type.

THE MORTGAGE LENDING PROCESS

Q. *It seems as though the mortgage loan process keeps getting more and more complicated. Why is it so confusing?*

You're right. The mortgage lending process can be a tangled maze. For example, when a first-time homebuying couple receives word that their loan closing will be delayed pending Fannie Mae approval, their response might be, "We don't care who that Fannie person is, we just want to get our loan!" Had someone explained to them that the secondary market is vital for the recycling of the lender's funds (and in turn could pass on greater loan affordability to them) they might be a bit more patient.

It is important that buyers and sellers alike understand the delicate inner workings of the primary market, secondary market and private mortgage insurer. I'll refer to this as "the triple challenge" and show you how an increased knowledge of its function can help clarify the mortgage lending process.

Q. *Who are the three main players in the mortgage market and how do they work together?*

The players in the "triple challenge" are the primary lenders, the secondary market and the private mortgage insurance market. The early years of mortgage lending found local lenders working alone, holding loans originated "in portfolio." This meant that when ABC Bank made a mortgage to the Brown family, the bank held that loan in its loan portfolio of investments, collecting the monthly payments from the first month through the 360th month, or until otherwise paid in full. This was actually quite beneficial for the Browns, as they developed an ongoing business relationship with the lender. If hard times arose and loan payments fell behind, they had a much better chance of negotiating with their friendly banker to help them over the rough spots than with someone who was unaware of their personal situation and perhaps less empathetic.

Q. *Why did lenders change from the portfolio practice?*

Keeping the loan in portfolio for 30 years was not necessarily in the lender's best interests. As interest rates fluctuated (typically moving upward), it became increasingly evident to many lenders that they should recycle these mortgages in order to receive not only higher interest rates, but also increased loan origination fees. Thus, in the late 1930s the secondary market was born.

The first player in the secondary market was the Federal National Mortgage Association (FNMA), lovingly called Fannie Mae. She was soon followed by a sister, Ginnie Mae, the Government National Mortgage Association (GNMA); and later by a brother, Freddie Mac, the Federal Home Loan Mortgage Corporation (FHLMC). Although each of the siblings serves a particular market segment, the scope of their duties is very similar. Their job is to recycle lent funds from primary markets, e.g., ABC Bank, in order to return funds to circulation at the local level while creating additional collateral and investment vehicles for the secondary market. For example, if ABC Bank had some $5 million worth of mortgage loans written to Ginnie Mae's specifications, they could be sold to Ginnie with the lender taking a slight reduction on the face value received for the privilege of converting the loans to cash. Ginnie would use these loans, and their monthly payments received, as collateral for issuing GNMA pass-through securities to purchasers. In other words, if the Brown's loan was sold into

GNMA in the secondary market, and the Browns subsequently purchased some GNMA pass-through securities, they would actually be purchasing their own flow of cash! (See Figure 1.1.) This approach, although on a much larger scale, has assisted thousands of lenders nationwide in increasing their lending capabilities while increasing their profit margins.

Q. *Was the addition of private mortgage insurance really that much of a necessity as far as the secondary market was concerned?*

Yes, over time. With more and more loans being sold into the secondary market, it was time for Fannie, Ginnie and Freddie to hedge against potential losses on the loans purchased—so private mortgage insurance became the third integral part of the triple challenge.

Private mortgage insurance (PMI) typically insures the top 20 percent of the new loan against the borrower's default. This was exactly the payment assurance needed by the secondary market. General guidelines of private mortgage insurance companies were added to the secondary market's existing list of loan requirements. Local lenders then added these criteria to their buyers' qualifying guidelines.

Q. *If the linking of the three groups was so positive, why have you termed it a "challenge"?*

Although the melding of primary lenders, secondary market and private mortgage insurance players has done much to increase the options and scope of lending in the United States, it still has some shortcomings. The biggest challenge is the one affecting buyers. Tough underwriting guidelines can prove too restrictive for some of today's first-time buyers, forcing them into ill-fitting programs or rejecting them altogether. With the median-priced home exceeding $100,000, median family income well under $40,000 and typical households having to save for 2.3 years just to accumulate a down payment, things have to change.

Q. *What is changing to make homebuying a reality for a larger segment of Americans?*

Figure 1.1   How the GNMA mortgage-backed securities program works.

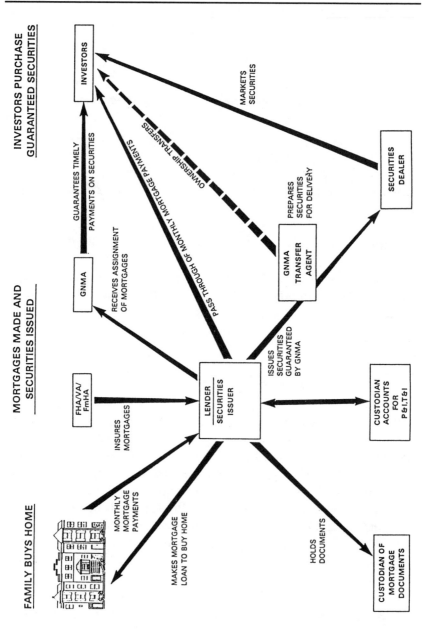

Several things. First, affordable housing programs have expanded. These common-sense programs allow lower down payments, higher qualifying ratios, and even nontraditional employment. (These programs will be explored further in later chapters.)

Second, borrowers have become more savvy about real estate. They're negotiating points and fees with lenders and hiring buyer agents to represent their interests, but most of all, they're not easily taking *no* for an answer. If a lender does reject them for a loan, they're uncovering little-known underwriting facts that will give them added leverage, troubleshooting gliches on their credit reports and learning the importance of prequalifying with a mortgage professional before looking for a home.

Last, lenders realize that it's not a perfect world. People get behind on their bills, lose their jobs and maybe even have to declare bankruptcy. That's why some lenders are bridging the gap between what the secondary market requires and what appears a good and logical business risk by keeping some loans in portfolio —the process has come full circle.

It's truly a whole new world in lending—one that should result in many more Americans achieving the American dream of home ownership!

THINK LIKE AN APPRAISER—SELECTING THE PROPERTY

Q. *Since lenders will evaluate the property with an appraisal, what's the best way to find a home the lender will approve?*

Most mortgage appraisal guidelines specify that the property be located in a stable neighborhood where values are strong. Even after all these years, the top three criteria of the homebuying process are still location, location and location. Let's look at four reasons why this is true:

1. Stable property will generate a stronger appraisal for the transaction. Since most loans are contingent upon securing a certain loan size based on appraised value, a favorable appraisal can make or break the sale.
2. Private mortgage insurance (and homeowner's insurance, too) will be more readily available if the home is in a good neighborhood.

3. The borrower will be able to consider a wider variety of loans if the home and the neighborhood are of good quality.
4. A home in a good neighborhood will have a strong potential for appreciation, making resale value the best it can be. This factor can also be important to the lender should the loan default.

Q. *If the stability of the neighborhood and the quality of the home are so important, what kinds of things should a prospective homebuyer consider before purchasing?*

An in-depth review of the property and surrounding area would help the borrower evaluate the strength of the purchase. Here are some things to consider:

Information by "Looking Around"

Check the traffic flow. Make several trips to the property during different days of the week and various times of the day to make sure accessibility is good. If commuting is a concern, make sure traffic flows well to and from the property.

Take different routes to access the property. Make sure there are no unsightly concerns near the property such as wrecking yards, dumpsites or overgrown vacant lots.

Check for noise pollution. Properties easily accessible to main highway arteries risk higher levels of noise bleeding into the neighborhood. Test the noise level from inside and outside the home. Take a stroll up the street to uncover any dog kennels, handyman garages or day-care centers.

Is outside lighting good? Incidents of crime and traffic accidents increase if neighborhood lighting is poor. Check the home's exterior lighting as well, especially near entrances and garage doors.

Analyze the condition of streets, sidewalks and services available. Is there ample street and sidewalk drainage? How many fire hydrants are there and how close is the nearest fire department? These factors will affect your homeowner's insurance as well.

Information by "Asking Around"

If the opportunity is available, make personal contacts with the neighbors before making an offer. They are often a great source of unbiased information about the neighborhood. Here are some possible questions to ask them:

- Do they feel that the area is generally quiet?
- Where do they shop near the area and why?
- What about the quality of schools?
- Do they think they would have any trouble selling their property? If so, why?
- Would they buy there again? If no, why not?
- Have they seen much crime or vandalism in the neighborhood? If so, was police and ambulance response satisfactory?

Checking with several residents can give a well-rounded view of the area, as well as help sidestep any prejudiced remarks.

Information by "Checking Around"

It's wise to verify material facts before you select a property. If you're working with a real estate agent, he or she can provide much of the following information for you.

Check the public records. Although the title report you receive at closing will reveal items of public record, it's wise to double-check for any current or pending assessment to the area such as for sidewalk repair or water or sewer line addition.

Check the level of crime for the area. The city police department can provide an overview of the type and volume of crime (if any) in the area. By calling the nonemergency number for the police department and stating the location of the property and the cross streets, the public service officer can provide you with an analysis for the area. Some police departments even do "safety checks," coming to the property to offer suggestions for exterior lighting and burglar protection.

Confirm general property value. Ask real estate agents or appraisers to confirm that property values in the area are stable and have not recently softened. A copy of comparable sales from the multiple listing service, which can be obtained from an agent, should help confirm this. A neighborhood with eroding property values might make the house difficult to sell and could be especially tough if you purchased using a small down payment and needed to sell in a short time.

Analyze the property itself. A good way to begin is by asking the seller to provide you with a property disclosure sheet, itemizing the contents and condition of the property, including the working order of all heating and cooling units and appliances. Be sure to test the air conditioner in the winter and the heating system in the summer. Turn on all appliances to guarantee their working order, and move throw rugs and other obstructions so you get a complete view of the property.

The buyer may be tempted to jump at purchasing a home based on the gleam of the imported ceramic tile counter tops, the quality of the parquet floor or the lush garden-like backyard. But by looking around, asking around and checking around, the borrower will help ensure the financial investment made is a sound one. For a property checklist, see Figure 1.2.

USING A FINANCE CONTINGENCY CLAUSE

Q.   *When a buyer does find a home he or she likes, what kinds of financing contingency clauses should go in the purchase agreement?*

If the purchaser can't buy without adequate financing, it's imperative to make the purchase contingent upon receiving suitable financing. If financing cannot be obtained within the parameters spelled out on the purchase agreement or in the time frame specified, the buyer would not have to complete the sale and, barring other conditions, the earnest money deposit would be returned.

The buyer should be specific, stating exactly what maximum size loan (usually a percent of the sales price) is needed, the type of loan with a maximum rate of interest, term of the loan and maximum amount of discount points the buyer will pay.

Using this information, a financing contingency might read as follows: "Purchase contingent upon the borrower applying for and receiving a 90% FHA [Federal Housing Administration] thirty (30) year fixed-rate loan, with interest not to exceed 10%. The

Figure 1.2   Home Inspection Checklist

MECHANICAL SYSTEMS

HEATING
Age, condition, and operation of main
system_____
_____
_____

Thermostat(s)_____
_____

Room-by-room heating_____
_____

COOLING
Age, condition, and operation of main
system_____
_____

Thermostat(s)_____
_____

Room-by-room cooling_____
_____

ELECTRICAL
Adequacy of service_____
_____

Light switches_____
Door bells_____
Exterior lighting_____

PLUMBING
Overall_____
Water heater_____

WASTE (SEWERS OR SEPTIC)
Flush toilets_____
Consult owners on condition_____
_____

Obtain service record_____

APPLIANCES

Range_____
Oven (all controls)_____
_____

Dishwasher (run full cycle)_____
_____

Refrigerator/Freezer_____
_____

Compactor_____
Disposal_____
Washing machine_____
Dryer_____
Other_____
_____

INTERIOR SPACES

WALLS, CEILINGS, AND FLOORS
Overall condition_____
_____

Water stains_____
Cracks_____
Settlement_____
Decay_____

BASEMENT AND CRAWL SPACES
Walls_____
_____

Floor_____
_____

Water penetration_____
_____

KITCHEN
Cabinets_____
Countertop_____
Floor_____

Figure 1.2 Home Inspection Checklist *continued*

BATHROOMS

Toilets (tank and operation)_____
_____
_____
Floor (around tub, shower, and toilet)_
_____
_____
Shower (check controls)_____
_____
Tub (check controls)_____
_____
Tile_____

GARAGE

Doors_____
Floor_____
Walls_____

EXTERIOR CONDITIONS

Roof_____
Siding_____
Windows/Doors_____
_____
Steps and stairs_____
_____
Decks/Porches_____
_____
Pool and accessories_____
_____
Sprinkler_____
Landscaping_____
_____
Drainage_____
_____

buyer will pay up to two (2) discount points to obtain the loan." A real estate agent can help buyers structure the language to use in the agreement.

THE BASICS OF LOAN DISCLOSURE

Q. *What does a lender have to tell a borrower about the lending process and the loan?*

A mortgage lender is required to make certain disclosures to a borrower at application or within three days after application. The disclosures describe costs incurred with the loan, the effective interest rate being charged and the possibility that the lender will transfer the servicing rights on the loan (also called "selling the loan").

Good Faith Estimate

The Real Estate Settlement Procedures Act (RESPA) requires disclosure of estimated settlement costs to homebuyers based on the parameters of the loan. Settlement costs, itemized on Department of Housing and Urban Development's (HUD's) settlement statement, include fees to be paid at closing; these can vary based on changes in the loan that occur between time of application and closing. In addition, the lender is required to provide the borrower with HUD's *Settlement Cost Guide* booklet describing the home-buying process.

Truth in Lending

The purpose of the federal Truth-in-Lending Law and regulations is to ensure that borrowers are aware of the terms and cost of credit so that they can knowledgeably compare loan programs and lenders. For example, the lender must disclose the annual percentage rate (APR) of the loan, defined as the cost of credit to the borrower expressed as a yearly rate. The finance charge disclosed includes any charge paid directly or indirectly by the borrower and imposed by the lender as a condition of extending credit.

Transfer for Servicing

This document shows the lender's intent regarding servicing (collecting payments) of the loan after closing, and tells what percentage of loans they have transferred servicing on in the past.

Lenders must also give adjustable rate mortgage applicants a worst-case scenario of how the monthly payment could adjust over the life of the loan. This requirement will be discussed further later in this book.

THE LOAN APPLICATION PROCESS

Q. *What does the applicant need to provide to the lender in order to qualify for a mortgage?*

Here's a checklist of the basics. Additional information needed from the self-employed buyer is discussed in Chapter 2.

While the lender may need more documentation, items included in this checklist are those likely to be requested, if applicable to the borrower's situation.

Property Information

☐ Copy of the purchase agreement; if a construction loan, copy of plans and specifications (The lender also may need information about the sale and the property in order to complete the loan application. This could include the number of units, for example, single family or duplex, the year built and how title will be held.)

☐ Legal description of the property

☐ Multiple listing service (MLS) information sheet, if available

Borrower Information

☐ A list of the borrower's home addresses for the past seven years

☐ Name and address of landlords for the past two years, if the borrower is a renter

☐ Names and addresses of all employers for last two years (Borrowers should make sure to give the address of the personnel office, since this might be different from the office location; any employment gaps should be pointed out and explained.)

Asset Verification

☐ IRS W-2 forms and perhaps even federal income tax returns from the past two years (A buyer needs to demonstrate two years of full-time or part-time employment in the same line of work; however, time spent in technical career training (such as a physician's medical internship) could count toward the two-year requirement.)

☐ Two most recent paycheck stubs

☐ Bank statements for the past two months

☐ Checking account numbers and locations

☐ Savings account numbers and locations

☐ Credit union account numbers and locations

☐ Mutual fund account numbers and locations

☐ IRA, 401(k) information

☐ Explanation of any other income the borrower wishes considered toward qualifying, including the following:

- Child support. The buyer needs to show proof of receipt, through a printout from the courts or 12 months of cancelled checks. (Payments must have been received for at least 12 months on time and must be scheduled to continue at minimum another 36 months to count as qualifying income, depending on the loan program.)
- A bonus. This can be counted if the buyer has received it for the past two years (the lender will average it).
- Overtime. If the buyer's employer will guarantee that it will continue, overtime can be included as an income source. Since many employers won't or can't do this, it may be tough to count as qualifying income, but might be used as a "compensating factor."
- Social Security and disability payments. The buyer must provide a copy of the award letter and a recent check stub or copy of a bank statement, if deposited there electronically through a direct-deposit program.
- Pension income. The buyer should provide a check stub and any forms showing duration of payments.
- Rental property income. This information can be provided in income tax returns from the past two years verifying rental income. (Only 75 percent of rental income is counted, but 100 percent of the expenses are deductions. For example, if rental income is $500 per month and the mortgage is also $500, the lender considers this a net loss each month of $125, since only 75 percent of the income is counted for qualifying.) The buyer should bring leases, if possible.

☐ Copies of documents and explanations of any other money owed to the borrower (e.g., receivable contracts)

Debt Verification

☐ Payment book or monthly billing statement for all debts (If neither can be found, the lender needs the name and address of the creditor, account number, monthly payment amount and the approximate amount owed in order to verify.)

☐ Documentation of current mortgages and home equity loans, including any recently paid off mortgages (If the buyer is in the process of selling a home, the new lender should receive a copy of the HUD-1 closing statement on that home before closing on the new home.)

☐ If renting an old home, a copy of a one-year lease, signed by the new tenant, prior to the closing of the new home

☐ Documentation of car payments

☐ Information about outstanding student loans

☐ A complete copy of any divorce decree or separation agreement to document alimony or child support

☐ Clarification of divorced persons' debts (For formerly joint debts that the other spouse is now supposed to pay, the buyer may need to prove that he or she isn't paying those bills, unless the debt was refinanced and the buyer's name was taken off the obligation. This is required even though the divorce decree says it's not your obligation. Proof can include six months of canceled checks from the former spouse to show that he or she is paying that obligation, and on time—otherwise, the debt may go against the borrower's long-term debt ratios for qualifying. This varies based on the loan program.)

☐ Information about any payments made as a direct withdrawal from a checking account or credit union

☐ A copy of any bankruptcy proceedings, if applicable, with status and explanation

☐ A gift letter or explanation of funds source for closing costs

☐ If a Veterans Administration (VA) loan, original Certificate of Eligibility and DD214

☐ Explanation letter for any late payments, judgments, liens, bankruptcy or foreclosure

☐ If nonresident, copy of Certificate of Resident Alien Status ("green card")

☐ A check for the application fee and credit report

Q. *Outside of what we've just covered, what other questions on the mortgage loan application should the borrower be prepared to answer?*

A section of the uniform residential loan application, called "Information for Government Monitoring Purposes," monitors the lender's compliance with the equal credit opportunity, fair housing and home mortgage disclosure laws. It also monitors the number and types of minorities being afforded the opportunity to apply for a home loan.

The section requests that you state your race, nation of origin and sex. While it's not mandatory that the applicant answer these questions, if the borrower declines to answer them, the lender is required to complete the questions based on meeting the applicants or by their surnames. Since this information becomes part of a national database to help monitor fair housing laws and reduce discrimination, it's advisable that the applicant answer the questions in this section.

One more point regarding the loan application: It should go without saying that information given the lender should be truthful and complete. Penalties for falsifying information are stiff. Intentional and negligent misrepresentations can result in criminal penalties and monetary damages under Title 18 of the United States Code.

Q. *If the lender wants to know information, can't he or she just dig for it?*

First of all, the borrower is expected by law to give all pertinent information to the lender. Morever, this "find it out yourself" attitude usually catches up with the borrower. By checking credit, verifying assets and employment and noting facts of public record, there's usually very little that escapes the underwriting process. Up-front and honest is definitely the best policy if the borrower wants the loan to come together.

THE LOAN UNDERWRITING PROCESS

Q. *What happens after the application is taken?*

Several things. The borrower's employment, income and funds on deposit for the down payment and closing costs are all verified. An appraisal may also be ordered at this time. Depending on the loan type, other documentation may be requested as well. Figure 1.3 summarizes the process and shows some common causes of delays.

This phase is called "underwriting the loan." It's perhaps the most difficult part of the loan process, since information must be thoroughly collected and analyzed in order to decide whether the loan will be made.

The underwriter, or loan endorser, carefully reviews the borrower's documentation and decides whether he or she would be a sound lending risk. If segments of the borrower's employment, credit or overall financial picture are vague or appear to be contradictory, the underwriter will request more information. This decision process can take days or weeks to complete.

The underwriting phase may also include the approval of the borrower and the property for private mortgage insurance, if required on the loan. This insurance protects the lender from the borrower's default, usually on the top 20 percent of the loan, and requires a separate approval based on the private mortgage insurance company's underwriting guidelines.

Underwriting guidelines for the major loan types will be discussed later in this book.

Figure 1.3　　The Loan Underwriting Process

Common Time Delays in New Financing	Financing Sequence

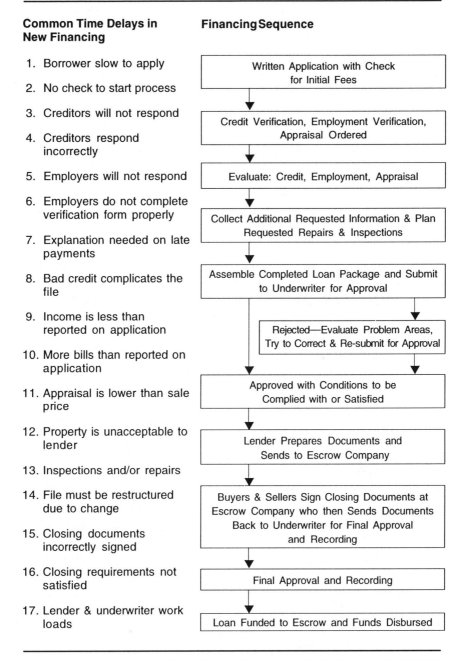

Common Time Delays in New Financing	Financing Sequence
1. Borrower slow to apply	Written Application with Check for Initial Fees
2. No check to start process	
3. Creditors will not respond	Credit Verification, Employment Verification, Appraisal Ordered
4. Creditors respond incorrectly	
5. Employers will not respond	Evaluate: Credit, Employment, Appraisal
6. Employers do not complete verification form properly	Collect Additional Requested Information & Plan Requested Repairs & Inspections
7. Explanation needed on late payments	
8. Bad credit complicates the file	Assemble Completed Loan Package and Submit to Underwriter for Approval
9. Income is less than reported on application	Rejected—Evaluate Problem Areas, Try to Correct & Re-submit for Approval
10. More bills than reported on application	
11. Appraisal is lower than sale price	Approved with Conditions to be Complied with or Satisfied
12. Property is unacceptable to lender	Lender Prepares Documents and Sends to Escrow Company
13. Inspections and/or repairs	
14. File must be restructured due to change	Buyers & Sellers Sign Closing Documents at Escrow Company who then Sends Documents Back to Underwriter for Final Approval and Recording
15. Closing documents incorrectly signed	
16. Closing requirements not satisfied	Final Approval and Recording
17. Lender & underwriter work loads	Loan Funded to Escrow and Funds Disbursed

Adapted with permission of Gary Everett, Steve Scott & Co. Realtors®, 910 NW Harriman, Bend, OR 97701.

Underwriting Roadblocks

Q. *Can a borrower get a loan even if he or she doesn't meet the underwriting guidelines?*

It depends on a lot of factors: the size of the down payment, the borrower's creditworthiness and whether the lender is selling the loan to the secondary market. Later chapters that discuss the major loan types will include information on these and other compensating factors. If a borrower has one or more of these pluses in his or her favor, the loan may be made even though all of the underwriting guidelines aren't met.

Q. *What major roadblocks can come up during the underwriting process?*

Many problems occur with verifying employment, down payments and income from such sources as child support and alimony. Borrowers sometimes change their financial pictures midstream in the loan process. Whether pro or con, these changes can invalidate the paperwork done up to that point.

It may seem bizarre to mention, but after the borrower applies for the loan, he or she should not change jobs or give notice to quit! If loan processing takes more than several months, the lender may reverify everything, including employment.

The same is true with taking on new debt. Just because the application has been taken doesn't mean that the lender won't know if the borrower purchased a new washer and dryer using time payments. A credit inquiry from the appliance dealer will show up on the credit report, and even adding a new small monthly debt may be enough to tip the scales against the loan.

In short, the rule of thumb for borrowers to follow after application and before closing is simply, *don't change a thing!*

Problems can also occur when verifying the borrower's funds, called "verification of deposit". The lender wants to make sure that the down payment has not been borrowed or gained by illegal means. That means that the lender is likely to verify that the money has been accumulating in an account, usually stationary for upwards of 90 days.

Funds that mysteriously disappear and reappear may send up a red flag, putting the validity of the funds into question and perhaps causing the lender to deny the loan. So if funds have increased or decreased radically (through transfers of accounts to other banks, and so on), the borrower should make sure the lender understands the reasons why.

Any documentation required to verify child support, alimony and debts incurred in a previous marriage may seem deep and cumbersome, but complying with paperwork requests may make the difference between getting and not getting the loan.

If anything changes—and that includes changes for the better—the buyer should make sure to notify the lender. Salary increases to become effective within 60 days of loan closing may be considered for qualifying, and additional down payments can make the buyer stronger in the eyes of the lender.

THE LOAN CLOSING

Q. *So after all the documentation is collected and the underwriter approves the loan, then the closing occurs?*

That's correct. The lender, or an appointed closing officer, such as a title company or attorney, prepares the closing statement, checks the title report, prepares the mortgages and deeds to be recorded and closes the transaction. Figure 1.4 shows a sample closing statement. It is good to familiarize yourself with these, since many could be negotiating points with the seller.

In addition, balances for any outstanding loans will be checked and the seller will give his or her permission to pay off that loan. (This permission can be granted through something similar to the estoppel letter shown in Figure 1.5.)

WHAT TO DO IF THE LENDER SAYS "NO"

Q. *If there are glitches in getting the loan, what can the buyer do if the lender still says "no"?*

As discussed earlier in this chapter, a lender can reject a loan application for myriad reasons. The following are some ways in

Figure 1.4   Sample Closing Statement

| SELLER'S STATEMENT | | | BUYER'S STATEMENT | |
DEBIT	CREDIT	ITEM	DEBIT	CREDIT
		Total Purchase Price		
		Binder Deposit		
		First Mortgage		
		Second Mortgage		
		Prorations & Prepayments:		
		Rent		
		Interest - 1st Mortgage		
		Interest - 2nd Mortgage		
		Prepayment Penalty		
		Insurance		
		Mortgage Insurance		
		Insurance Reserves		
		Taxes - City		
		Taxes - County		
		Tax Reserves		
		Expenses		
		Attorney's Fees		
		Escrow Closing Fees		
		Escrow Holding Fees (Long-term)		
		State Tax on Deed		
		Recording		
		Mortgage		
		Deed		
		Title Insurance		
		Brokerage		
		Miscellaneous		
		Total - Debits & Credits		
		Balance Due		
		Seller & from Buyer		
		Grand Totals		

continued

RECONCILIATION STATEMENT		
	RECEIPTS	DISBURSEMENT
Bank Loan (less points/origination fees)	_____	_____
Deposit	_____	_____
Check from Buyer at Closing	_____	_____
Brokerage Fee	_____	_____
Check to Seller at Closing	_____	_____
Seller's Expense	_____	_____
Buyer's Expense	_____	_____
Grand Totals	_____	_____

which a buyer can attempt to piece the sale back together if previous efforts to get the loan approved have failed.

Identify the Source of the Problem

If the Problem Is Borrower-Related　The borrower may ask the lender reanalyze the borrower's financial situation, based on answers to the following questions:

- Have any debts been paid off since the application was taken?
- Does any of the buyer's income now fall within the two-year track-record time frame? Could this income be used to help the buyer qualify for the loan?
- Could any assets be converted to cash?
- Would the borrower be willing to forgo this year's vacation in lieu of cash?
- Could any bonuses be advanced from the employer? Raises in income that are scheduled to occur within 60 days of closing may also be counted by the lender

Figure 1.5   Estoppel letter

Lender: _____   Owner's Name: _____
Lender's Address: _____   Property Address: _____
_____   Loan Number: _____

To Whom It May Concern:

You are hereby directed to furnish _____ and/or
their agent _____, with the following information
regarding my loan.

_____

_____

Effective Date: _____

Type of Loan

FHA   _____   Original Loan Balance: $_____
VA   _____   Present Loan Balance: $_____
Conv.   _____   Interest Rate: _____
Other   _____   Term: _____

Monthly Payment

Principal and Interest: _____   Assumption Policy: _____
              Taxes: _____   _____
          Insurance: _____   _____
        FHA Premium: _____   _____
       PMI Insurance: _____   Pay-Off Penalty: _____
       Total Payment: _____   _____

Is this loan in default? If so, please explain: _____
_____
_____

                        Loan Officer: _____
                               Date: _____

The borrower may ask to have the loan held in portfolio so that underwriting exceptions can be made. The success of this approach depends on the lender and its programs.

Another approach would be to identify the borrower's strengths and ways to showcase them. Be realistic: If a problem is so overwhelming that only time will correct it (such as a severely damaged credit rating), getting any loan right now might be impossible.

If all else fails, the borrower may wish to seek a less restrictive loan program or a more lenient lender. (This is usually a last resort, since precious time and money already have been expended in obtaining the loan; moving the loan may cause duplication of costs.)

If the Problem Is Property-Related   Determine strategies for repairing the property. Identify the person who has the most to gain by the sale going through. That person might be willing to pay for repairs. This person may be someone besides the buyer and the seller; for example, the seller's sellers, who may need to have the primary sale closed before theirs will close.

Another approach would be to determine a creative time frame for completing needed repairs. One option might be to close now and hold funds in escrow. You may be able to escrow two times the amount of the highest bid in order to complete repairs later, for example, in better weather.

You might also consider options other than cash. Perhaps the buyer could use "sweat equity" in lieu of cash for repairs.

The lender might also be more likely to make the loan if the loan-to-value ratio were different, or if the buyer paid a higher rate of interest.

The bottom line is, "it ain't over till it's over!"

CONSUMER BOOKLETS TO THE RESCUE

Q. *It seems as though there's a lot to learn about the homebuying process. Are there any consumer booklets you'd recommend?*

The following are some useful homebuying fact booklets, which can be obtained free of charge:

- *Unraveling the Mortgage Loan Mystery*
  Federal National Mortgage Association
  Drawer MM
  3900 Wisconsin Ave., NW
  Washington, DC 20006

You may wish to request a list of other homebuyer pamphlets available through FNMA.

- *A Consumer's Glossary of Mortgage Terms, Self Test* (For buyers wishing to determine how well they would do in qualifying for a mortgage) and *What Happens After You Apply for a Mortgage*
  Mortgage Bankers' Association
  1125 15th St., NW
  Washington, DC 20005
- *The Mortgage Money Guide* (Comparisons of homebuying options)
  Federal Trade Commission
  Bureau of Consumer Protection
  Pennsylvania Ave & 6th St., NW
  Washington, DC 20580

Other publications can be obtained for free or at a nominal cost (to $1.50) through the federal government's Consumer Information Center. To obtain a free catalog, write to the Consumer Information Center, P.O. Box 100, Pueblo, CO, 81002.

CHAPTER 2

QUALIFYING FOR THE MORTGAGE

Homebuyers should have a good idea of the amount of the mortgage for which they qualify *before* they start looking for their dream house, much less start shopping for the mortgage. Few documents hold as much power over buyers' financial futures as their credit reports. This chapter will address the basics of credit reports. It makes sense to order a copy of your report in the early stages of home purchase planning. Buyers should never assume that their credit report is spotless because they have been financially responsible. Mistakes on credit reports are common and take time to correct.

Once assured that creditworthiness can be sufficiently documented for lenders, the buyer can think about loan qualification. This chapter explains prequalification and qualification, and includes some special hints for self-employed borrowers.

CREDITWORTHINESS: THE BACKBONE OF MORTGAGE LENDING

Q. *Judging from the emphasis placed on verifying the type and amount of borrower debt, it seems lenders are very critical of the buyer's creditworthiness.*

Good credit is important in securing a home loan. In fact, many lenders will tell you that bad credit is one of the major reasons mortgages are denied. In an era of conspicuous consumption when consumers are using more "plastic," lenders are placing much greater emphasis on how well loan applicants manage the credit they have before granting them more. And since the lender must pull a credit report from at least two of the three major credit reporting agencies to compare and evaluate credit, errors and adverse information are more likely to be uncovered. For names and addresses of these national companies, see Figure 2.1.

Poor credit can be caused through a buyer's irresponsibility; more often, however, it arises innocently, from unchecked and uncorrected errors on an individual's report.

Major Credit Reporting Agencies

Q. *If the national credit reporting system is comprised of three major agencies, don't they share the same credit information on individuals?*

Not currently. While the three major national companies have recently started to electronically exchange their creditor data, efforts will not be system-wide until late 1995. Until then, your credit picture could take on a different complexion in all three reports. Subsequently, if a creditor erroneously reported information to all three agencies, there would be three different sets of errors to correct!

WHAT THE CREDIT REPORT SHOWS

Q. *What kind of information does the credit report contain? Does each major agency have different information categories?*

While each agency has its own reporting format, all three release information in the following categories:

- Identification: This section includes the borrower's name, address, Social Security number, employer, date of birth and spouse's name, if applicable.
- Credit history: This section lists all open and paid accounts, the current payment history of each creditor reporting to the bureau and prior payment history (which includes any late payments). By law, adverse information can remain on the report for seven years; bankruptcies can remain on for ten years. These negative postings may not come off automatically and their removal should be monitored by the consumer.

Figure 2.1   Credit Reporting Bureaus

EQUIFAX
Box 740241
Atlanta, GA 30374
1-800-685-1111
(8am - 5pm ET)
(Can charge report to a major credit card)

TRANS UNION
Box 390
Springfield, PA 19064-0390
(502) 425-7511
(24 hours daily)

TRW
Box 2350
Chatsworth, CA 91313-2350
Dallas, TX 75374-9029
(214) 390-9191
(24 hours daily)
(Each consumer can receive one annual complimentary report from TRW)

- Collection: This section includes any creditors who have turned over an account to a collection agency.
- Public records: All items of public record affecting financial obligations (such as bankruptcies, liens, judgments, divorce decrees, child support adjudications and so on) are included in this section.
- Inquiries: This section notes who has checked the consumer's credit back as far as 18 to 24 months. Anyone accessing a consumer's credit without a valid business reason could be in violation of the federal Fair Credit Reporting Act, fined up to $5,000, and imprisoned for one year.

SPECIAL CONSIDERATIONS FOR MARRIED AND DIVORCED PERSONS

Q. *Can a divorced person have a credit report solely in his or her name, apart from the ex-spouse?*

Every person has the right to obtain an individual credit history no matter what his or her marital status. Anyone, whether married, single or divorced can have his or her own individual credit report and references. Joint liabilities will appear on both spouses' reports.

Q. *Should a divorced person make special arrangements to ensure that his or her credit rating is not adversely affected by the change in marital status?*

It's especially important to check credit after a divorce, making sure obligations are sorted out, creditors are notified and the report is listed solely in the consumer's name. Ideally, this should be done before the divorce gavel raps, but usually is not.

Imagine the nightmare created when someone applies for credit after divorce, only to find that the car and corresponding payment awarded to the former spouse is still showing as a joint obligation! Ideally, the former spouse should requalify for that debt and have the posting removed from the other person's credit report. Again, this is not likely to happen. At the very least, a copy of the divorce decree will be requested by the mortgage lender, showing the allocation of assets and liabilities. This could easily add time to the loan qualifying process.

Q. *Could a person who is married to someone with bad credit get a loan in his or her own name?*

A married individual can secure a mortgage in his or her own name provided he or she meets the required income, assets and creditworthiness guidelines. Again, federal law prohibits discrimination based on marital status; therefore, one spouse's adverse credit cannot be used to deny a loan to the other spouse.

MAJOR AREAS OF CREDIT EVALUATION

Q. *What major credit areas does the lender evaluate before making a loan?*

When it comes to determining an applicant's creditworthiness, a lender examines the three *C*s: character, capacity and credit.

Character can be evaluated through objective factors such as length of residency at each address, terms of employment and a report free of financial judgments, liens and other matters of public record.

Capacity is increasingly important these days, since many consumers carry heavy debt comprised of many minimum payments. The lender evaluates the amount of debt compared to income, ways the new obligations may change the debt picture and the borrower's general economic stability.

Credit is the third measure. The lender evaluates existing credit relationships including bank loans, credit cards and so on. He or she pays close attention to limits, how the current balances relate to those limits and how long those accounts have been active. For example, a credit card held by the borrower for less than six months but currently at the maximum could indicate that the borrower could have trouble handling additional debt. If the lender does make the home loan, it may require a large down payment to lessen the risk.

What Constitutes "Good Credit"?

Q. *If credit is so vital to getting a loan, what specifically does a lender consider to be "good credit"?*

While credit interpretations vary from lender to lender, most lenders use guidelines to determine "good credit." In reviewing the applicant's credit for the past 24 months, with the greatest emphasis placed on the past 12 months, the lender should see the borrower's "intent to have excellent credit" in the borrower's management of revolving credit, installment credit and housing debt.

Revolving Credit   Examples of revolving credit include credit cards. No payments should be 60 days or more past due and no more than two payments should be 30 days past due. The reasons for any late payments must be explained satisfactorily.

Installment Credit   One example of installment credit is a car loan. No payments should be 60 days or more past due and no more than one payment should be 30 days past due. Any late payments must be thoroughly explained.

Housing Debt Housing debt could include a first or second mortgage, or rent: No payments can be past due. This can be proven by the borrower's cancelled checks for the last 12 months, loan payment history from the mortgage servicer or a credit report reference, or the borrower's year-end mortgage account statement, if it contains a payment receipt history.

Contrary to popular belief, good credit does not necessarily mean a perfect nor spotless credit report. It must, however, be fairly close to these guidelines, and not contain any adverse or derogatory information, such as liens, judgments, collections or recent bankruptcies.

ENSURING THE BEST POSSIBLE CREDIT REPORT

Q. *What errors could consumers expect to find on their credit reports?*

While errors can be found in a variety of forms, frequent mistakes occur in three areas:

- Misposting due to similar names
- Multiple entries of the same credit account or previously closed accounts still showing active
- Accounts that are disputed or improperly reported by the creditor

Q. *When is a person's name likely to be confused for another's in credit reporting, and how can one protect against it?*

If you're a junior or senior, or have a common name like Smith, Brown or Jones, you are most likely to have someone else's credit on your report. While names, addresses and Social Security numbers are generally used to report credit to the correct name, errors still occur. Upon hearing that someone else's credit was found on his or her report a homebuyer might remark, "Well, if it's good news, I'll keep it!" The problem is that an additional account, yours or not, could signal extra debt to the lender, which might not be good news for qualifying.

To avoid the name mix-up, it's good to use your full name including spelled-out middle or maiden names (or both!), when applying for credit.

Multiple Credit Entries

Q. *Is there anything wrong with multiple entries of the same account showing up on your credit report?*

Yes. Since the lender may consider that there's a possible monthly minimum repayment on each card (or usually a minimum of $15, if the amount is unknown) for the purpose of loan qualifying. In addition, the lender evaluates not just what is owing, but the amount of potential credit available to the borrower.

For example, two entries of the same $3,000 open line of credit with a zero balance could mean $6,000 potential debt from the lender's point of view. For the purpose of qualifying, the lender may consider a minimum monthly payment owing on each account, active or not. These monthly payments would be included in figuring the applicant's long-term debt for qualifying. The lender's rationale is that, upon closing the loan, the borrower could potentially take on new debt on these accounts, making it tough to repay the mortgage.

Closing Out Accounts

Q. *Would it help to qualify by closing out accounts and cutting up credit cards that are no longer in use?*

It may. It's important to go through the process thoroughly. Otherwise, these credit lines may not be canceled and could resurface on credit reports again.

Here's a system I've found to work: Notify the creditor in writing that you wish to close the account. It's best to send the request by certified mail, return receipt requested. That way you know it was received. A credit card, cut up, can be sent along as well. In the letter, ask the creditor to post the account "closed at customer's request." This clarifies that the account was closed voluntarily and not by the creditor for adverse reasons. Also inform the creditor that the credit report will be checked in 30 days to make sure that the account has been removed. This ensures that the request is handled promptly!

Removing Errors from the Report

Q.   If an error is found on the report, how can it be rectified?

Some of the greatest credit reporting nightmares come in the form of disputed or improperly reported items. Freeing these errors from your report may be tedious, but it can be accomplished. Here's how:

1. File a consumer dispute form with the reporting bureau, stating that you disagree with the report. By law, they must investigate the complaint in a timely manner (usually in 30 days or less) and report back to the consumer.
2. Write to the creditor as well, pointing out the mistake. If the dispute is resolved, have the creditor send letters to all three credit bureaus, asking that they change the information (if they initially received it). In addition, the consumer can ask the creditor to send a corrected copy of the report to all parties who accessed the report during the time the error appeared.
3. If a satisfactory conclusion is not reached with the creditor, the consumer can place up to a 100-word explanation on his credit report telling the consumer's side of the story. This explanation will remain on the report for six months, and can be extended for increments of six months.

After correcting an error on a credit report, it's good to request a copy of the corrected report from the credit reporting agency in approximately 30 days to show that the changes were made.

Q.   If there are three major credit reporting networks, do errors have to be corrected with all three?

Ideally, yes. Remember bureaus are just beginning to share information; but it's likely that if an error was reported to one agency, any information the other two have from this creditor may be incorrect as well. For the best chance of cleaning up the error, poll the other two agencies and follow the same troubleshooting process with them.

The Credit Appeals Process

Q. *If a problem can't be adequately rectified with a credit agency, is there an appeals process?*

Since credit reporting agencies are monitored under the federal Equal Credit Opportunity Act, a consumer could file a complaint with the Federal Trade Commission, Attn: Correspondence Dept., Room 692, Washington, DC, 20580.

Too Many Credit Inquiries

Q. *Could a buyer have a problem if too many credit inquiries appear on his or her credit report?*

A mortgage lender might be hesitant to make a loan to someone who had an abundance of credit inquiries in the past six months. This could serve as a red flag that the party was denied credit, is accumulating open lines of credit to borrow against or is leveraging assets prior to declaring bankruptcy. This could also indicate that the borrower is checking the credit report repeatedly in anticipation of an adverse posting. Nevertheless, the lender may want a written explanation as to why the inquiries occurred.

A lender may even pull a credit report on a loan applicant shopping for rates and points over the phone. This later shows on the credit report as an inquiry. When the applicant has a lender do a formal application for a mortgage, the lender may ask for an explanation of the other inquiries to clarify that the applicant was neither turned down for nor extended credit.

Checking Someone Else's Credit

Q. *Could just anyone check someone's credit?*

While the law requires that there must be a "valid business reason" to check someone's credit, it does not require that the creditor obtain written authorization from the consumer before the report is accessed. In fact, the consumer may not even be aware that his or her credit has been checked! If the consumer later contested that a valid business reason did not exist to check his or her credit, it would be up to the creditor to prove the validity. A federal fine of $5,000 and up to one year in jail applies if the law is breached.

Q. *Do credit reporting agencies have services that alert the consumer when someone accesses his or her credit?*

Due to the growing importance and interest of creditworthiness, special services such as TRW's Credentials Service alert subscribers when a credit report is requested or when anything adverse is posted to credit. In addition, subscribers can receive their own current credit reports by calling a toll-free number and giving a pass code. These services are provided for a small annual fee.

GETTING A MORTGAGE AFTER MARRED CREDIT

Q. *Would a lender ever make a loan to someone who had bad credit in the past?*

Possibly. Lenders know that it's not a perfect world and occasions may arise when credit blemishes are impossible to avoid. On a case-by-case basis, a lender might make a loan to someone with marred credit, particularly if it was caused by loss of job, poor health, death in the family or some other circumstance outside the applicant's control. For example, a borrower might still get a loan if he or she had been in a partnership that went bankrupt due to the actions of the partner. To grant an exception, the loan underwriter could request written documentation to verify the facts.

Q. *If someone's credit was so bad that the lender suggested the borrower get outside help to untangle it, whom might the borrower suggest?*

A nonprofit organization called the Consumer Credit Counseling Service would be a good suggestion. They evaluate income, ability to pay, analyze debt load and request that the individual surrender his or her monthly income to them, from which they will pay creditors. Their goal is to help reduce debt and make it manageable. The only cost is any voluntary contribution the consumer wishes to make. Locations of centers throughout the United States can be found in the yellow pages of the phone book under "credit."

Establishing Credit

Q. *What's the best way for a person with no credit to establish a credit rating?*

The answer is, very carefully! While amassing large numbers of credit cards may seem to be a great way to establish credit, adding monthly debt to a buyer's long-term debt ratio may hurt loan qualification prospects.

There are several prudent ways to establish credit:

- Obtaining a major credit card may make sense if the borrower has room for the monthly payment in his or her long-term debt qualifying ratio and will control spending so not to run up a huge balance.
- If the buyer is purchasing in several months, he or she could put the down payment in a bank account and obtain a loan against it. By placing this money with a lender as collateral, a loan can be made against the funds and repaid to establish credit. Three to six months is a good minimum time frame to show a credible payment pattern.
- If a borrower does not believe in credit and pays cash for everything, that practice could be documented to establish creditworthiness. For example, most power companies, utility companies and small retailers will be glad to verify that the applicant pays in cash and on time when he or she purchases. The more documentation that can be shown to the lender, the better.

Checking Your Own Credit

Q. *How far in advance of loan application should someone check his or her credit?*

Sixty to 120 days before beginning the house-hunting process is a good time to examine credit. This can alert the buyer to what creditors have reported, allow unused accounts to be closed and correct any errors that appear in the information.

Q. *How much does it cost to check one's own credit?*

For less than $20, a credit report can be received from one of the three national credit reporting agencies. (As stated earlier, TRW offers a free credit report to all consumers.) If someone has been denied credit or employment in the past six months due to adverse credit, the report is free. It's good to access all three reports the first time credit is examined to receive the complete picture. It's a small price to pay for peace of mind.

Q. *Is this the same report the lender will pull at the time of loan application?*

No. An individual receives a "consumer credit" or "in-file" report. While it's not as in-depth as the "mortgage credit report" the lender requires at loan application, it will give you a good overview of what the report contains.

THE CREDIT-CHECKING PROCESS

Q. *How does one locate a credit reporting agency, what information needs to be provided to them and what will the consumer receive?*

The process is as follows:

1. Call or visit the credit reporting agency. To find a reporting agency, check the yellow pages of your phone directory under "credit reporting agencies" for the affiliate nearest you, or contact the companies listed in Figure 2.1. The applicant must provide his or her full name, Social Security number, current address, any previous addresses for the past five years, date of birth, name of employer and the same information for a spouse, if applicable. The request must be signed and dated. Joint reports may require both signatures.
2. Provide identification to the reporting agency. This will be a picture ID card if the visit is in person. If the

request is made over the phone and the report is to be received by mail, each reporting agency has its own checklist of required information. For example, TRW requests that one of the following must be provided in a mail inquiry in order to guarantee that the consumer is making the request: a photocopy of a recent billing statement from a major creditor showing a current address, a copy of a utility billing or copy of a photo ID card, such as a driver's license. Equifax allows your request to be charged to a major credit card; TRW will send one annual complimentary report copy.

3. If applying in person, the consumer can see the report in a matter of minutes. By mail, it may take five to seven working days. Either way, detailed instructions are provided on how to decipher the many symbols and notations on the report.

BE AN INFORMED CONSUMER

With all the knowledge gleaned from a consumer's credit report, you can see why the lender puts such great value on it for making a lending decision. And after the borrower has gathered information, he or she will at least know what everyone else already knew about them!

PREQUALIFYING: A HOMEBUYER'S STAPLE

Q. *What are the benefits of a buyer being prequalified for a loan before viewing property? Has this become more of a norm in the last several years?*

It's fair to say that prequalifying has become a staple in the world of homebuying. It can tell buyers if they're financially ready to buy and what they can afford, and alert them to roadblocks that could hinder a purchase such as adverse credit or income that can't be verified.

Sellers feel more assured that the prospect viewing their home is a bonafide purchaser with the financial capacity to buy. A prequalified buyer also makes a seller feel that his odds are better than average that the sale will close, and may even decide to take the property off the active market because of it. Most sellers won't do this until the buyer has received official "loan approval" from the lender later in the loan process. In addition, many sellers may choose to keep the property available for showings until closing so that secondary or "back-up" offers could be taken should the first offer fail.

Some builders feel so strongly about buyers being prequalified that they may request a lender to be present at open houses they hold for new construction.

Real estate agents find strength in working with prequalified buyers. Prequalified buyers often are more motivated, since they know the price range of the property they should view, look for properties offering the type of financing they qualify for and are aware of what to expect in the homebuying process. For these reasons, the best time to prequalify is before the buyer begins viewing properties.

Q. *Who can prequalify a buyer?*

Any real estate professional knowledgeable in real estate finance (lender, real estate agent or builder/developer) can prequalify a buyer. Most real estate agents use some type of thumbnail qualifying techniques before they show property. To ensure that the buyer's qualifications are adequately researched, many real estate agents and other real estate professionals rely on a lender to prequalify the buyer.

To maximize efforts, it's a good idea for the buyer to prequalify with the lender where the loan will be obtained, if known at this stage.

Q. *Does prequalifying always have to be done in person?*

Prequalifying can be done either in person or on the phone. In fact, some prospective buyers may be prequalified over the phone (virtually without their knowledge) when they call a lender to shop for interest rates and points on loans. In other words, the strength of the borrower's qualifications may have something to do with the interest rate and discount points quoted for a certain loan. In a busy homebuying or refinancing market, it also lets the lender set priorities for his or her business, based on the strength of the potential applicant.

Q. *Doesn't prequalifying the buyer also have something to do with the fact that the real estate agent typically has represented the seller and needs to prescreen potential buyers?*

Yes, this is part of it. But changes in practices for real estate agents have altered the way agents view prequalifying buyers, putting heavier emphasis on lender input.

Here's why: If an agent represents the seller, the agent legally needs to tell the seller everything within his or her knowledge about the buyer, including what is known about the buyer's ability to qualify for a loan. Knowing this, it stands to reason that some buyers would prefer to give their financial information to a lender and let the lender give the agent the parameters of what they can qualify for. After analysis, the lender could respond, "Yes, the buyer is qualified for a loan of approximately $80,000, based on a 10 percent down payment, with interest not to exceed 9 percent". This gives the agent and the seller the appropriate information about the buyer without airing personal, nonpertinent information such as a previous divorce or unpaid debts.

It's also common today to have an agent representing a buyer as a buyer's agent. This means that the real estate agent is looking out for the interests of the buyer, including making sure that they are qualified to obtain a loan. In most cases, the borrower's financial situation is best analyzed by a mortgage professional. Using the expertise of the lender also alleviates some of the agent's liability that could be extended with interpreting a credit report or in analyzing the amount and type of income and debt the borrower is carrying.

These scenarios show why a large majority of real estate agents rely heavily on having borrowers prequalified early on with the lender.

Information Needed for Prequalifying

Q. *What information is needed to prequalify a buyer?*

In general, prequalifying explores four primary areas: the buyer's credit, income, debt and general ability to repay the mortgage.

The prospective buyer is asked to itemize his or her monthly income and all other revenue sources the buyer wishes to have counted for qualifying, such as alimony, child support and so on. He is asked about his debt, such as car payments, credit cards, lines of credit and alimony or child support. Using this information and the amount of the down payment available, the lender or agent can determine the loan size for which the borrower may qualify.

Prequalifying Example   Mary's gross monthly income is $4,000. In prequalifying, the lender needs to determine how much of that gross income can be used for principal, interest, property tax and insurance payment (PITI).

The secondary market standard is that up to 28 percent of Mary's monthly gross income can go toward her total housing payment, and up to 36 percent of Mary's monthly gross income can go toward paying her house payment plus other long-term debt. To truly put things in perspective, however, the lender needs to consider the amount of other long-term debt (debts that can't be paid off in ten months or are continuous in nature) Mary is carrying.

Multiplying $4,000 × 36 percent, the lender finds that Mary's total long-term debt cannot exceed $1,440 per month. After subtracting her car, student loan and credit card payments (totaling $700), the lender determines that Mary's principal, interest, taxes and insurance (PITI) payment can not exceed $740 per month.

The lender then subtracts an estimated 20 percent for monthly property taxes, insurance and private mortgage insurance from the $740, leaving $592 for Mary's principal and interest payments. To convert that monthly payment into a maximum loan amount, the lender divides by the monthly mortgage factor per $1,000 for a 30-year term (using 8 percent interest in this case). (Refer to the payment table in Figure 2.2 or see Appendix C: Amortization Factors.) $592 ÷ $7.34 (the cost of 8 percent mortgage money per $1,000) = 80.653. Converted to thousands, Mary can potentially afford a loan of approximately $80,653.

Q.   *Is a credit report part of the prequalifying process?*

Yes, it is. It's interesting to note that while the lender or real estate agent does not need written approval to do this, because under credit reporting law it is legally justified as a "valid business reason," most will still have the buyer sign an authorization to check credit. In addition, many real estate agents feel their legal liability is extended by interpreting the buyer's credit, and that checking credit is better left to the lender.

After the information is gathered, the borrower is told what maximum mortgage he or she could consider, what type of loan might best suit his or her needs and any potential roadblocks seen in qualifying for a loan.

Preapproval: A Higher Level of Prequalifying

Q. *I've heard the term "preapproval" used to refer to the prequalifying process. How is this different from regular prequalifying?*

While practices can vary from lender to lender and among loan programs, preapproval is designed as a more in-depth level of prequalifying. In addition to the credit report, the borrower provides the lender with deeper initial information such as copies of his or her last three bank statements, last two pay stubs and past two years of income tax returns.

Using that information, the lender preapproves financing for the buyer for a mortgage amount of X, based on a maximum interest rate of Y. Of course, this preapproval is based on everything staying the same in the applicant's financial picture. The borrower now knows what he or she can afford, and can use the information to market his offer to the seller, giving the buyer the strength of a cash buyer.

Preapproval programs serve as a great transaction tool for buyers, additional security for sellers and real estate agents and a good marketing tool for lenders.

Qualifying Ratios: The Bottom Line

Q. *After the lender gathers information from the borrower and fills in the application, can he or she give a quick "guesstimate" as to whether the borrower will qualify?*

Figure 2.2   Loan Payment Table (Monthly Payment for Each
$1,000 Borrowed)

Interest Rate	15 Years	20 Years	30 Years
4.00%	$ 7.40	$6.06	$4.77
4.50	7.65	6.33	5.07
5.00	7.91	6.60	5.37
5.50	8.17	6.88	5.68
6.00	8.44	7.16	6.00
6.50	8.71	7.46	6.32
7.00	8.99	7.75	6.65
7.50	9.27	8.06	6.99
8.00	9.56	8.36	7.34
8.50	9.85	8.68	7.69
9.00	10.14	9.00	8.05
9.50	10.44	9.32	8.41
10.00	10.75	9.65	8.78

Note: Chart represents principal and interest only.

This table helps you calculate your monthly housing costs (not including property taxes, insurance and any mortgage insurance premium). Each factor represents the principal and interest cost for each $1,000 borrowed. For example, if you're considering a $100,000 30-year mortgage at 8%, you would multiply 100 x $7.34 = $734 per month principal and interest payment.

It is to be hoped that this isn't the first time the borrower has talked to the lender about loan qualifying. Remember how important the prequalifying process is to the loan? If properly prequalified before she looked at properties, the borrower should have relatively little concern that she can now get a loan.

As was done in prequalifying, the lender will tally the gross income, divide it by 12 months (to determine monthly gross income) and then multiply that by the percentage allowed for the borrower's housing debt as well as total debt payments, based on the type of loan in which the borrower is interested.

Qualifying Example   Mary makes application to the lender for a $70,000 conventional loan, using a $7,000 down payment (10 percent) on the $77,000 property she wants to buy.

Step 1   The lender calculates that the principal and interest payments on $70,000 at 8 percent would be $513.63. (To arrive at this figure, the lender uses a formula similar to that in the chart in Figure 2.2 and multiplies the loan amount by the factor per thousand, $70,000 × 7.3376 = $513.63 principal and interest per month.)

Step 2   Adding a monthly figure for taxes, insurance and private mortgage insurance, the lender estimates the total PITI on this purchase to be $650 per month.

Step 3   Based on the lender allowing up to 28 percent of Mary's gross monthly income of $4,000 to be used for housing debt, the projected payment fits well within the housing ratio: $4,000 × 28 percent = $1,120 maximum allowable housing debt. In fact, by dividing Mary's proposed house payment by her gross monthly income, the lender determines that her housing ratio is a strong 16 percent ($650 ÷ $4,000 = 16 percent). Note: It's good for borrowers to have low numbers on qualifying ratios! That means that a low proportion of their gross monthly income is going to pay debt.

Step 4   The lender needs to determine whether Mary can qualify based on the amount of her long-term debt. Using a long-term debt ratio of 36 percent, the lender finds that for Mary to qualify, her maximum monthly long-term debt can't exceed $1,440. Adding her car, student loan, and credit card payments (totaling $700) to the $650 estimated house payment, her total long-term debt of $1,350 fits within the $1,440 boundary. In fact, by dividing Mary's long-term debt by her monthly gross income, the lender finds that her long-term debt ratio is 34 percent ($1,350 ÷ $4,000 = 34 percent).

If Mary has good credit, verifiable employment and adequate funds to close, it looks as though she can get the loan! For a sample qualifying worksheet, see Figure 2.3.

Remember, this is a brief example of the deeper calculations the lender would make on a conventional loan. Other loan programs would use different qualifying ratios and formulas, and might

Figure 2.3   Conventional Quick Qualify

What Can You Afford?

	COLUMN A	COLUMN B
Annual gross income	$ _____	
Divide by number of months:	÷12	
Monthly gross income:	= _____	= _____

(Record it in both columns.
Perform operations only on figures
in the same vertical column.)

Lenders will allow 28% of monthly gross
income for housing expense.   x .28
Maximum monthly housing expense allowance
(column B):   = _____
Many lenders allow 36% of monthly
gross income for long-term debt: x .36
Long-term monthly expense allowance: = _____
Figure out your monthly long-term
obligations below, and subtract it
from the allowance: − _____

> child support .... $ _____
> auto loan .... + _____
> credit cards .... + _____
> other .... + _____
> other .... + _____
> total long-term obligations: .... = _____

Monthly housing expense allowance: = _____

Look at the last amount in columns A and
B above. Record the smaller amount. $ _____
About 20% of the housing expense
allowance is for taxes and insurance,
leaving 80% for payment of mortgage
(principal and interest):   x .80
Allowable monthly principal and interest
(PI) expense: = _____
Divide this amount by the appropriate
monthly payment factor found on the
table in Appendix C: ÷ _____

                                                         = _____
Multiply by 1,000:   x 1,000
Affordable mortgage amount (what
the lender will lend): $ _____

include different mortgage insurance costs to obtain the loan. Following chapters will address the basics of qualifying for each major loan program, complete with qualifying sheets.

Q. *What a mess it would have been if Mary hadn't prequalified and fell in love with a house she couldn't afford!*

Exactly. Mary's options then would have been to find more money for her down payment, find ways to alleviate some of her debt or perhaps be forced to fall "out of love" with that house, into a cheaper one.

Mary is a prime example of what heavy long-term debt can do to the ratios. While her front-end housing ratio was great, her substantial monthly debt payments made the other ratio less attractive. Several more credit card payments and she might not have qualified at all.

QUALIFYING THE SELF-EMPLOYED BORROWER

Q. *Is it usually tougher for the self-employed buyer to get a mortgage?*

It depends on the circumstances and the type of loan desired. Since the self-employed buyer's cash flow and profitability is often tough to predict, guaranteeing income can be difficult to prove to the lender. In addition, the so-called low documentation/no documentation (low-doc/no-doc) loans of the 1980s, many of which were made to self-employed borrowers, have shown significantly more defaults than standard documentation loans. Self-employed borrowers, designated as anyone who owns 25 percent or greater interest in a business that employs them, are challenged by the mortgage loan process for two reasons:

1. Income tax write-offs whittle down the self-employed borrower's net income. While this is favorable come April 15th, it's a negative factor in qualifying for a mortgage loan. An applicant currently making a $1,200 mortgage payment may find it impossible to qualify for even a $600 loan payment on a new loan. Even after the lender adds back some deductions for the purpose of qualifying

(such as IRA deposits and depreciation), the applicant may not qualify.

2. Self-employed applicants must provide extensive documentation to the lender. This is a mandate from the secondary market, which purchases loans, the reason being that there is greater room for a borrower to embellish verifications if he or she is employer and employee. In addition to the standard items a loan applicant must furnish, the self-employed borrower may be required to provide the following:

- Two years of signed copies of complete income tax returns (with all schedules attached), a balance sheet for the previous two years (audited, or prepared by an accountant or professional tax preparer) and a year-to-date profit and loss statement for the sole proprietor
- If the business is a corporation, S corporation or a partnership, signed copies of the past two years of federal business income tax returns (with all schedules attached), a year-to-date profit and loss statement and a business credit report

Since many self-employed entrepreneurs are not the best bookkeepers, pulling these records together may prove tough, if not virtually impossible, for some applicants.

Q.   *What "red flag" areas do lenders monitor to make sure the self-employed borrower is revealing his or her entire financial picture?*

Fannie Mae monitors several areas to detect documentation concerns.

Red flags include income and deductions showing only round numbers for example, $500 or $1,000, on tax returns, a taxpayer in a high tax bracket who prepares his or her own return and a self-employed borrower who shows no estimated tax payments being paid.

Q.   *How is the self-employed person's income calculated to qualify for a loan?*

A rough formula would be as follows: Using income tax returns, add up the applicant's income after expenses (but before taxes) for the past two years. Then calculate the year-to-date income after expenses (but before taxes) for this year. Finally, divide the total of those sums by the number of months involved to get the average monthly income.

Q. *What other requirements must a self-employed person, working on commission, fulfill to qualify?*

For the applicant who works on commission, the lender needs W-2 forms and completed, signed tax returns for the past two years. The income is then averaged over the time period reported.

If the borrower's sole compensation is from commission, a year-to-date income statement will also be required.

Low-Doc/No-Doc Loans

Q. *Are low- or no-documentation loans still available to self-employed borrowers?*

While far less available today than in the 1980s, a few lenders do still make so-called low-doc/no-doc loans, usually with a minimum 25 percent to 30 percent down payment.

These types of loans do not require the same level of documentation and verification that a standard qualifying loan does. The abbreviated format for qualifying could include checking the borrower's credit, verifying down payment funds and total assets and doing an appraisal on the property. In fact, some lenders are willing to waive verification of assets entirely if the borrower were to use a 40 percent down payment!

Depending on the type of low-doc loan, the applicant may be asked to disclose his or her income, but it's not verified by the lender. The lender's rationale is that the large down payment lessens part of the risk of default. In addition, many of these loans are kept in the lender's portfolio, may require high origination fees and may carry higher interest rates than traditional loans do.

Creative Financing for the Self-Employed Borrower

Q. *What other types of loans might a self-employed borrower use?*

Another way the self-employed buyer might qualify would be by using a 75 percent first mortgage and a 10 percent down payment, and having the seller carry 15 percent of the purchase price in seller financing. Called 75/10/15 financing (and discussed in depth in Chapter 9), the borrower may be less scrutinized in taking a 75 percent loan, may sidestep the cost and requirements of private mortgage insurance, and may more readily qualify, since rates and points may be lower.

Q. *What kinds of creative financing could a self-employed borrower try?*

Seller financing is always an option, even though the seller may require the same credit report or other income verification a lender does.

A second suggestion might be to apply for a business loan rather than a mortgage. If a borrower is well established with a lender who understands his or her business workings, the borrower might use a commercial loan to fund the purchase.

While rates can vary, two points over prime is reasonable interest to expect to pay, with most loans being adjustable rather than fixed rate.

Loan amortizations may be short-term (10 to 15 years), but the borrower could negotiate a roll-over option with the lender.

A third option would be to take loans against assets, such as certificates of deposit, stock, life insurance and the like. The benefit is that you keep the asset intact while pulling cash out. The leverage techniques section later in this book goes into greater detail on these ideas.

Q. *What tips can you give self-employed borrowers to give them a better chance of getting a mortgage?*

A lender may waive the year-to-date profit and loss statement in the early months of the year, since the year is young and there's not enough history. In addition, a lender who holds others of the borrower's loans may limit some documentation, especially if the lender does not sell the loan to the secondary mortgage market and keeps the loan in portfolio (in-house) instead.

TIPS FOR GENERATING EXTRA CASH

Q. *What course of action do you suggest for the applicant who finds that he or she does not have enough income and down payment strength to qualify for a loan?*

Here are some possible suggestions:

- Sell an asset, such as a car, boat or motorcycle, or have a giant garage sale!
- Put a lien on an asset. Borrow against a car, boat, life insurance, stock, certificates of deposit or other personal property. (Be careful not to create more long-term debt in the process!) The borrower could also lien, with permission, a relative's asset to create cash. This is best accomplished when the borrower is a co-owner of the asset, such as stocks, bonds or certificates of deposits.
- Refinance an asset such as personal property (either free and clear or with existing debt on it) to free up cash.
- Receive a gift letter for the down payment or closing costs from a relative, or perhaps an employer, depending on the type of loan.
- Barter a service, use sweat equity as either part of the down payment or closing costs. For example, a roofer may make roof repairs in lieu of using the seller's cash for repairs
- Forgo a vacation and work instead! This could generate extra income. If a bonus is in the borrower's future, now might be a good time to request it. The borrower may even be willing to take a little less for the privilege of receiving the bonus early
- Transfer the use of an item. A buyer could allow a builder to use his or her backhoe in exchange for the builder paying more points on the loan. (This type of transfer would be regulated by the type of loan selected)

- Use receivables coming to the buyer. Notes carried that pay out over time could be assigned to the seller as part of the purchase price
- Use a coborrower or cosigner to help reduce the loan amount for which the borrower needs to qualify.
- Have the seller or other third party place extra funds with the lender in a pledged account to add extra collateral to the loan and therefore reduce the lender's risk. This is examined in depth in Chapter 9.

TIPS FOR REDUCING DEBT

Q. *What could an applicant do to reduce debt in order to qualify for a mortgage?*

The following suggestions might assist the buyer in debt relief:

- Pay off a debt. Use cash or another asset to alleviate the debt or sell an asset that has debt against it.
- Pay down a debt. Since the secondary market views long-term debt as anything that can't be paid off in ten months, the borrower could pay the debt down below that point. Lenders can choose to be more restrictive on what's considered long-term debt, so check with the lender.
- Refinance a high-rate loan.
- Consolidate your loans. Doing this may allow the borrower to take several high-rate loans and wrap them into one lower interest rate loan, and even lower the monthly payments by extending the loan term.
- Destroy credit cards. The borrower should ask the lender if and how this might benefit the borrower's ability to qualify.

Before changing a cash or debt position, the borrower should consult the lender to see how what's proposed could help or hurt the credit picture.

CHAPTER  3

COMPARISON SHOPPING

Most people spend several months searching for their dream homes and make a very careful, sometimes painstaking, decision. This only makes sense. After all, for most people, the purchase of a home is by far their biggest investment, the lion's share of which is usually the mortgage (the rare exception to this rule is seen with buyers who can pay cash). Therefore, it also makes sense to spend time shopping for a mortgage. Choosing the right mortgage can save borrowers thousands on a home purchase.

This chapter provides the tools to use in comparing mortgage choices. We start with the broadest of comparisons—might renting be a better option than buying—and, for those who have the option—is it better to pay cash for the home rather than use mortgage financing?

The mortgage market can be confusing. This chapter will make general comparisons on such issues as points, interest and lenders. The specifics of loan programs will be discussed later in this book.

RENT OR BUY?

Q. *Before someone considers purchasing a home, shouldn't they decide if it's the right economic move for them?*

Absolutely. For most people, a home provides not only a physical shelter but also a tax shelter and built-in savings plan. Since mortgage interest and property taxes are tax deductible and equity builds as the real estate appreciates, home ownership usually makes good economic sense.

Some circumstances might make renting a more logical option. For example, if it is likely that the buyer would need to sell the property quickly and recoup down payment and closing costs, purchasing might be unwise. Or if the real estate sales market is sluggish with values rapidly declining, renting might be a better bet.

Buyers can take precautions to limit potential losses even when they do make short-term purchases. The buyer can obtain a low down payment loan with low points and a higher interest rate; choose property in a stable, appreciating neighborhood; or both.

PAY CASH OR GET A MORTGAGE?

Q. *Should buyers always take out a loan just to get tax benefits when they purchase a home?*

Certainly not. Buyers must first decide what they want to achieve through home ownership, and then determine what financing options are best for their situations. Following are some of the pros and cons of paying cash versus financing a home.

Benefits of Paying Cash

- The cash buyer pays no mortgage payments. This is especially important to some buyers who still have nightmares over the number of homes lost to foreclosure during the Great Depression.
- The person who buys a property with cash pays no mortgage interest. Mortgage interest can more than double a property's purchase price if the loan runs full term.
- The cash buyer doesn't spend money, time or effort obtaining a loan. Closing costs are minimized to deed preparation, recording documents, and so on.
- The buyer who pays in cash doesn't need to obtain the property appraisal required with most mortgage loans.
- The cash buyer can take out a loan later, using the value of the property as collateral.
- Cash can give the buyer greater purchasing power in the marketplace, since a cash purchase is free of financing contingencies and finance-related costs.

The Downside of Paying Cash

- The cash buyer uses precious cash to buy the home, potentially depleting reserves for other purchases and emergencies. By obtaining a mortgage, the borrower employs the first tenet of real estate leverage: purchase using OPM (other people's money), even if it *is* the lender's!

- No mortgage interest means loss of tax advantages. Also, if consumer loans are needed later to finance other purchases, that interest is not tax deductible like mortgage interest.
- The cash buyer can't take advantage of tax-deductible closing costs. With a mortgage, a buyer can finance some fees into the loan to provide greater purchasing leverage.
- The cash buyer who does not obtain an appraisal could be purchasing an overpriced property. Should the property need to be sold in a short time, it might not bring the full price paid.
- By taking out a loan later, the buyer becomes not only the borrower but the seller as well for the purpose of paying costs. These additional fees might include title insurance, discount points and other closing fees.
- Mortgages applied for later might be considered refinances and might not be as liberal as an initial mortgage in interest rates and fees. In addition, this might prohibit the borrower from getting all the cash he or she needs out of the property. The purchaser would also need to anticipate whether he or she could qualify, should a loan be necessary later.

There's nothing to say that a buyer can't find exactly the right financing that gives tax advantages while not being so financially burdensome as to disrupt his or her sleep at night. This will be discussed further in this chapter.

SHOPPING FOR A MORTGAGE AND A LENDER

Q. *When the buyer's offer is accepted, what steps can be taken to find the best loan?*

Shopping for a loan is a lot like buying a car—it has to be priced right, comfortable and be able to last as long as needed! That's why it's increasingly important to shop not only for the actual loan, but for the lender as well.

A good lender will set the stage for a positive win-win loan experience. The loan officer not only will provide all the information the borrower needs to make an informed decision about which loan to choose, but will do everything possible to troubleshoot potential obstacles to bring the transaction to a speedy and successful closing. A lender may provide the information to help the buyer compare loan types, as shown in Figure 3.1.

Some of the best resources for finding the right lender are friends, family members and coworkers who have recently financed a home. The smart borrower will ask them questions:

- Who did they use?
- What kind of loan did they get?
- How long did it take to close? This might not be the best indicator of lender ability, since other circumstances might delay a closing.
- How have they been treated since the closing? Ask questions about payments, receipt of coupon books and inquiries about other services.
- Did the lender primarily refinance loans, rather than initiate new ones? This could indicate that a new loan might have to wait in the processing line behind large numbers of refinances, which are relatively easier to process.

As an additional resource, the borrower should ask real estate agents to provide names of lenders they know are reputable. Often this will be based on the types of loans in which lenders specialize, which is great information to have.

Don't overlook the fact that not all lenders make all types of loans. Additionally, a lender may make a certain loan type, but not specialize in it. For example, a lender who does just one or two VA loans a year might not be the best resource for a marginally qualified borrower who needs little-known underwriting leverage to qualify. Borrowers should ask about the volume of loans lenders make in the loan type desired before making formal application.

Q. *What's the difference between using a mortgage broker and a mortgage banker or other type of lending institution?*

Figure 3.1   Loan Type Comparison

To apply, Contact: J.Fred Volk
600 E. First, Ste. 900
Casper, WY 82601
(307)237−6655

| Property Location:
2510 E. 15th St, Ste 12 | List Price:
$55,000 |
| Real Estate Office:
Real Properties | Host:
Judi Fox |

FHA:	30 year	15 year	VA: 30 year	15 year
Total Loan	**$55,311.00**	**$54,774.00**	**$56,100.00**	**$56,100.00**
Aprox. Clos. Costs	$1,125.00	$1,125.00	$1,125.00	$1,125.00
Down Payment	$1,300.00	$1,300.00	$0.00	$0.00
Aprox. Prepaids	$666.71	$631.25	$624.43	$612.74
Discount Points	$0.00	$0.00	$280.50	$280.50
Cash Req	**$3,091.71**	**$3,056.25**	**$2,029.93**	**$2,018.24**
Prin & Int PMT	$386.74	$492.32	$392.26	$504.24
Taxes & Insurance	$57.06	$57.06	$57.06	$57.06
FHA Mort. Ins.	$22.38	$11.19		
Total PMT	**$466.18**	**$560.57**	**$449.32**	**$561.30**
Interest Rate	7.5000%	7.0000%	7.5000%	7.0000%
Discount	0.0000%	0.0000%	0.5000%	0.5000%
Term (in Months)	360	180	360	180

| Approx. Ann. Taxes | $349.69 |
| Aprox. Ann. Ins. | $335.00 |

FHA ARM (1−5 caps)	30 year
Total Loan	**$55,311.00**
Aprox. Clos. Costs	$1,125.00
Down Payment	$1,300.00
Aprox. Prepaids	$621.96
Discount Points	$0.00
Cash Req	**$3,046.96**
Prin & Int PMT	$314.05
Taxes & Insurance	$57.06
FHA Mort. Ins.	$23.05
Total PMT	**$394.15**
Interest Rate	5.5000%
Discount	0.0000%
Term (in Months)	360

| Max P&I (life): | $535.64 |

Figure 3.1 Loan Type Comparison *continued*

To apply, Contact:	J.Fred Volk 600 E. First, Ste. 900 Casper, WY 82601 (307)237−6655

Property Location: 2510 E. 15th St, Ste 12	List Price: **$55,000**
Real Estate Office: **Real Properties**	Host: **Judi Fox**

	30 year	15 year	1 Year Conv. ARM: 30 year (2−6 caps,convertable)
CONVENTIONAL:			
Total Loan (90% LTV)	**$49,500.00**	**$49,500.00**	**$49,500.00**
Aprox. Clos. Costs	$1,653.50	$1,653.50	$1,653.50
Down Payment	$5,500.00	$5,500.00	$5,500.00
Aprox. Prepaids	$624.12	$603.29	$578.23
Discount Points	$0.00	$0.00	$123.75
Cash Req	**$7,777.62**	**$7,756.79**	**$7,855.48**
Prin & Int PMT	$333.49	$435.97	$250.81
Taxes & Insurance	$57.06	$57.06	$57.06
Private Mortgage Ins.	$14.03	$8.25	$18.15
Total PMT	**$404.57**	**$501.28**	**$326.02**
Interest Rate	7.125%	6.675%	4.5000%
Discount	0.000%	0.000%	0.2500%
Term (in Months)	360	180	360
Approx. Ann. Taxes	$349.69		
Aprox. Ann. Ins.	$335.00		

	7 YEAR	5 YEAR
BALLOONS (BASED ON 30 YEAR):		
Total Loan (90% LTV)	**$49,500.00**	**$49,500.00**
Aprox. Clos. Costs	$1,653.50	$1,653.50
Down Payment	$5,500.00	$5,500.00
Aprox. Prepaids	$606.07	$606.07
Discount Points	$0.00	$0.00
Cash Req	$7,759.57	$7,759.57
Prin&Int PMT	$304.78	$304.78
Taxes & Insurance	$57.06	$57.06
Private Mortgage Ins.	$14.03	$14.03
Total PMT	**$375.86**	**$375.86**
Interest Rate	6.2500%	6.2500%
Discount	0.0000%	0.0000%
Term P&I Based on (in Months)	360	360

Reprinted by permission of J. Fred Volk, Wallick and Volk, PO Box 685, 222 E. Eighteenth Street, Cheyenne, WY 82001. 307-634-5941

Mortgage brokers, as their name denotes, "broker" mortgages as a middleman. They locate borrowers who need mortgage money and place them with investors who want to make loans. The mortgage broker receives a fee for making a successful match.

Unlike other types of lenders, mortgage brokers do not work with their own cash—they merely place borrowers with lenders.

One plus in working with a mortgage broker is that they have access to a variety of investors and a myriad of loan types. They can help marginal borrowers locate financing with investors willing to take more risk.

Mortgage bankers, on the other hand, not only originate loans but also close the loan using their funds. They make their profit by charging fees and points and also by selling the loan in the secondary market.

Mortgage bankers also profit by servicing loans or selling the servicing rights on loans they originate. Servicing is the process of receiving monthly loan payments and collecting and accounting for the taxes and insurance on mortgages. Many large mortgage banker companies today have separate loan servicing divisions that contribute greatly to corporate profit.

Q. *Can a borrower be forced to apply for a loan with a certain mortgage company because the builder of the home requests it?*

No. This is considered restraint of trade and is illegal. While it's not a bad idea to consider a lender the builder knows and does a high volume of business with, since the loan might get special attention, that lender should not be the borrower's sole option.

QUESTIONS TO ASK BEFORE CHOOSING A LOAN

Q. *Once the lender has received information about the borrower and has discussed possible financing programs, what general loan questions should the borrower ask the lender before choosing the best loan?*

The following are some questions a borrower might ask to clarify his or her loan choice:

- Is the loan assumable? If so, under what circumstances and would the interest rate change? How would that be determined?
- Can the private mortgage insurance (PMI) on the conventional loan be removed? If so, what are the current requirements? If the removal guidelines are strict now, they probably won't get any better with time!
- Can the buyer pay taxes and insurance outside of the loan payments? This is determined by the type of loan and lender requirements, but is great for the borrower's cash flow!
- Is there any prepayment penalty on the loan? Is there any minimum amount of prepayments required; for example, must it be paid in $100 increments?

INTEREST RATES, LOAN TERMS AND DOWN PAYMENTS

Q. *Is the interest rate the major consideration when shopping for a loan?*

While one of the first options consumers consider in making an affordable home purchase, the interest rate is certainly not the only factor in mortgage financing. The following is a quick checklist of questions the borrower should ask, followed by an explanation of each.

- What are the borrower's financing goals? The borrower should estimate the time he or she will own the property. Short-term owners could use an adjustable rate mortgage (ARM) for short-term savings; elect for a higher interest rate with fewer discount points, which would not be recouped if the property were sold in a short time; or use a loan containing a balloon provision.

  Long-term owners could use a 15- or 10-year fixed-rate loan to build equity quickly and sidestep interest over the life of the loan; pay higher points to reduce the interest rate; or use a permanent buydown to reduce the interest rate for the life of the loan.

- If and when the borrower does sell, how important will it be to get all equity out immediately? If this is important, the borrower may wish to choose a loan that is assumable and would be market competitive when assumed.
- Will anyone else be participating as a coborrower or co-signer on the loan? The answer to this question may dictate the type of loan available to the borrower, as not all loans allow multiple borrowers.
- How much savings does the borrower wish to use as a down payment? Is that including, or in addition to, the closing costs? This can help determine the size and type of loan.
- How much of a monthly payment is the borrower prepared to make? The answer to this question should be based not only on what the borrower can afford, but also on the size of the monthly payment he or she is mentally prepared to make.
- What are the borrower's current mortgage or rent payments? A lender may hesitate to approve a loan with radically larger payments than a consumer is accustomed to paying without showing a substantial income increase. A severe payment difference may increase financial pressure on the borrower, perhaps enough to cause the loan to default.
- Would the borrower mind if the payment amount fluctuated? If so, it's probably not wise to take on an ARM or similar interest-sensitive loan.

Should Buyers Wait for Interest Rates To Drop?

Q. *Does it make economic sense to wait for interest rates to drop before purchasing property?*

It does if the borrower has a reliable crystal ball! Drops in interest rates usually are accompanied by increases in purchase prices, making any interest rate savings a washout.

The Cost of Waiting Using 4 percent annual inflation, a $100,000 priced home today would become $104,000 over one year. If interest rates during that year were to jump just 1 percent from 8 percent to 9 percent, principal and interest payments would be $103.20 more per month ($734 per month on the $100,000 loan at 8 percent interest, compared to $837.20 per month on the $104,000 loan at 9 percent).

If the borrower multiplied that difference by the 360 months of the loan, that's an extra $37,152—a dear price to pay for waiting!

15-Year Versus 30-Year Loans

Q. *How does one choose between a 15-year and a 30-year loan?*

Many factors go into deciding which loan term best suits a buyer's needs and qualifying abilities.

Interest Savings in Choosing a 15-Year Loan The monthly principal and interest payments on a 15-year, 9 percent loan for $100,000 would be $1,015, compared to $805 per month on a 30-year loan. While total payments on the 15-year loan would amount to $182,700, the 30-year loan would cost a whopping $289,800, a difference of $107,100 more! In fact, when the 15-year loan is paid off, there will still be $79,300 owing on the 30-year loan! (More than three quarters of what was initially borrowed!)

Q. *Are there other financial benefits to using a 15-year versus a 30-year loan?*

Interest rates may be lower on the 15-year loan, depending on the lender and the loan program. Because equity builds faster on a 15-year loan, a low down payment shouldn't cause a problem if the borrower has to resell in a short period of time.

Q. *If a 15-year mortgage makes such good financial sense, why doesn't everyone use it?*

First, not everyone can qualify for a 15-year loan. Because of the shorter amortization time, the monthly payment is larger. Going back to the earlier example comparing costs for the 15- versus 30-year loan: To qualify for the 30-year loan's $805 payment, the borrower would have to have $2,875 income per month to meet a lender's 28 percent housing ratio requirements. To qualify for the 15-year loan's $1,015 payment, however, the borrower would need $3,625 income per month, or $750 more than needed for the 30-year loan.

Second, some borrowers enjoy the peace of mind that comes with a lower monthly payment, especially if they were to fall on tough financial times. In fact, approximately 80 percent of all loans made are 30-year loans. Borrowers could make prepayments on the 30-year loan to retire it early, if the loan program allowed, but with the 15-year loan they'd be saddled permanently with the higher payment.

The exception to this school of thought is found in homeowners who are refinancing their existing loans. A much larger percentage of those individuals are using 15-year loans, and in some cases, 10-year terms, to reduce their purchasing costs.

Don't forget that if the borrower is making a higher monthly payment, that money will not be available for other investments. This could mean lost financial opportunities.

And finally, not everyone can access a 15-year loan on every mortgage available. Availability can vary based on the lender and the program.

Lenders are usually more than happy to project costs to help buyers decide which loan term best suits their needs. Total borrowing costs for different loan terms can be compared by using the chart in Figure 3.2.

Pros and Cons of Small Versus Large Down Payments

Q. *How does a borrower weigh the advantages of making a small versus a large down payment, other than what the lender might require on a certain loan?*

As discussed earlier, it may not be in the short-term buyer's best interest to invest lots of money in the property. Too small of a down payment, however, coupled with low property appreciation, may create a deficit if the owner needs to sell in a very short period of time. If the borrower knows this and is willing to take the risk, he or she should be prepared to make up the shortfall when he or she sells.

Figure 3.2   Comparing Interest Costs by Loan Term

The following table illustrates a $100,000 mortgage at $8\frac{1}{2}$ percent interest as paid to maturity under five different loan terms. Although the payment difference between 30- and 15-year loans is $216, the interest saved over the term of the loan is $99,556!

Terms	Monthly Payment	Months Paid	Total Cost	Interest Cost
30-year	$ 769	360	$276,809	$176,809
20-year	$ 868	240	$208,278	$108,278
15-year	$ 985	180	$177,253	$ 77,253
10-year	$1,240	120	$148,783	$ 48,783

A second consideration is that the borrower may want to make a large down payment if it means securing a lower interest rate or sidestepping the costs of fees or PMI. This will be discussed in depth in Chapter 4. A large down payment may even loosen some loan underwriting requirements, since the lender's risk is reduced.

DETERMINING LOAN COSTS

Q. *How does the borrower determine which loan program is most cost effective, especially where loan costs and fees are involved?*

Unlike comparing interest rate differences that are fairly obvious and straightforward, comparing loan costs and fees can get complicated. This is because it's not just the loan costs that are being compared, but also the loan program terms.

Fixed Rate Versus Adjustable Rate

The lender offers a 90 percent conventional, fixed-rate loan at 9 percent interest that will have total closing costs of $2,500. Costs for a 90 percent ARM at 6 percent interest, however, are $2,900; the loan also can be converted to a fixed-rate loan at any time during the first five years of the loan.

At first glance, it's virtually impossible to tell which is the better buy. The borrower needs to compare the two loan programs based on how long he or she anticipates keeping the loan, what the conversion fees might be and how the rate would adjust if the loan were converted to a fixed rate.

Lenders will prepare comparisons such as these if provided with the necessary information to plug into the scenario. This is the best way for borrowers to make sure they are not being led astray based only on bargain interest rates and low closing costs. A loan comparison worksheet is shown in Appendix A.

Q. *What are the major categories of loan costs?*

Loan costs vary depending on the type and size of loan. The following are some general loan cost categories that pertain to most buyers:

- Down payment (minus any earnest money deposit)
- Out-of-pocket costs: fees for appraisal, credit report and so on, often paid at the time of loan application
- Title insurance: a one-time fee that varies among states and with the size of the loan
- Two months' escrows: two months' impound of property tax, homeowner's insurance, and PMI, if the loan so requires
- First-year PMI: the first annual insurance premium on the loan, if required, paid in cash if not financed into the loan, as allowed by some PMI companies
- First year's homeowner's insurance: a paid receipt showing payment or funds advanced to the lender to pay directly to the insurance company
- Discount points, if applicable
- Prorated loan interest: interest paid by the day for the closing month, to a maximum of 30 days
- Two months' cash reserves: an equivalent of two months of mortgage payments left over in cash as fin ding (required on conventional loans; not giv lender, just verified to be on hand; can be in 401(k), IRA, or the like.)

Fees to Negotiate

Q. *What loan fees can be negotiated with the lender?*

As with many things in this world, closing costs and discount points can be negotiated. But it's doubtful the borrower will get a premium, unless there are trade-offs with the lender.

For example, the lender may be much more willing to reduce closing fees or require fewer discount points if the borrower is well qualified and is making a substantial down payment. In addition, if a higher interest rate is being charged, that, too, could offset other concessions the lender might be willing to make.

The lender may be willing to entice a borrower by offering low fees when the company is seeking a larger business market share or introducing a new program. In addition, a lender may give incentives to faithful past customers, or to encourage a new borrower who may bring additional business to the bank.

Low fees, however, can be smoke and mirrors obscuring an overall higher interest rate or other lender benefit. As in the previous question, asking the lender to compare different financing options is the best approach in determining the true cost of borrowing.

Q. *What types of loan costs generally vary widely from lender to lender?*

Fees are as different as the lenders who charge them. The major differences can be found in the following four major categories of fees.

1. Loan Origination Fees. Many companies don't charge this fee, but some do. It's usually considered another point (1 percent of the loan amount) and can make a seemingly great loan package a bad choice. If charged, this is also a fee that may not be thoroughly explained up front.
2. Excessive Escrow Fee Collection. Most loan companies collect two months of escrow impounds or reserves at closing for taxes and insurance. Some companies collect three months, which can drive up the amount of cash the borrower needs at closing. This is definitely an area

where negotiation may help, unless the loan type mandates a certain reserve amount.

3. Separate Application Fees. Most companies include the application fee in the out-of-pocket expense quote; others have this as a separate fee (of several hundred dollars), which many not be explained until the borrower applies for the loan. Borrowers should ask about this when calling to check for rates and costs, since the amount can vary significantly among lenders.

4. Miscellaneous Fees. Often called "fluff fees," these miscellaneous fees can include document preparation fees, tax-checking fees and courier charges. The borrower should make sure they are itemized and try to negotiate to lower them.

DISCOUNT POINTS

Q. *What are discount points and how are they used?*

One point is equal to 1 percent of the loan amount. Points are used to increase the lender's financial yield on the loan. For example, if the lender has the choice between making a loan at 8 percent and one at 8.5 percent interest, it's pretty obvious which one he or she would choose.

Points bridge the gap between interest rates, allowing the lender to make the loan at a lower interest rate. While the value of points can vary depending on financial markets, most lenders consider that it takes roughly six to eight points to lower the interest rate by 1 percent. This can be illustrated through the following example.

If a lender quotes that it will take three points (3 percent) to lower a 9 percent interest rate to 8.5 percent on an $80,000 loan, that's $80,000 × 3 percent, or $2,400 payable in cash at closing to bridge the financial gap in interest by one-half percent.

Most loan types allow the seller and buyer to negotiate payment of points in the purchase agreement. See chapters on specific loan types for further clarification.

Determining How Many Points To Pay

Q. *If the lender gives the borrower the option of how many points to pay for a certain rate of interest, what's the best way to decide?*

The prime factor to consider is the time the borrower will own the property and keep the loan. The following is a formula to help determine the "dollars and sense": Calculate the difference in the monthly payment amounts and the difference in the cost of the points, and divide the amount paid in points by the amount saved by the lower monthly payment to obtain a "break-even" mark for holding the property. Below is an example.

Points Versus Interest Savings Mr. Fredericks is getting a $90,000 mortgage for 30 years. The lender tells him that there are two choices: A 9 percent interest rate with zero points for a payment of $724.16 per month, or an 8.875 percent interest rate with one-half point ($450) and monthly payments of $716.08.

The mortgage payment difference is $8.08. The difference in points is $450. If Mr. Fredericks pays $450 now, he can save $8.08 every month he has the loan.

To calculate the breakeven point, he would take the expense ($450) and divide it by the monthly savings ($8.08). It would take 55 months to break even.

Therefore, if Mr. Fredericks will keep the house and the loan for 55 months or more and not refinance, it may make sense to pay the one-half discount point. But if it's anticipated that the house would be sold or refinanced in the next five years, the loan with no points may be more economical.

Keep in mind that this example is a relatively simplistic analysis, and doesn't take into consideration time-value of money, tax ramifications or the long-term savings of the lower interest rate.

Q. *Could a borrower ever negotiate points with a lender?*

Possibly. Lenders determine points primarily based on the price they have to pay for funds, the type of loan involved and other lender competition in the marketplace. If the lender does decide to charge fewer points, one or more of the following offsetting factors is probably in the picture:

- Is the borrower willing to pay a premium rate of interest? Remember, points bridge the gap in the lender's financial yield on the loan.
- How strong is the borrower? If the lender could risk losing the applicant by not being competitive enough on the points, there may be a concession.

Remember, points are merely one piece of the borrowing puzzle. No amount of discount point concessions is worth dealing with a slow loan processor or unscrupulous lender.

Q. *Are points tax deductible on mortgage loans?*

For the purpose of acquiring residential real estate, discount points are tax deductible in the year paid. The IRS specifies that in order for points to be deducted, they must not exceed points generally charged in the area.

In March of 1994, the IRS surprised everyone when it changed its policy to reflect who could deduct points on mortgages. The new ruling allows buyers to deduct points on mortgages—even if paid by sellers. Previously, points were deductible only if the buyer paid them at closing.

The change comes after the IRS decided that the buyer really pays the points, even if the seller helps share the expense. The rationale was that the seller typically increases the sales price to include the points.

Not only are points non-deductible for sellers, the rules are retroactive after December 31, 1990, benefiting people who bought homes in 1991, 1992 and 1993. Buyers can file an amended return with the IRS on Form 1040X and write "discount points" in the top right-hand corner of the form. The buyer also needs to attach a copy of the settlement statement received at closing.

This new ruling creates one negative for buyers should they sell, since the capital gain may be larger due to the points.

For example, if a buyer paid $100,000 for a home and the seller paid $2,000 in points for the buyer, the basis of the home for tax purposes is $98,000 (since the points are deducted). But a taxpayer wouldn't be faced with that gain if a more expensive home were purchased, or if the over age 55 one-time $125,000 exclusion on capital gains was taken when the property was sold.

These changes for deducting points have no affect on refinancing. Owners who refinance must deduct points over the life of the loan, not all at once.

For example, if a borrower paid $3,600 worth of points to obtain a 30-year loan with a lower interest rate, he or she could deduct only $10 for each of the next 360 months or $120 per year. For this reason it may help to minimize points paid to refinance a loan.

USING BUYDOWNS

Q. *How does one buy down an interest rate?*

Buydowns are prepaid interest used to reduce the interest rate on a loan temporarily or permanently. The buyer or other party pays this money at closing, allowing him or her to qualify at the lower interest rate and reduce the monthly payment.

Buydowns can bring the interest rate down for a short period called a temporary buydown, or permanently lower the interest rate for the life of the loan. One of the more familiar approaches is the 3-2-1 buydown, where the interest rate is 3 percent lower than the note rate of the loan for the first year, 2 percent lower during the second year of the loan, and 1 percent lower during the third year of the loan, after which it stays at the note rate—the interest the borrower agreed to pay—for the life of the loan.

Q. *If buydowns are used, the borrower only has to qualify at the buydown rate?*

This varies based on the type of loan. Conventional loans sold to the secondary market let the borrower qualify at a maximum of 2 percent below the note rate, with a minimum floor of 7 percent interest. Borrowers using FHA loans qualify at a maximum of 2 percent below the note rate, and even if VA borrowers use buydowns to reduce the interest rate, they still must qualify at the note rate interest.

Buydowns will be discussed further in chapters on each loan type.

DETERMINING LOCK-INS

Q. *When would it make sense for the borrower to lock in the interest rate?*

With fluctuating interest rates, this has turned out to be the real estate $64,000 question. Locking in an interest rate means that if interest rates rise during a specific timeframe (usually 45–60 days), the rate quoted will remain the same. Again, this depends on a variety of factors. The following are answers to the basic questions one might ask to decide whether it is advantageous to lock in an interest rate:

- If the borrower doesn't lock in and the rate increases, could he or she still qualify for the loan? Logic dictates that if a bump in the rate will disqualify the borrower, locking in is not only prudent, it's advised!
- How long is the lock-in and how far away is the closing? A 45-day lock will be moot if a closing isn't projected for 60 days.
- Is there a fee for locking in? When is it paid? Is it refundable? This often applies to fees for extended rate lock-ins that extend an interest rate guarantee to 60, 80 or 110 days. It's therefore wise for the borrower to know what's being paid, when it's paid and under what circumstances, if any, it can be refunded.
- How long will the borrower keep the loan? Should he or she pay more points up front to get the lower interest rate, or less points and go with a higher interest rate? (Isn't it amazing how many decisions are based on how long someone will keep the loan and the property?) Again, the standard answer: Short-term ownership favors less points paid at closing and higher interest rates. Long-term ownership favors more points paid at closing to receive lower interest rates.

The borrower can check several sources before deciding to lock in the interest rate.

- Check with the lender. What have been the interest rate trends on that particular type of loan and what is projected?
- Check financial indicators: the federal discount rate, the rate at which banks borrow money from the Federal Reserve; actions of the Federal Reserve Board (which tightens or loosens monies in circulation); and especially the ten-year treasury note market, which has a big impact on determining short-term interest rates. These can be monitored through local papers or the in-depth coverage in *The Wall Street Journal.*
- Don't forget the role international events play in interest rates. As the U.S. shifts to a global economy, international crises play an even bigger part in the volatility of U.S. interest rates. In fact, many lenders advise that if negative world news is brewing, it probably makes sense to lock in the rate.

CHAPTER 4

CONVENTIONAL LOANS

This chapter is designed to give you a current base of information regarding single-family conventional loan housing programs. Research for this chapter comes from lenders' programs in many states, from a variety of economic climates and real estate markets, as well as current secondary market guidelines. Check with individual area lenders to apply information in this chapter to loan programs currently available.

The term *conventional loan* refers to any mortgage that is neither insured nor guaranteed by the government. It stands to reason, then, that conventional loans were the first traditional loans made by local lenders. Loans were held in the lender's investment portfolio until they were paid in full or, heaven forbid, foreclosed upon. While this enabled the borrower to build a business rapport with the lender, it was usually not in the lender's best financial interests. With rates fluctuating, particularly upward, the lender received below-market interest on the loan, while not being able to recycle the funds to lend other borrowers.

It's fair to say that the advent of the secondary market in the late 1930s was most welcome! Now lenders could sell their loan packages to the secondary market, recycling lent funds (for a slight discount off the loans' interest), bringing funds back home to be lent out.

Today, although some lenders still accept loans to be held in-house, a majority sell their loans to the secondary market.

In this chapter, we'll investigate the advantages and disadvantages of conventional lending and uncover little-known facts regarding underwriting that can help the borrower get the loan.

PROS AND CONS

Q. *What are the advantages of a conventional loan?*

The advantages are as follows:

71

- The interest rate is "fixed" for the life of the loan to eliminate worry over escalating interest and payments.
- Lenders may be willing to keep the loan in their own lending portfolio, thus allowing more underwriting flexibility.
- Lenders may be willing to negotiate or eliminate certain loan fees.
- Many lenders allow comortgagors on conventional loans.
- A lender may allow collateral other than or in addition to the real property being mortgaged.
- A lender may be willing to finance personal property along with the real estate loan (such as a "package mortgage" including appliances). This might be found when a newly constructed property is sold furnished by the builder.
- Many appraisals need meet only the guidelines of the lender's own board of directors' guidelines or the secondary market (if applicable), instead of the strict appraisal standards of FHA and VA.
- If PMI is required, its premiums are usually less expensive than with ARM programs or FHA mortgage insurance.
- With regard to PMI, the lender may decide to self-insure the loan, increasing the interest rate to compensate for any potential loss.
- The lender can assist the borrower in funding a portion of the closing costs in exchange for a higher interest rate. (We'll cover "premium pricing" later in this chapter.)

Q. *What are the disadvantages of the conventional fixed-rate loan?*

The disadvantages are as follows:

- The interest rate is set for the life of the loan, disallowing the purchaser any decrease in rates should they fall.
- Interest rates are ultimately determined by each lender and can run at higher market rate levels than those of FHA and VA.
- Origination fees and other loan costs are determined by the lender's individual guidelines and by market demands

and needs, and could therefore be higher than those of similar programs in the marketplace.

- Since mortgage documents for fixed-rate loans can vary depending on state and lender, a lender could specify certain clauses to be included in a mortgage document. These include the alienation (or due-on-sale) clause, prepayment penalty and acceleration clause.
- Most loans with greater than an 80 percent loan-to-value ratio generally will require the borrower to provide PMI if the loan is to be sold in the secondary market.
- Conventional loans may require larger down payments than those of government programs.
- Some lenders may require application and processing fees at the time of loan application, some of which may be nonrefundable, based on individual lending policies.
- Many lenders will take only a first mortgage position, which might eliminate some creative financing options for the buyer.

Q. *Who makes the rules regarding what a lender can and can't do in conventional mortgage lending?*

It depends. If a lender wants to sell his or her loans into the secondary mortgage market, that involves one set of rules. If borrowers on those loans used less than a 20 percent down payment and PMI is required, that's another set of rules. In addition, local lenders might be more restrictive still, based on their boards of directors' underwriting demands.

Since a majority of all conventional loans are sold to the secondary market, those guidelines set the stage for a high percentage of lending.

PROFILE OF A CONVENTIONAL-LOAN BORROWER

Q. *Is there a standard profile of a borrower who could best benefit by using a conventional fixed-rate loan?*

You might have trouble describing the characteristics of a conventional loan borrower, since he or she could look like most anyone interested in getting financing!

There are, however, some general characteristics that describe many conventional buyers. The buyers

- usually have at least a 5 percent down payment, unless they are making the purchase with a gift of 20 percent or more from a third party.
- have money for closing costs.
- have good to excellent credit ratings.
- can qualify for loans using standard ratios and market-rate interest.
- don't usually need a lot of special loan underwriting considerations.
- desire a fixed-rate mortgage (for financial or emotional stability).
- have fairly light debts in proportion to their income.
- don't want a prepayment penalty on the loan.
- might ask the lender to keep the loan in portfolio (particularly if they have been a long-time customer, or are using a large down payment).
- can wait the standard 30 to 50 days it takes to close the loan.
- may have jobs where income increases are either rare or nonexistent.
- have room in their qualifying and loan payments for PMI insurance.

If this profile fits a prospective buyer, maybe there's a conventional loan in their future!

SECONDARY MARKET GUIDELINES

Q. *If a borrower's loan was sold to FNMA or FHLMC in the secondary market, what kind of qualifying ratios would be required?*

FNMA and FHLMC Loan Underwriting Guidelines for Fixed-Rate Loans

For owner-occupied, single-family residences, and for second home and investor loans, PITI can't exceed 28 percent of the borrower's gross monthly income and PITI plus long-term debt (any debt that extends ten months or more) can't exceed 36 percent of the borrower's gross monthly income. The maximum loan-to-value ratio is 95 percent on single-family residences, 80 percent on second homes and 70 percent on investor loans (FNMA, fixed-rate only; FHLMC negotiates investor loans individually).

On owner-occupied and second-home purchases with subordinate financing (a second mortgage), the first mortgage cannot represent more than 75 percent of the lesser of the sales price or appraised value. This requirement also applies to owner-occupied refinances.

Maximum loan-to-value ratio based on size of primary residence is as follows:

Number of Units	*Loan-to-Value Ratio*
1	95 percent
2	90 percent
3	80 percent
4	80 percent

Appendix A includes a qualifying sheet for conventional loans to help assist in calculating loan payments quickly.

Adjustable-rate mortgage qualifying ratios are shown in Chapter 6.

Guidelines for Condominiums and Townhouse Purchases

Q. *What about loans for condominiums and townhouses? Are they underwritten the same way as detached housing?*

Lenders will generally lend up to 95 percent loan-to-value ratio for fixed-rate loans on owner-occupied condos and townhouses, but only up to 90 percent when an adjustable rate is used. Condos and townhouses as second-home purchases usually require a 20 percent down payment.

There are no specified minimum square footage restrictions in the secondary market, since lending is based solely on the unit's marketability. The development project must be FNMA or FHLMC accepted or have lender warranties. In addition, the project cannot have heavier investor concentration (nonowner-occupied units) than a certain percentage of the total (usually approximately 40 percent).

What Counts as Long-Term Debt?

Q.   *You mentioned that the secondary market considers long-term debt to be any debt that can't be paid off in ten months. Could the lender choose to be more restrictive?*

Yes. This could occur if the lender found the borrower to be marginally qualified or determined that payments were substantial and could affect the repayment of the loan, especially in the early months of the loan. An example would be a $450 car payment with five payments remaining.

The lender could also choose to be more restrictive if area defaults were high. A lender erring on the side of caution could allocate a minimum payment of 5 percent of the outstanding balance or a minimum of $10 per month to revolving debts for the purpose of calculating long-term debt. Short-term obligations or others that don't have set monthly payments may be considered to have at least the interest due monthly.

When lenders are more restrictive, it often will be to consider debts that can't be paid off in six months, rather than ten.

Contributions Help the Buyer Qualify

Q.   *What contributions does the secondary market allow the seller to make?*

A contribution, also called a financing concession, is the payment of a cost that is typically paid by the buyer, but instead is paid by the seller or other third party.

Such items can include transfer taxes, cost of title insurance policies and surveys, recording fees, tax stamps, attorneys' fees and any seller-paid buydown or seller-paid financing costs.

Seller contributions that can be made over and above the following limits are those that occurred when market interest rates shifted and the seller used points to buy down the interest rate.

Lender-paid buydowns and lender-funded transaction costs do not have to be counted against what the seller can contribute to the buyer.

If contributions exceed the following limits, any excess will be subtracted from the sales price before the loan amount is calculated:

Secondary Market for Owner-Occupied Property
3 percent of the property value on a 95 percent loan
6 percent of the property value on a 90 percent loan

Maximum Second-Home Contribution Limits
FNMA: 6 percent of property value on an 80 percent loan
FHLMC: 6 percent of property value on all loan-to-value ratio loans

Addresses for FNMA and FHLMC regional offices are listed in Appendix B.

The Government National Mortgage Association is the last player in the secondary market. Because GNMA deals with government-insured and guaranteed loans, we'll cover these underwriting guidelines in Chapters 7 and 8.

Guidelines for the Property

Q. *We've talked so far about borrower qualifications. What are the standard property guidelines for the secondary market?*

Although properties are approved on a case-by-case basis, properties must generally meet the following guidelines:

- The property should be in an area with properties of comparable value and quality.
- Streets must be dedicated and properly maintained.
- Land value cannot be excessive compared to the improvements on the property.

An estimate of value from an appraiser is used to substantiate all loans sold to the secondary market.

PREMIUM PRICING: LENDER CONTRIBUTIONS

Q. *You mentioned that the lender could contribute to the buyer's closing costs and that those contributions could be in addition to what
a seller would contribute. Do lenders do this very much?*

When the lender contributes to payment of the buyer's costs, it's
called *premium pricing.* That is a subtle indication that it's not
truly gratis! The trade-off is that the borrower does have to pay less
out of pocket to purchase the property, but the lender will more
than likely recoup those contributions by charging a higher
interest rate on the loan.

In an active loan market with low interest rates and plentiful
refinancing, lenders may have more than enough borrowers and
may not rely on premium pricing to put loans together. But some
lenders who desire a bit more of a market share, or are looking for
marketing draws, find this to be a valuable tool.

Using Compensating Factors When Ratios Don't Fit

Q. *If a borrower's ratios exceed the standard guidelines, could he or
she ever qualify for a loan?*

Possibly. While secondary market qualifying guidelines set the
standard for granting loans, there can be exceptions to the rules.
Examples might include a borrower with a history of handling a
higher-than-average rent payment, especially if other long-term
debt was relatively low, or a borrower who consistently saves
a high percentage of his or her annual income. Situations such
as these are what the secondary market terms "compensating
factors."

Fully documented compensating factors can be used to approve
conventional fixed-rate loans with loan-to-value ratios of 90
percent or less when borrowers do the following:

- Make a large down payment
- Purchase a property that qualifies as "energy efficient"
- Demonstrate the ability to devote a greater portion of
  their income to housing expenses

- Can show a consistent pattern of saving, maintain a good credit history or have a debt-free position
- Can demonstrate a potential for increased earnings because of education or job training
- Have short-term income (Social Security income, child support, and so on) that traditionally is not counted in qualifying because it would not continue three years beyond the date of the mortgage application
- Purchase a home due to corporate relocation of the primary wage-earner and the secondary wage-earner (with a previous work history) is expected to return to work
- Have substantial net worth

Fully documented compensating factors can be used with 90 percent or greater loan-to-value ratios if, in addition to meeting one or more of the criteria listed earlier, borrowers meet one of the following conditions:

- Have financial reserves, part of which must be in the form of liquid assets that equal at least two months of PITI payments, that can be used to carry the mortgage debt
- Demonstrate that they are able to carry a substantial housing payment, new housing expenses don't exceed their old and they have good prior mortgage payment and acceptable credit
- Have a total long-term debt ratio of 30 percent or less, excellent payment histories on prior mortgages, and acceptable credit

Having one or more of these compensating factors can serve as strong leverage for the borrower who needs a little extra "oomph" in qualifying for a loan.

LITTLE-KNOWN UNDERWRITING FACTS

Q. *Are there ever any differentiations between what local lenders allow and what the secondary market will accept?*

There certainly are. In fact, some of the following little-known facts can help put loans together (if the borrower knows what to ask for, of course):

- The lender will allow qualifying ratios to be exceeded by 2 percent on the housing and long-term debt ratio if a purchaser is buying an energy-efficient house.
- The secondary market will allow the seller to take the borrower's existing property or an asset other than real estate in trade as part of the down payment on the new property, as long as the borrower has made a 5 percent cash down payment on the new loan.
- The seller can give the purchaser credit toward the down payment for a portion of previous rent payments made under a rental purchase agreement. The minimum original term of the rental must be 12 months, and only those rents that exceeded the market rent, as determined by an appraiser, can be counted. For example, if market rent is $800, but the purchaser actually paid $900, the monthly credit toward purchase would be $100.
- A borrower can pool his or her funds with funds received as a gift from a relative who lives with him or her in order to come up with the minimum 5 percent cash down payment. Both parties must reside in the new residence. In addition to these funds, the borrower could receive an additional down payment gift from a relative or a gift or grant from a church, municipality or nonprofit organization.
- When the loan-to-value ratio for a mortgage is 80 percent or less, the full down payment may come from a gift from a relative or a gift or grant from a church, municipality or nonprofit organization. This means that one of these parties would make the entire 20 percent down payment and the borrower would not have to make any other down payment from his or her own funds.

Q. *What should a prospective borrower do with all these great underwriting exceptions and little-known facts?*

Use them, of course! A borrower can read through the compensating factors and little-known facts and see what might fit his or her circumstances.

Then, if the lender doesn't qualify the borrower, or claims that borrower resources are marginal for the loan size, the borrower could bring up this "ammunition" to see if it could lend additional purchasing leverage. It can't hurt!

Q. *Does the secondary market have any maximum loan limits for loans it purchases?*

Yes. These are recalculated every year to reflect increases in purchase prices. Single-family one-unit dwellings have current maximum loan limits in excess of $200,000, with multiple unit financing available in excess of $300,000. The borrower should check with the lender to determine the current maximum loan amount available for the property he or she wishes to purchase.

Loans in excess of these secondary market loan ceilings can still be made by a lender. These are called "jumbo loans" and are sold separately to investors rather than through the usual secondary market channels.

Because these loans are not the standard size, the borrower may have to pay a higher interest and other lender incentives.

Q. *Does the secondary market limit making loans based on the amount of properties held by an owner?*

Yes, with clarification. The secondary market will allow a borrower to have any number of properties with financing on them as long as the property purchased is a principal residence.

The borrower can have no more than four properties currently financed if the new property being purchased is a second home or investment property.

These guidelines apply to all properties held by the borrower, not just those purchased by the secondary market, but do not apply to properties that are free and clear with no outstanding financing.

BORROWERS WITH BANKRUPTCY OR FORECLOSURE HISTORIES

Q. *Can someone who has previously declared bankruptcy apply for a loan to be sold to the secondary market?*

A bankruptcy must have been discharged fully and the borrower must have reestablished good credit. Usually, a two-year period between discharge of the bankruptcy and the mortgage application is required; but an exception may be made after one year if the lender is able to document that extraordinary circumstances caused the bankruptcy (such as extended illness not covered by health insurance).

Q. *What about borrowers who have had previous foreclosures? Can they get conventional loans?*

The secondary market usually won't purchase loans of borrowers who have had mortgage foreclosures less than three years earlier. Again, if extenuating circumstances can show that a foreclosure was beyond a borrower's control, an exception might be made. These circumstances might include a serious, long-term illness, death of a family's principal wage earner or loss of employment due to industry reduction. The borrower must have established good credit and show an ability to manage his or her financial affairs.

TYPES OF QUALIFYING INCOME AND VERIFICATION

Q. *What kind of income will conventional lenders accept and how is it verified?*

In general, the lender wants to determine the probability and stability of the borrower's income sources. This means verifying two years' tenure for all income, full-time or part-time.

The secondary market can verify income in two different ways. The lender could send out "verification of employment" forms for the employer to fill in and return, or the lender could use a streamlined verification method called TimeSaver, which allows the lender to contact the employer's personnel office by phone to verify employment, income and any overtime.

If a borrower is employed by a relative or family-owned business, federal income tax returns must be provided to the lender.

The following is a checklist of additional income sources that might be considered:

- ☐ Part-time income can be counted, provided it has been uninterrupted for the past two years and is expected to continue; seasonal work is acceptable and the borrower needs assurance that he/she will be hired back for the next season.

- ☐ Overtime and bonus income that has occurred for the past two years and which will probably continue can be counted. (If the employer doesn't say that the overtime will end, it can be considered to continue.) The lender will average the past two years' income; if the income is more than 25 percent of borrower's total income, income tax returns must be provided.

- ☐ Raises guaranteed to occur within 60 days of loan closing may be included for the purpose of qualifying.

Other income sources could include the following:

- ☐ Retirement income
- ☐ Military income
- ☐ Veteran's benefits
- ☐ Social Security income
- ☐ Alimony
- ☐ Child support
- ☐ Notes receivable
- ☐ Interest and dividend income
- ☐ Employer subsidized mortgage payments
- ☐ Trust income

☐   Unemployment benefits

☐   Rental income

☐   Auto allowances and expense account payments

VERIFYING THE BORROWER'S DOWN PAYMENT

Q.   *Does the lender have to verify that the borrower has the down payment?*

Yes. The lender can use methods similar to those previously mentioned for verifying employment: sending out a "verification of deposit" form to be signed by the depository institution where the funds are held, or the TimeSaver method that allows the borrower to provide the last three bank statements to verify the funds.

In addition to the down payment, the lender needs to verify that the required cash reserves are available in an account (usually equal to two months of mortgage payments) after the closing monies are paid out.

USING GIFTED FUNDS AS LEVERAGE

Q.   *It's great that a borrower can use down payment funds given by a relative or institution. But what kind of documentation has to be shown to the lender?*

A gift from a relative must be evidenced by a letter signed by the donor. It must specify the dollar amount of the gift and the date the funds were transferred; list the donor's name, address, phone number and relationship to the borrower; and include the donor's statement that no repayment is expected.

The lender must verify that the funds are in the donor's account or have been transferred to the borrower's account. This could mean obtaining a copy of the donor's withdrawal slip and the borrower's deposit slip, or a copy of the donor's canceled check.

If funds haven't been transferred prior to settlement, the donor can give the closing agent a certified check for the amount of the gift.

Because funds borrowed by a donor as a gift to a buyer might later put strain on the buyer to repay the amount, some lenders will want to check the donor's account history to determine the original source of the gift (for example, to ensure that the donor has been accumulating it in a savings account). The donor should be advised that this investigation could occur so that he or she won't be personally offended if it does.

If a gift or grant comes from a church, municipality or nonprofit organization, it must be evidenced by a copy of an award, gift letter or the legal agreement that specifies the grant or gift's terms and conditions. In addition, the lender must include a copy of the documents showing the transfer of the funds.

CITIZENSHIP NOT A REQUIREMENT

Q. *Does a borrower have to be a U.S. citizen to qualify for a loan to be sold to the secondary market?*

No, mortgages can be made to resident aliens. A lawful, permanent U.S. resident can qualify under the same terms and conditions as a U.S. citizen. He or she must prove residency with an Alien Registration Card or a green card.

Mortgages can be made to nonpermanent resident aliens as well, as long as the borrower occupies the property as a primary residence and the loan-to-value ratio does not exceed 75 percent.

REFINANCING WITH CONVENTIONAL LOANS

Q. *What kinds of refinancing guidelines does the secondary market use?*

Guidelines for Changing Loan Interest Rate or Term

- Loan-to-value ratio on owner-occupied properties can't exceed 95 percent.
- When subordinate financing (a second mortgage) is less than one year old, FNMA will not allow it to be paid off from the proceeds of a "no cash out" refinance.

- Junior liens (second mortgages) obtained through FHLMC must have had at least one year of payments from the origination date of the mortgage in order to be refinanced. If not, it is considered as a cash out and all applicable guidelines apply.
- Loan-to-value ratios on investment property and second homes cannot exceed 70 percent.

Guidelines for Pulling Equity (Cash) Out

Loan-to-value ratios on owner-occupied properties cannot exceed 75 percent. This option is not available on second homes or investor properties.

Q. *Does an owner who refinances have to requalify with the lender, just as with a new loan?*

A streamlined refinance procedure is available to the borrower who doesn't have to requalify based on ratios. This option is available only if the new loan will be placed with the same lender, the loan will remain a conventional loan and the borrower's income has not declined. In addition, the borrower's mortgage payment record has to be satisfactory for the past 12 months and the new mortgage payment can't exceed the old payment by more than 15 percent.

CLOSING COSTS

Q. *Does the secondary market require that the borrower pay certain closing costs?*

The secondary market requires that the borrower pay the following prepaid settlement costs:

- Interest charges and real estate taxes for any period after the settlement date
- Hazard insurance premiums
- Impounds for PMI, unless it is financed as part of the mortgage amount

Other costs may be paid by the buyer or seller, based on what they've negotiated. As discussed previously, however, these would be considered contribution amounts and would have maximum limits before being subtracted from the appraised value of the property, before the maximum loan was calculated.

Exceptions to contributions are third parties who are not participants in the sale, including the buyer's relatives or an employer. There are no restrictions as to the amounts they can pay, but the funds might need to be tracked as gifted monies. The borrower should check with the lender regarding specific examples of nonparticipant funds that could be used. For buyer and seller cost estimate sheets, see Appendix A.

Q. *Besides 20-year and 30-year amortization schedules, what other types of conventional loan programs will the secondary market accept?*

Besides the 30 types of ARM that the secondary market will purchase, some of which we'll discuss in the next chapter, lenders can originate myriad programs.

Programs vary from somewhat common construction-permanent financing to infrequently used leasehold estate loans, and everything in between! There are loans for cooperative housing, energy improvement, rehabilitation of properties and loans for manufactured housing.

Biweekly, growing equity and balloon mortgage programs give borrowers differing degrees of leverage to help them purchase; these concepts will be discussed in depth in Chapter 10.

Several of the more familiar programs include the employer-assisted Magnet loan, designed for corporations to assist their employees in purchasing homes, and the two-step mortgage in which the loan is fixed for five or seven years, depending on the program, and then adjusts to a new fixed-rate loan for the balance of the 30-year term.

COMMUNITY HOMEBUYER PROGRAMS

Perhaps the best secondary market programs for moderate income buyers are the community lending programs, also known as community homebuyer programs or 3-2 option mortgages.

These programs were born out of the federal government's Community Redevelopment Act to provide affordable housing to a larger sector of Americans.

These programs provide leverage for buyers by providing 95 percent loans. Borrowers need only 3 percent down payments, while family-member gifts, community bond programs, churches or nonprofit sources can provide the remaining 2 percent down payment.

"Sweat equity," work traded for down payments or closing costs, is also acceptable in the program.

Qualifying ratios are easier, too, for borrowers under this program; housing debt can comprise up to 33 percent, and long-term debt up to 38 percent, of their gross monthly income. These guidelines can be exceeded if strong compensating factors can be shown (such as a history of paying high rent). Unlike other conventional secondary market programs, this program can waive two-month cash reserves of extra mortgage payment monies.

Another feature of the community homebuyer programs is that borrowers receive education on homebuying and home affordability aspects. Buyers are requested to attend classes or complete workbook projects instructing them in how to purchase a home and how to trim costs of ownership, including energy efficiency and home maintenance.

As you might guess, the overall response to these community homebuying programs has been positive, and it appears that this type of home affordability program will become an American staple.

Q. *Are these lower-down payment conventional loans the start of a financing trend?*

It appears so. Several major mortgage companies are initiating loans requiring just 3 percent down to assist low and moderate-income borrowers. These pilot programs were initiated because the community homebuyers programs have been so successful and defaults relatively low.

As with the community homebuyer programs, 97 percent loans will require buyers to complete a homebuyer education course.

Fannie Mae has agreed to purchase these loans in the secondary market in loan amounts not to exceed 115 percent of area median income.

In addition, FNMA expects to purchase over $150 billion in mortgage loans over the next several years to assist low and moderate-income minorities and immigrants. These loans would target eleven "gateway" cities across the United States to provide affordable housing.

CHAPTER 5

PRIVATE MORTGAGE INSURANCE AND CONVENTIONAL LOANS

Lender guidelines and the rules of the secondary market restrict the ability of lenders to make high loan-to-value mortgages without some guarantee against borrower default. Private mortgage insurance allows lenders to increase their loan-to-value ratios and still sell their mortgages in the secondary market. If it approves the loan, the PMI company will issue a commitment to insure the lender. With this guarantee, the lender can increase the loan amount to as much as 95 percent of the property value. The borrower pays the PMI premium and gets the benefit of a smaller down payment.

The biggest challenge for most first-time homebuyers is raising the money for the down payment. Private mortgage insurance is therefore one key to affordable housing, making the dream of home ownership possible for many.

This chapter explains the cost of PMI and how it impacts the mortgage. The focus is in how PMI companies work with lenders of conventional loans. Federal Housing Administration has its own insurance program, which is covered in Chapter 8. VA loans, described in Chapter 8, are guaranteed.

THE BASICS OF PRIVATE MORTGAGE INSURANCE

Q. *Is there any way a lender would make a loan to a buyer who might be considered a marginal risk?*

The lender might require that the buyer purchase PMI to indemnify the lender for any loss caused by default during the early years of the loan. Typically, any loan-to-value ratio greater than 80 percent (particularly if the loan is to be sold in the secondary

90

market), will require the purchaser to include PMI as a requirement of securing the loan. Private mortgage insurance originated in the 1940s with the first large carrier, Mortgage Guaranty Insurance Corporation (MGIC), referred to as "magic." For this reason, early PMI methods were termed to "magically" assist in putting together a loan package otherwise unacceptable to the lender! Today, however, the field has broadened to include nine PMI insurance underwriting companies in the United States. (See Figure 5.1 for addresses and phone numbers.)

Q. *How does PMI work?*

PMI companies write insurance protecting approximately the top 20 percent of the mortgage against default, depending on the lender's and investor's requirements, as well as the loan-to-value ratio and the particular loan program involved. (For a claim illustration, see Figure 5.2.) Should a default occur, the lender would sell the property to liquidate the debt and would then be reimbursed by the PMI company for any remaining amount up to the policy value.

Q. *How does the buyer apply for PMI?*

Private mortgage insurance takes on the same qualities as any other insurance—the rates can be shopped for, amenities of policies may vary and certain types of restrictions in coverage do apply.

Although the buyer typically bears the cost of the PMI, the lender is the PMI company's client. Based on this fact, many lenders deal exclusively with only a select number of PMI companies. This rationale is based on the assumption that lenders can do a better job of placing loan risks with one or two companies, since they know the guidelines for those insurers. This supposed strength can turn into a weakness when one of the lender's prime companies turns down a loan because the borrower doesn't fit within its risk parameters. An unenterprising lender might follow suit and deny approval on the loan application without consulting even a second PMI company. Pandemonium results: the buyer is upset, wondering what's wrong with him or her; the lender is

---

Figure 5.1   Private Mortgage Insurance Companies

Amerin Guaranty Corporation
303 East Wacker Drive, Ste. 900
Chicago, IL 60601
(800) 257-7643
Fax: (312) 540-0564

Commonwealth Mortgage Assurance
  Company
1601 Market St.
Philadelphia, PA 19103–2197
(800) 523-1988
Fax: (215) 496-0346

G.E. Capital Mortgage Insurance
  Corporation
P.O. Box 177800
Raleigh, NC 27615
(800) 334-9270
Fax: 919-846-4260

Mortgage Guaranty Insurance
  Corporation
P.O. Box 488, MGIC Plaza
Milwaukee, WI 53201
(800) 558-9900
Fax: (414) 347-6802

PMI Mortgage Insurance
  Company
601 Montgomery St.
San Francisco, CA 94111
(800) 288-1970
Fax: (415) 291-6175

Republic Mortgage Insurance
  Company
P.O. Box 2514
Winston-Salem, NC 27102–9954
(800) 999-7642
Fax: (919) 661-0049

Triad Guaranty Insurance Corporation
P.O. Box 25623
Winston-Salem, NC 27114
(800) 451-4872
Fax: (919) 723-0343

United Guaranty Corporation
P.O. Box 21567
Greensboro, NC 27420
(800) 334-8966
Fax: (919) 230-1946

The Mortgage Insurance Company of
  Canada
1 Dundas Street West
Ste 1600, Box 12
Toronto, Ontario
Canada M5G 1Z3
(416) 977-6254
Fax: (416) 598-1967

---

apologetic while responding that the borrower didn't meet the underwriting guidelines.

Let's look at it from the lender's point of view. He or she desires the very best quality as well as an assurance that the PMI company will stand behind its loan guarantee commitment. And today, with tough times abound for many types of insurance companies,

Figure 5.2　　PMI Claim Illustration

Original Purchase Price	$100,000
Original Loan (10% Down)	$ 90,000
Principal Balance Due	$ 88,915
Accumulated Interest	
(excluding penalty interest and late charges)	7,850
Subtotal	$ 96,765
Attorneys' Fees	$ 2,420
Property Taxes	1,140
Hazard Insurance (Premiums Advanced)	710
Property Maintenance (Preservation Expenses)	350
Disbursement and Foreclosure Cost	525
Subtotal	$101,910
Less Escrow Balances and Rent Received	240
Total Claim	$100,670

Generally after a lender has instituted foreclosure and acquired evidence of marketable title to the property, a claim can be submitted. On receiving the claim, the insurer will decide whether to pay the entire claim and take title to the property or pay the coverage amount stated in the policy. The insurer will typically take title only in those cases when acquisition and sale by the insurer is likely to reduce the insurer's loss. When the insurer does take title, the lender will receive the full amount of the claim.

On receiving this claim, the insurer will attempt to determine the likely resale price. The expenses resulting from a sale would include the real estate agent's commission and other settlement costs, which on average would run at about 10 to 15 percent of the sale price. The insurer obtains this and other information in order to decide what option to take. From the lender's perspective, if the policy was written with 25 percent coverage, the claim payment option made by the insurer would have been $25,168, which means the lender could sell the property for approximately $80,000 and not suffer loss.

Reproduced with permission of Mortgage Insurance Companies of America.

lenders are putting an even higher priority on the strength and credibility of the PMI companies with which they do business. This was recently brought to my attention when a local lender told me of hundreds of thousands of dollars in PMI claims that appear to be currently uncollectible due to a PMI company's bankruptcy.

The lender has an increasingly difficult task to be fair to the borrower while shopping for the most effective method to soften liability. Sometimes, it may appear that a lender has no justification for doing what he or she does—but look deeper, it's undoubtedly there.

Q. *What can the buyer or agent do if PMI is denied by one insurer?*

If PMI is denied by one insurer, consider the following possibilities:

- The borrower can ask the lender to submit the application to another (or several other) PMI insurers. A list of those licensed to do business in the borrower's state can be obtained from the state's insurance commission. Note, however, that the first question asked by the subsequent PMI company may be, "Has this party ever been denied insurance?" It's difficult to tell just how much impact the answer to this question has on consideration of the application. If the lender refuses to shop for another insurer, the borrower may not only be teaming up with the wrong PMI company, but the lender also may leave much to be desired!
- The borrower can ask the lender to hold the loan "in portfolio." Since PMI is primarily a strong requirement of the secondary market, a local lender may not require it should he or she decide to keep the loan in-house. The buyer might entice the lender to keep the loan by increasing the note rate, increasing the origination fees or transferring accounts held with other lenders. Nevertheless, sidestepping PMI in a 30-year loan (not to mention getting the loan in the first place) is well worth a few more dollars up-front.
- The borrower can explore ways to decrease the loan-to-value ratio so that PMI will not be required by the secondary market. If increasing the down payment is out of the question, the seller could be asked to carry a second for 15 percent of the sales price; the buyer would then secure a 75 percent loan, while coming in with a 10 percent down payment. The secondary market will currently pur-

chase loans with subordinate (second mortgage) financing if the first mortgage does not exceed 75 percent loan-to-value. The lender, however, will consider the debt service payment to the seller on the second mortgage in the qualifying ratios for the first mortgage. The lender will also want to see a copy of the security document on the second mortgage that its impact can be considered in the loan underwriting of the first mortgage, especially regarding large monthly payments or balloon payments.

- A gift letter donor could be located for the down payment, leaving the borrower's funds to be used as an additional amount down; or the borrower could team up with a relative or friend to create a coborrower situation.

Sometimes the denial from the PMI company may be a way for a lender to escape from an obligation he or she was not crazy about in the first place. That's why asking what the true problem is will help you get to the root of the matter.

THE COST OF PRIVATE MORTGAGE INSURANCE

Q. *What does PMI cost?*

Costs vary from insurer to insurer, as well as from plan to plan. PMI fees can be paid in several ways, depending on the PMI company used. Typical payment plans are "annuals" and "singles."

The annual plan has the borrower paying the first-year premium at closing, then an annual renewal premium is collected monthly as part of the total monthly house payment. This annual payment is remitted annually to the PMI company and is the traditional way private mortgage insurance has been paid.

Q. *How is PMI calculated?*

The calculation method can be best explained through an example, such as the following:

The Barkers are told that the PMI company being used to insure their $100,000 loan requires an up-front first-year premium of one-half of 1 percent of the loan amount ($100,000 × .50% = $500 at closing). In addition, their monthly PMI premium of .34 percent (added to their PITI payment) will be $28.33 ($100,000 × .34% = $340 annual premium, divided by 12 months = $28.33 per month). Every month thereafter, until the loan is paid off or the borrower petitions the lender to have the PMI removed, that premium will be paid by the borrower.

OPTIONS

Q. *How does the singles premium plan for PMI differ from the traditional method?*

The singles payment plan allows the borrower to pay a one-time single premium, instead of a first-year premium and an annual renewal premium. Since single premiums typically are financed as part of the mortgage loan amount, no out-of-pocket cash is used for mortgage insurance at closing. While this is good news for cash-poor borrowers, it's not without a cost. The premium will have interest tacked onto it since it's financed with the loan. Even though interest is deductible and the traditional PMI monthly payment is not, the borrower should evaluate if this makes economic sense, particularly if the property will be held a long time.

Q. *If a borrower did finance the PMI into the loan, could he or she ever get it back?*

Possibly. The single payment plans offer the choice of refundable or nonrefundable premiums (with the exception of Pennsylvania and South Carolina, where nonrefundable premiums are not available). A refundable premium allows the borrower the opportunity to receive money back on any unused portion in the event mortgage insurance coverage is discontinued before the loan is paid in full.

The first-year cost on a nonrefundable premium is slightly less than that of a refundable premium, thereby giving the borrower a small up-front savings. If coverage is discontinued on a loan with a nonrefundable premium, the borrower has no opportunity for a refund.

Q. *Does the borrower have to pay the PMI premiums? (especially the up-front cost)?*

This is more custom than law. According to most PMI companies, there is no requirement as to who pays the premiums. Secondary market guidelines, however, require the borrower to pay the impounds for recurring premiums. But if the loan is not being sold to the secondary market and the buyer is a bit short on cash to close, the borrower could negotiate with the seller (or other third party) to assist with the initial PMI fee. Since it does become part of the monthly principal and interest obligation, the lender will consider it as part of that monthly payment for qualifying purposes. It may not happen frequently, but there may be times when including the payment of monthly PMI premiums makes a difference in the amount of loan the buyer can afford.

Q. *Does PMI insure only first mortgages?*

No. Some PMI insurers will take on second mortgage risks. Be prepared, however, to pay some heftier premiums for second mortgage insurance.

Q. *Can PMI ever be removed?*

It depends. Although PMI serves to protect the lender only on the top portion of the loan, many loans never have it removed.

There may be several reasons why PMI insurance is not removed from a loan: First, and most important, PMI is removed on a case-by-case basis. Just as each property is unique, so is each borrowing situation. And lenders, as well as PMI companies, feel that since they lent funds and insured the loan in the first place, PMI should be left intact unless the situation can remain stable once it is removed. This is why PMI premiums are still being made on some old loans. The choice to short-rate premiums back to the mortgagor is based on the particular program as well as the insurer.

Many people assume loans, not knowing that PMI is a part of them. Even if they do see it as an itemization on their mortgage receipts, they may not know that they could petition to have it removed.

The request to remove PMI may be submitted to the wrong party, such as the servicing agent instead of the owner of the loan. The borrower should determine who owns the loan and make a request to the owner. If the loan has been sold, many times an assignment of ownership will show on public records. Although it's best for the borrower to ask the lender what the current PMI removal guidelines are, based on the lender and where the loan has been sold, here are some standard guidelines:

- Borrower's payments must have been timely.
- A current appraisal justifies that the loan balance is currently 80 percent or less of current market value.
- Borrower's payments must be current.

Remember, PMI removal is based on a case-by-case decision from the lender, who may be working with his or her own board of directors' guidelines.

Q. *How could a buyer best be apprised of the PMI guidelines and regulations?*

The best buyer is an informed buyer. Even though removal guidelines may change somewhat with a particular PMI company and the secondary market during the life of a loan, if the borrower knows the general guidelines up front, decisions can be made *before* taking on a potentially adversarial situation. The borrower should ask the lender the following questions simultaneous to applying for PMI insurance:

1. How many companies' programs will be shopped?
2. How does the selected policy compare overall to others in the marketplace, evaluating the following criteria:

- Rates
- Size of policy (particular loan-to-value ratio insured)
- Current guidelines for removing PMI insurance (such as percentage of equity needed in property or other determinant)
- Ways current guidelines could be expected to change (such as this particular company's history of changes, whether

there are any guaranties against changes and who makes the final decision for removal, e.g., a board of directors?)
- Documents from the lender, outlining the procedure of requesting removal of PMI

Although asking these questions prior to closing the loan won't guarantee an error-free situation, they will bring up facts that need to be known regarding PMI—up front, where it counts!

PMI APPROVAL GUIDELINES

Q. *What can the borrower expect the PMI company to look for in approving him or her for PMI insurance?*

PMI companies look at many of the same questions posed by the lender. In addition, however, they pay particular attention to the answers to the following questions, which have proven to increase the risk factors of default on the loan. Here are some "red flag" questions from PMI insurers:

- Are payment increases scheduled in the loan, and if so, is it feasible that the borrower can meet them?
- Does the loan have a discounted "teaser" rate, such as in some ARMs?
- Are there any temporary buydowns that may mean increased interest, and payments, later on?
- Is the loan-to-value ratio high (particularly for the type of loan used, as well as for the marketplace)?
- To what financial degree is the seller contributing, if any? (Most PMI companies allow up to 3 percent of the sales price for a loan with an over 95 percent loan-to-value ratio, and 6 percent when the loan-to-value ratio is 90 percent and under. Although the appraiser is expected to adjust for seller contributions, the amounts specified are the maximum amounts allowable by most PMI insurers.)
- How much cash does the borrower have on hand? (PMI companies are putting much more emphasis on reserves as a cushion against delinquent payments.)

- Is the economy of the area sound? (Insurers are often wary of single-industry situations.)
- Is there an oversupply of housing in the area? (This might indicate declining market values.)
- How stable is the borrower's employment?
- Is the borrower a professional or unskilled laborer? (While this may appear to be a form of discrimination, blue-collar workers statistically are attributed to higher levels of loan defaults.)
- Is the borrower using a gift letter to fund any part of the purchase?

Q. *What part does the property play in receiving PMI approval?*

Cautious of the impact weak properties have in contributing to defaults, PMI companies are scrutinizing properties much more closely. The following questions address some appraisal "hot buttons":

- How is the neighborhood rated? (Unexplained or unacceptable appraisal explanations of fair and poor neighborhoods indicate factors that may weaken the borrower's commitment to the property. This may negatively affect the insurability of the loan.)
- Who appraised the property? (Most PMI companies reserve the right to declare appraisers and appraisals unacceptable.)
- How does the property compare to others in the area? (If a property is valued at 90 percent or more of the highest property value in the neighborhood, it is considered to be a high-risk property. It may typically suffer from overimprovements and longer marketing times.)
- Is the property physically sound and in good repair? (A low rating in this category may cause the property to be uninsurable.)
- What were the comparable properties used in the appraisal, and where were they located? (Typically, PMI companies will allow no more than one of the three required comparables to be supplied by the lender or developer from his own files unless justified by the ap-

praiser. In addition, except for rural locations, at least two of the three required comparables must be located within one mile of the appraised property, or the difference in location must be fully explained. This one-mile range normally encompasses the neighborhood of the property.)

- Was there a sales concession in the sale? (This might be a chattel item, such as a car or boat, that is included by the seller to consummate the transaction. The value of the item will be deducted from the sales price and appraised value by the PMI company if it has not been deducted by the appraiser.)
- Appraisals generally are valid for one year on both resale and new construction; recertification of value is required on new construction if the appraisal is more than four months old at time of closing.

Q. *So PMI has its own set of qualifying guidelines, one for the borrower and one for the property?*

That's correct. If the borrower or the property doesn't "fit" within one PMI company's guidelines, the lender should take a proactive position to find one that accepts the risk, if possible.

While qualifying for PMI may seem to be an extra hoop for the borrower to jump through, the application and paperwork is handled entirely by the lender. And considering the number of borrowers who couldn't purchase at all because they don't have a 20 percent down payment, the minimal effort and cost that PMI insurance adds doesn't seem like a very great price to pay.

CHAPTER 6

ADJUSTABLE RATE MORTGAGES

The adjustable rate mortgage (ARM) products of the early 1980s gave ARMs an initial "black eye" in the financial marketplace. Many of these early loans were actually RRMs (renegotiable rate mortgages), meaning that on an anniversary date, the mortgagor would have to renegotiate with the mortgagee. This was no easy task, since inflation and interest rates were skyrocketing. Many consumers couldn't qualify for the higher loan rates, forcing them into compromising situations with lenders, which sometimes included selling the property or losing it altogether.

The ARMs of today are much better products, with caps (maximum limits set on interest rate adjustments) and strong secondary market underwriting guidelines, as well as mandatory rate disclosure regulations for lenders. Like any mortgage loan program, ARMs best serve buyers with particular needs to be satisfied and problems to be solved. After we examine how ARM products work, we'll be able to determine which buyers and situations are best suited for this type of loan.

PROS AND CONS

Q. *What are the advantages of ARMs?*

Here they are:

- Lower interest rates (than for fixed rate mortgages) allow the buyer to qualify more easily for the loan or leverage into a more expensive property than he or she could otherwise afford.
- Rates adjust based on increases and decreases in the particular index used, which is a gauge of inflation in the economy. This creates an equitable situation for lender and borrower alike.

- Various indexes are available on which to base the ARM.
- Various adjustment periods are available to the borrower, e.g., six months, one year, three years, five years or ten years.
- Some ARMs can be converted to fixed-rate mortgages during a specific time frame in the loan (e.g., between months 13 and 60)
- Initial lower-than-market "teaser" rates may drastically reduce the borrower's monthly payment in the first year of the loan.
- Many lenders keep ARMs in portfolio, allowing the buyer to request special concessions of the lender, such as no PMI or no monthly reserve account for taxes and insurance.
- Adjustable rate mortgages may be assumable at the current note rate (with the exception of several programs).
- Adjustable rate mortgages are good to use in times of low inflation; they are also good for short-term ownership.

Q. *What are the disadvantages of ARMs?*

The disadvantages are as follows:

- There are no interest rate guarantees, since indexes fluctuate with the economy.
- The buyer's financial situation may change after the loan is cast, making payment increases financially prohibitive for the borrower.
- The buyer may overleverage, using an unrealistically low initial teaser rate to get into the loan.
- The loan may contain a "negative amortization" clause, allowing any shortfall of interest not paid monthly to be added back onto the principal balance. (This could cause a resale nightmare should the buyer have to move while the loan is showing negative amortization. It may also create an unsalable property, with the loan balance exceeding the market value.)
- The buyer may not fully understand ARMs and not be aware that the lender's program is using an unfavorable index as a base.

- The lender may be charging an unusually high margin, the lender's cost of doing business plus profit, which is added to the index to create the interest rate. This margin is set at loan origination and remains constant for the life of the loan.
- Convertible ARMs may have higher interest rates or margins as bonus to the lender. If the buyer chooses not to convert to a fixed-rate mortgage, this premium may defeat any cost savings with the ARM or perhaps make the program less cost-effective than a fixed-rate program might have been.
- Convertible ARMs have conversion fees for fixing the interest; the new fixed rate is not determined by the cost of the lender's current fixed-rate program. It is usually based on the note rate for that particular investor (e.g., FNMA securities) plus an additional $\frac{5}{8}$ percent interest.

THE BASICS OF ADJUSTABLE RATE MORTGAGES

Q. *What's the best way to learn how ARMs work?*

The best place to start in understanding the ARM is to have a working knowledge of its components:

- Index: A financial indicator that rises and falls, based primarily on economic fluctuations. It is usually an indicator of inflation and is therefore the basis of all future interest adjustments on the loan. Mortgage lenders use currently more than 20 indexes.
- Margin: A lender's loan cost and profit. The margin is added to the index to determine the interest rate.
- Initial interest: The rate during the initial period of the loan, which is sometimes lower than the note rate. This initial interest may be a teaser rate, an unusually low rate used to entice buyers and allow them to more readily qualify for the loan.
- Note rate: The actual interest rate charged for a particular loan program.

- Adjustment period: The interval at which the interest is scheduled to change during the life of the loan (e.g., annually).
- Interest rate caps: Limit placed on the up-and-down movement of the interest rate, specified per period adjustment and lifetime adjustment, e.g., a cap of "2 and 6" (2 percent interest increase maximum per adjustment, 6 percent interest increase maximum over the life of the loan).
- Negative amortization: Occurs when a payment is insufficient to cover the interest on a loan. The shortfall amount is added back on to the principal balance.
- Convertibility: The option to change from an ARM to a fixed-rate loan. A conversion fee may be charged.
- Carryover: Interest rate increases in excess of the amount allowed by the caps that can be applied at later interest rate adjustments.

Q. *How are rates set for ARMs?*

Rates are comprised of two components: the index and the margin. The index is an indicator of inflation and can come from a variety of sources. The margin is the cost of doing business for the lender, including profit, and is added onto the index to make the interest rate. This formula is used to determine each interest rate adjustment.

Q. *What are teaser rates and are they a good idea?*

A teaser rate is an unrealistically low introductory rate, less than what the current index plus margin would total. Lenders may offer these to introduce a new program to the marketplace or to boost business. The benefit to the buyer is the lower initial interest and payments (although some lenders qualify the buyer at the fully indexed second-year rate). The danger is that when the payments do adjust, their increase may cause "payment shock," causing the borrower to fall behind or default on the loan. The borrower should go into this type of payment schedule with eyes wide open, particularly if loan qualification is marginal.

Q. *What indexes does a lender use for ARMs?*

Although lenders can choose from more than 20 different indexes, it is not always possible for the consumer to request that a certain index be used with the loan program desired. The lender offers types of loans that the secondary market has agreed to purchase, which includes a predetermined index.

But a consumer could research various ARMs offered by several lenders to determine which programs contain the best combination of indices and program benefits. The informed buyer should be aware of the most common indexes:

Treasury Securities Index

- One-year treasury securities index: This index is currently the basis for approximately 75 percent of all ARMs. It's best to use when rates are high and likely to go down. The initial rate is usually 2 percent or more below the fixed rate. It can adjust quite rapidly, causing quick interest and payment changes. Buyers using this index would be well served to have strong caps.
- Three-year treasury securities index: This is best to use when rates are stable or expected to rise. This index sometimes has sizable gaps between its initial interest rate and that of fixed-rate loans. Over time, however, the gap may decrease, causing a loss of incentive for using an ARM.
- Five-year treasury securities index: This index offers good stability due to long periods between rate adjustments. A disadvantage is that many times the initial gap between this index and the fixed rate is slight. This index is best to use when rates are expected to increase.
- Programs are also available using the ten-year treasury securities index.

For current treasury securities index rates, contact a local lender, *The Wall Street Journal* or *USA Today,* or request *H.15* (a weekly newsletter) from Publications Services, Mail Stop 138, Board of Governors, Federal Reserve System, Washington, DC 20551.

The Federal National Mortgage Association also has a 24-hour hotline, (202) 752-6799, for current index quotes.

Treasury Bills Index

The six-month T-bill is the most volatile of the indexes mentioned here. This index is best to use when interest rates are very high, and rate decreases appear inevitable. The initial rate is usually 2 percent or more below the fixed rate; however, increases happen quickly, causing the buyer's payment to escalate. This index could be termed "fast," as increases and decreases occur quickly.

For current treasury bills index rates, contact a local lender, *The Wall Street Journal* or *USA Today* for information, or request the Federal Reserve bulletin described earlier.

Federal Home Loan Bank Board (FHLBB) Contract Interest Rate Index

The FHLBB index is based on the monthly average contract rate charged by all lenders on mortgage loans for previously occupied homes. It's good to use when this index appears to be at its low point in its cycle. It adjusts very slowly and is therefore preferential to buyers. In addition to averaging fixed-rate loan interest rates, other ARM indexes are also averaged and added into this index, allowing it to stay low. Unlike most other indexes, the contract interest rate index typically carries no additional margin.

For current FHLBB contract interest rate index rates, contact a local lender, *The Wall Street Journal* or *USA Today.*

Eleventh District Cost of Funds Index

The 11th district refers to the 11th District of the Federal Reserve Bank, headquartered in San Francisco, California. This index is generally one of the slowest to adjust, which makes it favorable from the borrower's point of view. Once rates increase, however, they are also slow to decline. That's why you might term this index "slow"—slow to rise, slow to decline. It's particularly good to use on the up side swing of inflation (when rates are rising), rather than when rates are predicted to fall. Be sure to ask the lender, however, how often interest rates can change. If adjustments are as often as monthly, negative amortization might occur, depending on the terms of the loan.

For current 11th district cost of funds index rates, contact a local lender, *The Wall Street Journal* or *USA Today,* or the Federal Reserve District in San Francisco, California.

DISCLOSURE PROVIDED BY LENDERS

Q.   *What does the lender provide to the prospective borrower to help understand the choices available in ARMs?*

The lender provides a great deal of information about ARMs.

First, the lender must give the borrower written disclosure about ARMs either at the time a loan application form is provided or before the consumer pays a nonrefundable fee, whichever comes first.

The lender must make educational material available to the consumer. Many lenders use the *Consumer Handbook on Adjustable Rate Mortgages,* published jointly by the Federal Reserve and the FHLBB.

In addition, the lender provides a worst-case scenario of where the loan could adjust during its life. This will show the borrower how high the monthly payment could go. If that payment is something he or she could not live with or would wake up nights worrying about, an ARM might not be the right type of loan.

As with all types of loans, most lenders are more than happy to prepare comparisons of various types of adjustable rate programs, itemizing up front and overall costs for the life of the loan.

Q.   *What are the requirements for notifying the consumer about ARM interest rate changes during the life of the loan?*

During the term of the outstanding ARM loan, notice must be given to the borrower of an adjusted payment amount, interest rate, index rate and loan balance. This notification must be made once each year during which there is a rate adjustment, regardless of whether there is a payment change. The notice must be mailed not less than 45 days before the new payment amount is due. Further, the disclosure must indicate the extent to which any increase in the interest rate has *not* been fully implemented (e.g., the index rate plus margin would exceed the rate cap). The notice must also state the payment required to fully amortize the loan if it is different.

MARGINS

Q. *If a consumer shopped for the most stable and reasonable index, would that loan result in the lowest interest rate?*

Not necessarily. The index could be a dream, while the loan's margin could be a nightmare! Even though searching for the best index is important, shopping for the lowest margin can make thousands of dollars worth of difference over the life of a loan.

Q. *Who sets an ARM's margin, and how does it affect the interest rate?*

As stated previously, the lender determines the margin, since it is the combination of his or her costs of making the loan, plus profit. The margin is set at the time of loan application and remains constant for the life of the loan. The index rate *plus* the margin combine to make the note or accrual rate, also called the fully indexed rate. So, even if the index is favorable, a high margin could counteract any expected interest savings!

Refer to the comparative example in Figure 6.1. In this example, the one-year treasury index is at 3.75 percent. This index, added to the lender's margin of 2.75 percent would make a note or accrual rate of 6.5 percent. (This note rate isn't necessarily the first-year rate charged by the lender, however, since he or she may give a lower or "teaser" rate to make the loan more attractive to the borrower.) In the example, the lender gave the borrower the 6.5 percent initial interest rate, which is effective until the first interest rate adjustment.

When it's time for the annual review of the interest rate on the loan, the borrower finds that the index has increased 2 percent, to 5.75 percent. After adding the margin of 2.75 percent to the index, the interest rate escalates to 8.5 percent, and the payment jumps to $766.83.

Figure 6.1   Mortgage Comparison—Adjustable Rate Versus Fixed Rate

	Fixed Rate Mortgage	Adjustable Rate Mortgage
Mortgage Amount	100,000	100,000
Interest Rate	9%	6.5%
Year 1	9%	8.5%
Year 2	9%	10.5%
Year 3		
Year 4		
Year 5		
Loan Term	30 years	30 years
Adjustment Period	N/A	1 year
Maximum Cap Per Period	N/A	2%
Lifetime Cap	N/A	6%

	Fixed	Adjustable	Cumulative Savings Adjustable Mortgage Over Fixed
1. Interest Rate, Year One	9%	6.5%	
2. Monthly Payment x 12	9,655	7,585	
3. Total Payments Made, End of Year One (#2, above)	9,655	7,585	2,070
4. Interest Rate, Year Two	9%	8.5%	
5. Monthly Payment x 12	9,655	9,193	
6. Total Cumulative Payments, End of Year Two (lines 3 + 5)	19,310	16,778	2,532
7. Interest Rate, Year Three	9%	10.5%	
8. Monthly Payment x 12	9,655	10,879	
9. Total Cumulative Payments, End of Year Three (lines 6 + 8)	28,965	27,657	1,308

While the index may wax and wane, the margin remains fixed for the life of the loan. So, all other points being equal, the loan with the higher margin will end up costing the buyer more.

Q. *Is there ever a time when it would benefit the buyer to take a program with a higher margin?*

Perhaps, if that program had other redeeming characteristics, such as low caps, a good index or a convertibility option to change the ARM into a fixed-rate mortgage. The benefits should financially outweigh the higher margin as far as the borrower is concerned.

Q. *What percent could you expect to be charged for a margin?*

Lenders quote margins anywhere from 1 percent to 4 percent.

Q. *Do all adjustable rate loans have margins?*

No. ARMs using the FHLBB contract interest rate index mentioned previously do not use one in addition to the index. However, this index is typically three-fourths percent, or more, higher than other indexes.

Q. *What factors would cause a lender to charge different margins on various programs?*

Some programs might allow an ARM to be converted into a fixed-rate mortgage while other programs might charge higher margins for the privilege of using a more stable index. Or a lender might have a loan program that makes other concessions that he or she needs to cover in the form of a higher ongoing charge (margin). Some lenders may be willing to negotiate slightly on margins if they could be shown trade-offs such as higher initial interest or loan origination fees, or the ability to do additional business with the borrower.

INTEREST AND PAYMENT CAPS

Q. *What would prevent the fully indexed rate from hitting astronomical heights?*

Caps. Caps are limits, specified per loan adjustment period (called adjustment caps) as well as for the life of the loan (called lifetime caps), that prevent interest rates from going through the ceiling. Just as they protect the upward movement, so too do they prevent the rate from falling to levels where the loan is no longer cost-effective for the lender.

Q. *Besides knowing what they are, what does a borrower need to know about caps?*

It's important to know what they apply to—the initial rate or the note rate? And, particularly if you're using a teaser rate, do the rate caps apply to the first adjustment?

Q. *Is it possible to find an ARM program that has no caps?*

It's possible, but not probable. The Competitive Equality Banking Act of December 1987 prohibits lenders from originating programs without lifetime caps. Instead of a program having an interest adjustment cap, it might have a payment cap, e.g., $7\frac{1}{2}$ percent per adjustment.

Q. *Where do most lenders set caps?*

The range swings are as wide as 1 percent to 3 percent for adjustment period caps, and from approximately 3 percent to 6 percent for lifetime caps. Some loans, however, may have flat rates stated for lifetime caps in lieu of interval amounts, such as "the rate cannot drop below 8 percent or exceed 14 percent during the life of the loan."

Q. *How do payment caps work?*

Just like the rate cap, a payment cap limits the amount a monthly payment can increase per adjustment period. A normal range of payment caps is anywhere between 5 percent to 12 percent, with 7.5 percent being the most common. This is because it takes a payment change of approximately 7.5 percent to offset 1 percent of interest increase in a loan. It's also possible to have rate caps and payment caps in the same loan.

Q. *Aren't payment caps better than interest rate caps because a buyer can gauge exactly what the maximum payment adjustment will be and budget for it?*

No, they may not be the best way to control the buyer's situation; in fact, they could do some harm. Critics of payment caps claim that they may be a prime cause of negative amortization in loans. This is caused when the interest increases, but the payment doesn't adjust to fully cover the additional interest. The shortfall is tacked back onto the principal balance, resulting in interest-on-interest and less equity in the property. Consider the example of a loan with payment caps of 2 percent per period and 6 percent lifetime, but the payment cap specifies a 7.5 percent payment increase per adjustment. If the fully indexed rate allows the full adjustment of 2 percent, while payments increase to cover only 1 percent, there is a 1 percent interest shortfall.

The alternative, of course, is to have the buyer pay off the negative amortization or increase the payment beyond the specified adjustment. Most lenders don't enforce the first option but do enforce the second, based on what the mortgage allows.

Q. *What kinds of questions should borrowers ask themselves before getting into an ARM with a payment cap?*

First of all, do they anticipate that their incomes will increase to cover the additional monthly payments? They should also ask themselves how much they could afford to have the loan increase —in other words, what is their threshold of pain?

Next, they should ask whether the loan has a maximum amount of negative amortization allowed. This is important so that leverage can be controlled, particularly any in excess of the property value. Within this should be the question of whether the property's value will increase enough to offset any negative amortization.

Finally, but perhaps most important, borrowers should measure the gap between the interest rate and the payment cap. As seen in the earlier example, the greater the difference, the greater the risk of potential negative amortization.

Obviously, payment caps, just as ARMs, need to be evaluated based on the desires and capabilities of the individual borrower.

NEGATIVE AMORTIZATION, CARRYOVER AND ADJUSTMENT PERIODS

Q. *Why would anyone want a loan with negative amortization in it?*

If handled prudently, negative amortization doesn't have to be a time bomb. For example, if the property is appreciating and the borrowers are able to increase monthly payments over time to make up for the interest shortfall, it may not have any adverse effects. Remember, too, negative amortization is a form of leverage—used wisely, it's good business; used haphazardly, it's a keg of dynamite.

Q. *Obviously, most lenders aren't crazy about negative amortization. How do they handle it?*

Lenders deal with negative amortization in one of several ways. First, they limit the amount that can accrue on a loan, usually to a ceiling of 125 percent of the original loan balance. If the lender deems it necessary, he or she can ask to increase the monthly payments to extend the loan's term, or that the borrower make a cash payment to reduce the balance.

Most lenders today are lessening negative amortization up front by requesting larger down payments, particularly in programs where this problem of deferred interest is liable to occur. In addition, many are not marketing ARMs containing negative amortization.

Q. *How does carryover differ from negative amortization?*

Carryover is excess interest that can't be charged during an adjustment period because the caps prevent it; unlike negative amortization, however, carryover is not added onto the principal to increase its size. The amount of the carryover is noted on the loan and is applied by the lender at a subsequent adjustment period. For example, if the interest rate could jump a maximum 2 percent cap from 6 percent to 8 percent, but the total rate change would have been 3 percent to 9 percent, the extra 1 percent could be applied at a future adjustment. Carryover deals with the interest rate change, whereas negative amortization deals with the principal balance and the payment amount.

Q. *How can the borrower be protected from excessive carryover in a loan?*

The best answer, of course, is to avoid loans with carryover provisions. The next-best answer is to make sure that any carryover language contains limitations as to how much carryover can be applied and for what term it is effective. Most loans, for example, specify that carryover doesn't exceed the amount of the lifetime cap on the loan. The borrower should have the lender's rules clearly explained regarding carryover before entering into a loan agreement. Even though carryover has a different application than negative amortization, its overall impact is still the same— significantly higher interest over the life of the loan.

Q. *If the adjustment period on the interest rate is different from the payment adjustment, could this be another potential cause of negative amortization?*

Absolutely! Two potential types of adjustment periods can occur in ARMs—one for the interest rate and one for the payment. Although most ARMs adjust both simultaneously, some may adjust the interest rate monthly while adjusting the payment annually. If rates are rising, there could be a potential shortage of payment, resulting in the unpaid shortfall being added back onto the principal amount. Although most lenders do attempt to keep both adjustments in sync, some lenders using the 11th district cost of funds index adjust interest monthly and the payment annually.

Q. *Can the borrower choose the adjustment periods for his or her loan?*

It depends. Not all loans offer a choice of adjustment periods. This is based not only on the lender's decision, but also on the index used. For example, the three-year treasury note index program will have the interest and the payment adjustment period at the same time—every three years!

Borrowers should gauge the adjustment period to probable increases in income, if possible. A young doctor setting up practice and purchasing his or her first home might be wise to go with a three-year or longer adjustment period to allow time for getting the heavy start-up costs of the business out of the way, and for stabilizing income before any hefty payment increases take place.

Q. *How much impact would rate trends have on the adjustment period chosen?*

Quite a lot. If rates appear to be edging upward, a borrower would not want a program that adjusts monthly. To sidestep negative amortization, the borrower would not want a program where the rate adjusted monthly while the payment adjusted annually. With rising rates, the longer the adjustment period, the better. However, lenders may charge higher rates on longer-adjusting programs, so this should be a consideration. Most lenders prefer the one-year adjustment term and will usually reflect this preference in their rates and fees.

If rates appear to be falling, a quicker adjustment period may help to bring down the rate. Remember, too, as discussed previously, the particular index chosen has an impact on how rapidly the changes occur.

Q. *Is there a time during the year when rates have historically been higher? If so, wouldn't borrowers want to avoid having their loans adjust at this time?*

Not all indexes are based on one certain rate at a given point in time. They may reflect an average of rates over a period. There are peak borrowing times that may affect mortgage interest rates, even though it's hard to tell what direct impact they have on the index. This is late spring (from April through July), and again in the fall (late August through early October). One rationale here may be that first-time buyers get the itch to buy when everything is green and new in the spring, followed by families who need to move prior to school starting in the fall. During these peak buying times, lenders' origination fees tend to inch up. This is nothing more than the effect of supply and demand on the marketplace.

CONVERTIBLE OPTIONS

Q. *Wouldn't it be best for the borrower to choose an ARM that could be converted to a fixed rate, in case interest rates went wild?*

Although the convertibility option has gotten a lot of press since appearing in ARM programs, it is not for everyone. The convertibility option allows the borrower to convert the rate from adjustable status to a fixed rate, but not without a cost. Just as when a customer chooses cherry pie from an à la carte cafeteria line, there is a price to pay. The same is true of ARM options. Although the cost may not be readily apparent, it will be reflected in a higher lender's margin, a higher interest rate or steeper origination fees.

A borrower who chooses the convertibility option in a loan and fails to use it is tacking on useless costs that may make the ARM less cost-effective than a fixed-rate program. Loan options are like items in the cafeteria line—the more you choose, the more you pay. The conversion option can be the cherry pie in a loan program—eat the pie and the customer is glad to have paid the price—leave the pie on the table, and the customer has wasted money!

Q. *When would a convertibility option in an ARM benefit a borrower?*

Conversion options make sense in several circumstances. First, when interest rates are high but the borrower feels that they will go down. The reasoning is that a borrower can benefit initially by the adjustable rate being lower than a fixed rate; and, when rates do fall, he or she can lock into a reasonable fixed-rate program without requalifying or paying the costs of refinancing.

Second, convertibility options make sense when an ARM is chosen for its attractive initial rates, but the borrower feels that rates in general are edging up. This may apply to a borrower who needs the initial qualifying leverage of the lower rate, but may be leery of being locked long-term into an adjustable rate program. It's not just the cost of the convertibility option that is being weighed, but also the overall cost of the ARM loan package (including origination fees, margins and the particular index), compared to the costs of the fixed-rate package.

Ownership periods have a lot to do with convertibility options, also. Obviously, if a borrower chooses the ARM for short-term ownership, he or she may not benefit from paying extra for a convertibility option. On the other hand, if ARM programs are not the norm in a market area, having the convertibility option available to a new purchaser assuming a loan may be an entice-ment.

Q. *How long does a borrower have in which to exercise the conversion option?*

The conversion option period varies from loan to loan. One of the most common periods, however, is between months 13 and 60. Some lenders prefer exercise of the option only on the anniversary date (e.g., at years one, two or three). Most loans do state a maximum time during which the conversion must take place. If not exercised, the option is lost.

In addition, the conversion option may be void if the loan is assumed. This will usually be stated on an addendum rider to the ARM. It's critical that the borrower realize this before misrepresenting to a new assumptor that the loan can later be converted.

Q. *Can a borrower predict what the new fixed rate will be when he or she exercises the convertibility option?*

It depends. A few lenders may quote a predetermined rate, but most will wait to compute the new rate until the option is taken. Contrary to popular belief, when an ARM is converted to a fixed-rate mortgage, the borrower does not receive the lender's current 30-year interest rate for fixed-rate loans. Adjustable rate mortgages sold into the secondary market base the new rate on the 30-day commitment price of treasury securities *plus* an additional five-eighths percent. These commitment rates are typically higher than what you would expect to pay if you initially were to receive a fixed-rate loan. So this rate, coupled with an additional five-eighths percent, may lessen the attractiveness of the conversion to a fixed-rate loan, and of the convertibility option in general.

Q. *By now, we know enough to ask what the cost of converting the loan from ARM to a fixed-rate mortgage will be!*

Good for you! In the past several years, these costs have become much more tempered. In fact, most fees to convert the adjustable rate to a fixed rate range from $100 to $250, although loans held in portfolio might have substantially different fees. This is one question the borrower should ask up front before closing the

ARM. There should be no reason why a definitive answer regarding conversion fees can't be given at that time.

ASSUMPTION OPTIONS

Q. *What about assuming an ARM? Is it possible?*

Although it depends on the loan, many adjustable rate loans are assumable at the current rate and terms. Exceptions to assumability could be programs that have convertibility options. Once converted to fixed rates, they are no longer assumable.

Other adjustables that are not assumable include the two-step program and the so-called *Stable* loan (which will be reviewed later in this chapter).

The borrower should ask to see a copy of the current assumption guidelines *prior* to loan origination. Note, however, that although these are the guidelines in effect at that time, many institutions allow their boards of directors to change the assumption guidelines should the need arise.

Q. *Is it true that some lenders require the new assumptor of an ARM to be even more qualified than the original purchaser?*

This is very often true. Before releasing the original obligor, the lender wants to be guaranteed that the new assumptor is as qualified, if not more so, than the original borrower. Part of the rationale here is that the interest rate may have been adjusted substantially higher, creating even more of a risk for the lender. While the loan disclosure statement may state that the loan is assumable, it generally does not state the specific conditions for the assumption. The terms and conditions specified in the deed of trust, mortgage, addendum rider or note will give more in-depth assumption specifics.

Q. *I'm sure you can guess the next question—what are typical assumption fees on ARM loans?*

The answer to this question may sound familiar: They vary! New buyers should always check assumption fees with the lender before agreeing to assume a loan.

OTHER RISKS

Q. *Do ARMs contain prepayment penalties if the loan is paid in full prior to the due date?*

Not usually, but it could most likely occur if a loan had a low teaser rate to entice borrowers into a program. If rates did rise, causing borrowers to refinance into a competing lender's program, the first lender would stand to lose a sizable amount of money— thus the prepayment penalty. However, were the borrower to refinance with the same lender, the penalty might be waived. This is yet another point that makes for great negotiation in the early stages of choosing a lender and a loan program.

Private Mortgage Insurance

Q. *Doesn't PMI shield the lender from risk with ARMs?*

Yes, to a degree. Even though PMI is typically used to insure the lender from the borrower's default on approximately the top 20 percent of the loan, lenders have recently required borrowers under some ARM programs to insure lesser loan-to-value ratios.

Private mortgage insurance for ARMs can come at considerable cost. As with the fixed-rate PMI program, ARMs have the initial premium (paid up front or financed at time of loan closing), *plus* the recurring premium (based on a percentage of the declining principal balance of the loan), paid monthly with the PITI payment. The PMI premium rates for ARMs can be as much as 25 percent higher than for fixed-rate loans. For some borrowers, this may mean that what they have saved by using the ARM has been partially eroded by increased PMI costs. Be sure to add this increased cost when comparing adjustable programs to those of fixed-rate programs.

Q. *Can a borrower shop around to get the ARM buyer's PMI rates down?*

It certainly wouldn't hurt. But keep in mind that many times a PMI insurer will have lower rates for a certain program because its risk is minimized in some way, such as through tougher qualifying criteria for the buyer. Because many ARM buyers are already fairly leveraged, this is often the straw that breaks the camel's back. The borrower wouldn't want to put a high priority on securing lower PMI rates just to find that he or she has not qualified for the loan according to the PMI company's underwriting guidelines.

Don't forget the possibility of this option: Ask that the lender keep the adjustable rate loan in portfolio, since ARMs tend to be the most profitable of loans for lenders. In this way, the lender may choose to waive PMI insurance or to self-insure. Either way, it will probably mean less cost to the borrower.

THE QUALIFYING PROCESS

Q. *In general, isn't it easier to qualify for an ARM?*

Since interest rates for ARMs tend to be lower than for fixed-rate loans, this is typically true. Many lenders, however, work within the FNMA secondary market guidelines that require a borrower to be qualified at the first adjustment period rate if the loan has 2 percent annual adjustment caps, a term longer than 15 years and a loan-to-value ratio over 75 percent. The rationale is that equity in a higher-leveraged loan tends to build slowly, increasing the lender's up-front risk on the loan. The Federal Home Loan Mortgage Corporation uses an even more detailed approach to qualifying ARM borrowers, based on loan-to-value ratios and buydowns.

As an additional safeguard, FNMA requires that the borrower be qualified at a minimum rate of 7 percent on loans with start rates below 7 percent. This can defeat some of the qualifying leverage of bargain-basement low rates for borrowers.

Q. *What loan-to-value ratios can a borrower get on an ARM and what are the qualifying ratios?*

Traditionally, a borrower can get up to a 90 percent loan-to-value loan with qualifying ratios of 28 percent housing debt and up to 36 percent long-term debt.

If the interest rate on the loan is temporarily reduced by buying down the interest rate, the long-term debt ratio for qualifying will be reduced to 33 percent.

The borrower may be able to find a lender willing to make a 95 percent loan with an adjustable rate. Since this type of loan would increase the lender's risk, the borrower could expect tighter qualifying guidelines and higher PMI premiums.

As with all qualifying ratios, lenders could allow these ratios to be exceeded if fully documented with compensating factors. For example, a borrower who has a history of above-average income growth or a recent college graduate who has obtained professional employment with high growth potential might be allowed to exceed traditional ratios. For more information, see the qualification sheet found in Appendix A.

PROGRAM TYPES

Q. *How many different types of ARMs are there?*

Since ARMs are designed to "fit" borrowers' financial situations, more ARMs exist than can be enumerated here. There are currently 30 FNMA ARMs alone!

The following are some of the most common combinations of terms, caps and options a borrower might find. The first number in the cap is the maximum amount of interest rate adjustment per period, and the second number is how high the interest could go over the life of the loan.

- One-year treasury securities index, with caps of 1 and 5 percent with or without convertibility option to fixed rate
- One-year treasury securities index, with caps of 2 and 6 percent, with or without convertibility option to fixed rate
- Three-year index, with caps of 2 and 6 percent, convertible at first or second interest rate change date
- 3-1 ARM, fixed rate for the first three years, then adjusts on every anniversary date thereafter, with a cap of 2 percent per adjustment
- Cost of funds index, 6-month adjustments; caps of 1 and 6 percent, has a convertibility option
- One-year treasury securities index, with caps of 7.5 and 5 percent over the life of the loan; allows negative amortization

Q. *How does the two-step mortgage work?*

It may help to think of the two-step mortgage as a 30-year fixed-rate loan with one rate adjustment during its life. Tied to the ten-year Treasury index, the two-step has a fixed interest rate for the first five or seven years, depending on the program chosen. After that, the interest rate adjusts once to a new fixed rate, where it remains for the life of the loan.

Because the initial scheduled payment is lower, the two-step can help a borrower qualify for a larger loan than might have been allowed for a 30-year fixed loan. It's also good for short-term ownership.

Q. *What is the Stable mortgage?*

The Stable mortgage is an ARM tied to the treasury securities index, with caps of two and six, and which adjusts annually. The unique feature of the Stable mortgage is that it blends some of the features of the ARM with those of the fixed-rate loan. Thus, it's more stable than the standard ARM.

Here's how it works. The margin for a Stable loan is higher than with other adjustable loans, requiring that only 50 percent of the index be added to adjust the interest rate per period. The result is less volatility in payments than with a traditional ARM. But the trade-off is that the borrower would have a higher initial interest rate than with a standard ARM program.

Q. *Is the Federal Housing Administration's ARM a good program?*

Yes, the FHA ARM is a good program. First, it has 1 percent annual and 5 percent lifetime caps. These are becoming more and more rare in the marketplace, so it's good to find them within an affordable program. Second, the program contains no negative amortization. Many times with low caps, negative amortization defeats the other cost-effective qualities of a program. That's not a concern with the FHA ARM. And third, and perhaps most important, the qualifying and down payment requirements are the same as those under the standard FHA 203.b. loan-program.

If there is a shortcoming to the program, it may be in the index used. It's based on the treasury bills index. This index tends to adjust fairly quickly in times of rising inflation, although the caps of this program will prevent runaway interest.

The FHA ARM does allow the borrower to qualify at the initial rate and will even allow coborrowers on the loan who do not have to reside on the property. Therefore, it's particularly good for first-time purchasers, which is exactly what FHA loans should be about.

CALCULATION ERRORS

Q. *With changes on potentially hundreds, if not thousands, of loans held by a lender, do errors ever occur in adjusting rates?*

Yes, they do, and it's up to each borrower to monitor adjustments on his or her individual loan and query the lender if it appears an error has been made.

Each loan has its own set of variables, including the date the loan is to be recalculated, the index to use and how the interest is to be rounded off. In times of volatile rates, an error in one or all of these areas could change the outcome of the interest rate.

That's why it's wise for the borrower to check his or her loan documents to determine when adjustments are calculated and then check the particular index used on that date. This can be found in *The Wall Street Journal, USA Today* and most major newspapers. If the borrower checks index information on the renewal/adjustment date and compares that information to what the lender sends notifying of any adjustment, the borrower can help safeguard against errors. If the information is different, the original lender or current loan servicer (where payments are mailed) should be contacted. Most lenders have a review process in place to field and answer borrower inquiries.

Warning signs that a borrower may need to review the ARM include loans with frequent adjustment periods using complicated formulas, loans written prior to 1986 when guidelines were very loose or any loan that has recently been sold to another investor.

QUESTIONS TO ASK

Q. *When is the best time to use an ARM?*

As seen in this chapter, interest rate differentials alone are not enough to justify using an ARM over a fixed-rate loan. The deciding factor should be determined by analyzing the savings between loan programs. As a very broad rule of thumb, if the borrower can save at least $2\frac{1}{2}$ percent in interest by using an ARM, and will hold the property for less than four years, it may pay to go with the ARM. Obviously, the smaller the gap between the fixed and adjustable rates, the less attractive adjustable rates become. Consider the following example:

> Joe Singh knows he is going to be transferred in two years. He can get an ARM today of 6 percent instead of a conventional fixed-rate loan of 8.5 percent. The ARM might be cost effective for him, given his circumstances.
>
> Remember, however there are a lot of variables to compare in selecting a loan, including the up-front costs of borrowing on the two loans.

The smaller the gap between rates, the less attractive adjustable rates become.

Questions To Ask Before Taking Out an ARM

Q. *What questions about the loan should the consumer be able to answer before taking on an ARM?*

- What is the history of the particular index used by the lender? (Ask to see historical documentation.)
- Where do economists think interest rates are currently headed? If up, your interest savings may not be as great as you thought. If down, you may have an even bigger win than anticipated! (Be sure to compare the answer to this question to our previous discussion about index selection.)
- What are the terms of the loan? When does the ARM payment adjust? How will the new rate be figured? What is the maximum to which the payment could rise, and the minimum to which it could fall?
- What is the lender's margin? (Since this remains constant for the life of the loan, it has as much, if not more, impact on where the rate adjusts to as do interest rates.)

- Is there a convertibility option; if so, what does it really cost? (Take into consideration any higher interest rate on the loan as well as conversion fees.) Don't forget to ask how the fixed rate will be determined at the time of conversion. To answer these questions, the borrower should obtain a completed copy of the ARM loan disclosure statement. If the borrower has difficulty weighing the options, he or she should seek the expertise of a financial adviser.
- How long will the property be held? Remember, ARMs are usually most advantageous with short-term ownership (less than approximately four years during times of rising inflation).
- Will the ARM chosen be attractive as an assumable loan when the property is sold? Are there any bells, buzzers or whistles in the loan that would hinder the loan's transferability? What are current assumption fees, as well as policies and procedures for assuming this type of loan?
- What are the up-front costs of the loan? Do they offset any potential interest savings? Is there any creative way to finance these into the loan to eliminate out-of-pocket cash at closing? If so, how will that affect the monthly payment and any future resale value?
- Is the lender willing to hold the loan in portfolio? If so, how might that benefit the buyer?

Q. *Which loan is the best adjustable rate program?*

That's like asking how long someone's legs need to be—the answer to this, of course is, "long enough to reach the ground!" If a particular ARM program suits a buyer's needs, then that's the best loan. Apply the following questions to determine which type of ARM best suits the borrowers' needs:

- What are the borrower's goals in buying this property? If rapid equity buildup is desired, the borrower should stay away from any product containing negative amortization; if the goal is a first home purchase or tight qualification, perhaps a low introductory rate or rate adjustments that

occur every three or five years should be used; index and
margin will also be important.

- How long do the borrowers plan on owning the property?
  Short-term owners should consider a loan with good assumability, a slow-moving index upward, low up-front
  loan origination fees, low down payment and no negative
  amortization.

  Long-term property owners may be wise to avoid
  ARMs completely. If an ARM is selected, however, these
  buyers should select one with a good convertibility option
  with low conversion fees. Index and margin are very important to long-term owners, who could also use more
  leverage going in (including negative amortization), since
  they have more time to recover equity.

- How important will it be to get equity out immediately
  upon selling the property? Purchasers who will need all
  the equity should select a program that is readily assumable at a good market rate and should save the conversion
  option until interest rates hit the absolute lowest point of
  the rate cycle to make the loan more salable. This type
  could use a loan with negative amortization to keep
  equity low.

  Purchasers who won't need all equity, could use a program with more stringent assumption guidelines.

- Who else will participate in the purchase? If there is only
  one purchaser, then virtually all ARM programs are available. Many ARM programs sold into the secondary market may not allow coborrowers; among those that do, each
  has its own strict guidelines. Check each investor (FNMA,
  GNMA and FHLMC) for its own underwriting requirements.

- What are the borrower's current mortgage or rent payments? As mentioned previously, adjustable rate products
  are the most likely loan products to suffer payment shock.
  Research has shown that annual payment adjustments in
  excess of 30 percent are more than 70 percent likely to
  cause payment shock, resulting in slow repayment or possible default of the loan obligation.

- How much savings does the borrower wish to use as a
  down payment? If the borrower wishes to make only a

small down payment, high-rate PMI insurance will be required, as will squeaky-clean credit, strong income base and cash reserves of at least two or three months. This type of purchaser will have limited negotiating power with the lender, due to extreme leverage.

The borrower who is prepared to make a large down payment will have an easier time qualifying, and a portfolio approach will be more likely; he or she will be in a stronger negotiating position for lower margins and origination fees, and may request to pay taxes and insurance outside of the monthly payment.

- How much of a monthly payment is the borrower prepared to make? Consider affordability and desirability issues. For most ARMs, the housing ratio (depending on which investor buys the loan) must use an approximate maximum of 28 percent of gross income. The total debt ratio including all debts of ten months or more plus PITI payment, cannot exceed 36 percent of gross income. Many lenders, particularly in situations with high loan-to-value ratios, will consider any balance owing on an obligation as a long-term debt to be included in the total debt ratio.

- Would the borrower mind fluctuating payment amounts? If the answer is "yes," the borrower is not suited for any type of ARM; if the answer is "no," the borrower could decide the preferred (financially and emotionally) frequency of payment adjustment (e.g., every year, three years, five years or ten years) and choose the type of loan to match.

- What of the borrower's current assets, including personal and real property, could be mortgaged or sold to raise extra collateral cash if necessary? If the borrower's debts are low, he or she could borrow against an asset, but repayment may be considered in long-term debt ratio. In addition, an asset can be converted to cash to use as additional down payment to negotiate a loan with a lower margin or lower cap.

- What are the borrower's short-term and long-term liabilities? Balances are needed to determine this, as well as repayment schedules. If the borrower has lots of credit accounts and small liabilities, he or she may not be able to qualify for a high loan-to-value ARM, or may have to pay off some accounts to qualify. If the borrower has few debts, but is short on down payment or cash reserves, he or she should consider obtaining a gift letter or borrowing from a low-interest source, such as life insurance or a credit union.

Appendix A includes a mortgage checklist from the Federal Reserve Bank that is helpful in choosing the best ARM program to fit a buyer's needs. Also, see buyer and seller estimation forms in Appendix A.

Q. *What are the characteristics of the typical ARM purchaser?*

Although each buyer's qualification and profile will be unique, here are some characteristics that may assist you in determining if ARM financing is best. The buyers:

- can expect with some certainty that their incomes will increase;
- desire a home that is slightly out of their financial reach;
- desire short-term ownership;
- cannot qualify at market rates and need a lower initial interest rate;
- wish to buy property when conventional fixed-rates are high or when rates are expected to decline, particularly if the ARM has a conversion option;
- don't need the security, emotional or financial, of a fixed-rate mortgage;
- want the loan to adjust based on inflation and economic swings;
- need a better loan assumability feature than available with fixed-rate mortgages; or
- want to shop for index and adjustment period that best coincides with their needs in purchasing the property.

One last note: Many borrowers forget about using ARMs when interest rates for conventional fixed-rate loans are low. By offering borrowers extra purchasing power tailored financially to their individual situations, coupled with loan assumability when the property is sold, ARMs give added benefits fixed rates don't offer. Borrowers should not overlook them when shopping for an affordable loan.

CHAPTER 7

FEDERAL HOUSING ADMINISTRATION LOANS

This chapter contains basic information about FHA single-family mortgages. Since this information was gleaned from standard FHA guidelines, practices could vary slightly in certain states and cities.

The FHA was established in 1934 under the National Housing Act. It is part of the federal Department of Housing and Urban Development (HUD). Its birth paved the way to mortgage affordability for many Americans, who had previously been locked out of home ownership due to a combination of high interest rates and short-term loans, making payments costly. Programs of the FHA expanded loan terms to 30 years at interest rates typically below those of conventional loans.

FHA was also instrumental in determining the first set of construction and appraisal standards for inspecting property prior to loan approval. Many of the quality and safety standards that the housing industry uses today are by-products of early FHA guidelines.

Before 1983, FHA retained the right to control rate ceiling maximums on FHA loans. It's interesting to note, however, that since interest rates are no longer capped, FHA loan rates have remained generally lower than conventional rates. This is the result of supply and demand, default protection to the lender and discount points.

- Low down payments on FHA loans, as well as fairly liberal underwriting guidelines, make FHA loans attractive, thus creating demand
- Since the lender is insured for the life of the loan against borrower default, the lender can offset the lower interest received for the security of loan repayment in case of default

131

- Discount points charged by the lender help sweeten the pot financially, increasing the desired yield to the lender.

LEVELS OF FEDERAL HOUSING ADMINISTRATION LOANS

While FHA national loan underwriting guidelines establish basic guidelines for loan administration, regional FHA offices, as well as local lenders can choose to be more restrictive. See Appendix B for a national listing of HUD offices.

For example, if loan defaults in a local lender's market has been edging up, that lender might choose to be more cautious about risks taken in order to control the problem.

That's why it's important for the borrower to shop not only for the type of FHA loan, but for the lender who will make it. In general, lenders who do a high volume of FHA loans will be more in tune with little-known exceptions and underwriting allowances than a lender who does one or two FHA loans a year.

PROS AND CONS

Q. *What are the advantages of using FHA financing?*

The following are among the many advantages FHA loans afford borrowers:

- There is a low down payment requirement. On the standard Section 203(b) homeowner's program, the down payment is only 3 percent on acquisition prices of $50,000 or less. For acquisition amounts over $50,000, the down payment is 3 percent on the first $25,000 and 5 percent of the balance, up to the maximum loan amount allowable in the particular region.
- The entire down payment can be "gifted," or given to the borrower, by a relative.
- Closing costs can be financed into the loan.
- There are no reserve requirements of two months' PITI payments at closing as found with conventional loans.
- Loan rates are typically lower than for market-rate conventional fixed-rate loans.

- A seller or other third party is allowed to participate in paying the buyer's closing costs.
- Loans originated prior to December 1, 1986, are simply assumable, meaning that the purchaser does not need to formally qualify. Other FHA loans are assumable with qualifying.
- Loans are assumed at the note rate under which they were originated, with the exception of FHA ARMs, which are assumed at the loan's current rate of interest.
- FHA loans have no prepayment penalty.
- Since a new FHA loan pays off existing encumbrances, the seller receives all of his or her equity, less costs of sale.
- Qualifying guidelines assist the average buyer in the marketplace; some underwriting guidelines are actually less restrictive than those of conventional fixed-rate loans.
- The lender is insured against loss for the life of the FHA loan.
- It is possible to place subsequent mortgages after an FHA first mortgage. New financing could even be placed around an FHA mortgage originated before December 1, 1986.
- A second mortgage can be initiated simultaneous to a new FHA first mortgage.

Q. *What are the disadvantages of using an FHA loan?*

- Loans originated after December 1, 1986, are no longer assumable without qualifying.
- On loans originated before December 1, 1986, purchasers who do not receive a release of liability when selling may be secondarily liable should the loan default.
- Sellers may object to paying discount points or other closing costs attributed to FHA financing.
- Since a seller may be requested to pay fairly heavy costs to assist a buyer, the seller may want to sell only if full price is received.
- A mortgage insurance premium (MIP) is required up front, or can be financed into the loan, and an annual renewal premium is charged, payable in the monthly payment for the life of the loan.

- A 1 percent loan origination fee is charged on FHA loans.
- Appraisal guidelines for FHA loans may be more stringent than those of conventional mortgage appraisals.
- Loan processing for FHA loans may take longer than it does for conventional loans.
- Generally, borrowers are allowed only one FHA loan at a time.

THE BASICS

Q. *What is the basic FHA loan called?*

The primary single-family program is the Section 203(b) loan, which provides financing on one- to four-family owner-occupied dwellings. This includes condos, Planned Unit Developments (PUD), and new construction financing, all of which must be on FHA's approved list. Loans are available in rural and urban areas and have loan terms for 15 and 30 years.

Q. *Many people think that FHA loans are only for low-income buyers. Is this true?*

That's a commonly held misconception about FHA loans. Although there have been some FHA subsidized programs to assist low-income families, FHA's mission is to insure lenders on housing loans made to borrowers who do not meet the necessary down payment requirements or other conditions of conventional mortgages. With FHA loans, borrowers still need to meet monthly income guidelines sufficient to support housing obligations. Because the loans are insured by HUD, however, the lender is protected against the borrower's default and can offer more liberal terms and competitive interest than a buyer might otherwise be able to obtain.

Q. *Who is the typical FHA buyer?*

Although each buyer's qualification and profile will be unique, the following are some general characteristics. The FHA borrower:

- is only moderately qualified and needs a qualifying interest rate lower than required for a market-rate conventional loan
- needs leverage in qualifying, with lower down payment or gifted funds
- is working with a seller or other third party to pay part or all of the closing costs and prepaids
- requires a loan that is assumable
- desires an insured loan (with possibly some of the mortgage insurance eventually rebated)
- wants to place a second mortgage initially behind the FHA first mortgage, or later during ownership of the property
- is interested in leveraged programs of ARMs, GPMs or GEMs

Q. *What are the general buyer qualifications for FHA loans?*

Borrowers need to have a satisfactory credit record, the down payment required (or gifted funds available for the down payment), cash needed to close and steady, verified income to make the monthly payments without difficulty.

Citizenship Not Mandatory

Q. *Is U.S. citizenship mandatory for obtaining an FHA loan?*

While the borrower must reside on the property, U.S. citizenship is not a requirement for obtaining an FHA loan. Under the Equal Credit Opportunity Act, lawful permanent residents of the United States are entitled to the same credit benefits as any American citizen and may not be discriminated against due to national origin. Permanent and nonpermanent resident alien borrowers must show an established employment history and evidence employment will continue.

Borrowers Restricted to One FHA Loan at a Time

Q. *Why are FHA buyers restricted to one loan at a time?*

Several years ago, FHA experimented with allowing borrowers to have multiple, simultaneous FHA loans if the first loan did not have a high loan-to-value ratio. If the borrowers wanted to purchase again with an FHA loan, they could pay down the balance on the first home to 75 percent loan-to-appraised value.

Foreclosures persisted, so FHA now allows borrowers to have only one FHA loan at a time. Exceptions to this rule include the borrower who relocates from another locale and can qualify only by using an FHA loan, or whose family size has increased so that the present home no longer meets his or her needs.

Second Mortgage Simultaneous to a New First FHA Loan

Q.   *Would FHA ever allow a borrower to secure a second mortgage simultaneously to a new FHA first mortgage?*

Remarkably, the answer is yes. Secondary financing simultaneous to a new FHA first mortgage may be allowed if the combined amounts of the first and second mortgages do not exceed the applicable loan-to-value ratio loan. In addition, the second mortgage must not force a balloon payment before ten years, reasonable monthly payments must be made on the second mortgage and prepayment of the obligation must be allowed at any time.

Borrowers age 60 and older can obtain secondary financing with total loan-to-value ratios of the combined first and second mortgages up to 100 percent of the property's appraised value.

Q.   *When might a buyer use an initial second mortgage with a new FHA first?*

This situation would be most likely to occur when interest rates on the first mortgage are high and qualifying for an entire loan at that high rate could be difficult, as in the following example.

FHA interest is at 11 percent. Edith Olson can't qualify for a $60,000 loan at that interest rate, so she secures a $15,000 second mortgage at 9 percent interest simultaneous to closing a $45,000 FHA first mortgage.

Of course the FHA lender knows of the second mortgage and qualifies Edith for both sets of debt repayments. The two payments are melded together for the purpose of qualifying, and the lower interest rate of the second mortgage is just enough to leverage Edith into qualifying for both loans.

QUALIFICATION GUIDELINES

Maximum Mortgage Limits and Loan-to-Value Ratios

Q. *What mortgage limits are allowed under FHA loans?*

While a federal ceiling is currently set at over $151,000 for FHA loans (and is adjusted periodically), mortgage limits vary among geographic areas, because these limits are based on the area's median sales prices. Because these maximum loan amounts fluctuate, borrowers should consult a local lender for the current maximum FHA limit.

Q. *What are the maximum loan-to-value limits allowed under FHA?*

Federal Housing Administration loans are based on a percentage of total acquisition cost. Acquisition costs are defined as the sales price plus the amount of FHA closing costs the purchaser pays. This means that FHA will allow the buyer to finance closing costs into the loan.

To determine the maximum loan available, and conversely the down payment required, use the following formulas:

- For properties with total acquisition costs of $50,000 or less, multiply the total acquisition cost by 97 percent. This translates into a 3% down payment.
- For total acquisition costs greater than $50,000, determine the maximum loan amount by multiplying the first $25,000 by 97 percent (to calculate the 3 percent down payment) and multiplying the remainder by 95 percent (to determine the 5 percent down payment). Then add the two sums together. Remember that the loan can't exceed

the maximum limit allowable for the borrower's geographic area.

Apply this method to the following example.

Jeanette Jones is buying a $65,000 house. After adding the
$1,500 in closing costs allowable under FHA, she finds that the
total acquisition cost would be $66,500. The lender will finance
97 percent of the first $25,000 ($24,250) plus 95 percent of the
remainder, up to the area maximum loan ($41,500) for a loan
amount, not including FHA mortgage insurance, of $63,675.
That's $63,650, rounded down to the nearest $50 increment.
  In addition to the previous calculation, FHA also requires
that loans do not exceed a certain percentage of the sales price
(98.75 percent, if the sales price is $50,000 or under, and 97.75
percent if the sales price is over $50,000). This cap was
implemented several years ago to hedge against excessive closing costs being financed and to curb defaults.
  In this final step to determine a maximum loan, Jeanette
multiplies the sales price ($65,000) by 97.75 percent, or
$63,500, rounded down to the nearest $50. Since this amount is
less than the $63,650 figure calculated earlier, the maximum
loan is $63,500—the lesser of the two calculations. Under FHA,
Jeanette can add mortgage insurance on top of that maximum
loan if she needs to finance it into the loan. In addition, she will
need to put a $1,500 down payment on this purchase.

An easy-to-use worksheet for calculating the maximum loan
allowed under FHA is shown in Figure 7.1.

Quick Loan Calculation

Q. Is there a quicker way to calculate the maximum FHA loan?

Here's one shortcut that can be used to determine acquisition
costs for mortgages higher than $50,000:

Acquisition cost × 95% + $500 = maximum loan
$66,500 × 95% = $63,175 + $500 = $63,650 loan (rounded down
to nearest $50 increment)

Figure 7.1   FHA Maximum Mortgage Worksheet

Mortgages $50,000 and Less	**Mortgages Higher Than $50,000**
Step One	**Step One**

Mortgages $50,000 and Less		Mortgages Higher Than $50,000	
Sales Price	(1) _____	Sales Price	(1) _____
Application Fee	$ _____	Application Fee	$ _____
Recording Fee	$ _____	Recording Fee	$ _____
Notary Fee	$ _____	Notary Fee	$ _____
Title Insurance	$ _____	Title Insurance	$ _____
Transfer Tax	$ _____	Transfer Tax	$ _____
Loan Origination Fee	$ _____	Loan Origination Fee	$ _____
Total Costs	$ _____	Total Costs	$ _____
Allowable Closing Costs	(2) _____	Allowable Closing Costs	(2) _____
Total (1) + (2) =	_____	Total (1) + (2) =	_____
x 97% =	_____	Less $25,000 =	_____
Base Mortgage	$ _____	x 95% =	_____
		Add Back $24,250 =	_____
		Base Mortgage	$ _____

Step Two	**Step Two**

Step Two		Step Two	
Sales Price	$ _____	Sales Price	$ _____
x 98.75% =	_____	x 97.75% =	_____
Base Mortgage	$ _____	Base Mortgage	$ _____

Maximum base mortgage is the lower of step one or step two.

In addition, be sure to multiply the sales price by 97.75% to determine which of the two amounts would be the maximum loan allowed. That FHA goes by the lesser of the two calculations.

$65,000 sales price × 97.75% = $63,500 maximum loan.

FHA Borrowers Can Finance Closing Costs

Q. *So the borrower is only allowed to finance those closing costs he or she pays?*

That's correct. If the buyer isn't paying those closing costs, they can't be financed into the loan; Figure 7.2 shows what can occur in loan amount calculations when this happens. Each HUD regional office determines which closing costs are reasonable and customary for the area. These typically include fees for appraisal, inspection, credit reports, loan origination, deposit verification, home inspection (up to $200), title insurance, document preparation, property survey, attorneys, recording and testing (such as for water). Again, the FHA estimate of closing costs does not include discount points or prepaid items such as insurance prorations and property tax impounds required from the borrower to close.

Gifts

Q. *Could the borrower use gifts for the down payment on an FHA loan?*

Yes, if the gift comes from a relative. As with gifts for all types of loans, the funds must not be required to be repaid. In addition, the funds must appear in the borrower's account and be verified prior to loan approval.

Closing Costs

Q. *How could a seller financially assist a buyer?*

The seller can pay discount points, buydowns and other financial supplements for the borrower up to a maximum of six percent of

---

Figure 7.2   Calculating Maximum FHA Loan Amounts

Four Ways To Calculate Maximum FHA Loan Amounts

With a sales price and FHA value of $55,000, and $900 for the FHA estimate of closing costs, we can use the following formulas*:

1. Purchasers Are Paying Their Own Closing Costs and Prepaid Items.

$55,000	55,900	25,000	30,900	24,250	
+ 900	-25,000	x 97%	x 95%	+29,355	
$55,900	30,900	24,250	29,355	53,605	= $53,600
					Maximum Loan

Quick Method = $55,900 x 95% = $53,105 + 500 = $53,605 = $53,600 (round to nearest 50)

2. Sellers Are Paying All of the Purchasers' Closing Costs.

$55,000	55,000	25,000	30,000	24,250	
+ 0	-25,000	x 97%	x 95%	+28,500	
$55,000	30,000	24,250	28,500	52,750	= $52,750
					Maximum Loan

Quick Method = $55,000 x 95% = $52,250 + 500 = $52,750

3. Sellers Are Paying All of the Purchasers' Closing Costs & Prepaid Items.

$55,000†	54,600	54,600	25,000	29,600	24,250	
- 400	+ 0	-25,000	x 97%	x 95%	+28,120	
$54,600	54,600	29,600	24,250	28,120	52,370	= $52,350
						Maximum Loan

Quick Method = $54,600 x 95% = $51,870 + 500 = $52,370 = $52,350

4. Sellers Are Paying a Portion of the Closing Costs.

$55,000‡	55,450	25,000	30,450	24,250	
+ 450	-25,000	x 97%	x 95%	+28,927	
$55,450	30,450	24,250	28,927	53,177	= $53,150
					Maximum Loan

Quick Method = $55,450 x 95% = $52,677 + 500 = $53,177 = $53,150

*Don't forget the second step in determining the maximum loan amount: Multiply the sales price times 97.75 percent (for sales prices over $50,000) and 98.75 percent (for sales prices under $50,000), then compare it to the maximum loan amount in the first calculation. The lesser of the two will be the maximum loan.

† FHA can view prepaid items paid by the seller as a sales concession. In this example, the $400 is an estimate for prepaid items which is deducted from the sales price as a concession paid by the seller.

‡ In this example it is assumed that the seller is paying one-half of the buyer's closings costs (FHA estimate is $900 divided by 2 = $450).

the sales price. Past that point, deductions will be made dollar for dollar from the sales price before the maximum loan amount is figured.

Any charge considered to be a seller-paid closing cost for the buyer will be subtracted likewise from the sales price as well as being contributed to the six percent ceiling. See Appendix A for buyer and seller cost estimate worksheets.

No Cash Reserves Required

Q. *Does the borrower need two months of reserve PITI payment in cash as with other loans?*

There is no reserve requirement set by FHA on single-family one-unit dwellings. The lender could impose reserves of three months' PITI on multi-family occupied dwellings, such as two-unit to four-unit properties.

Qualifying Income

Q. *What are the qualifying income criteria for standard FHA loans?*

It's a common misconception that buyers who do not fit within the exact qualifying ratios will not receive FHA loans. Although the following ratios are guidelines, they are not absolutes; the loan underwriter will carefully weigh each individual situation before making a lending decision.

Housing Ratio   The following monthly expenses should not exceed 29 percent of the borrower's monthly gross income: PITI, including MIP); any homeowner association or condo fees; and any local improvement district or improvement assessments.

Total Debt Ratio   The following monthly expenses should not exceed 41 percent of the borrower's monthly gross income: Total mortgage payment, auto payments, installment charges, loans, child support or alimony or other obligations to run more than six months. (See Appendix A for a qualifying worksheet.)

Compensating Factors

Q. *What exceptions could the lender make on these ratios?*

Strong consideration to exceed the ratios could be given an applicant who uses a large down payment and has substantial cash reserves (three months of PITI), a history of light use of credit, excellent job history and no other large debt payments, such as car loans.

Also considered as compensating factors would be the borrower's track record of managing a large house payment, a new house payment that will increase only slightly (10 percent or less), or compensation or income not reflected in qualifying, but which could directly assist repayment of the mortgage. Changing circumstances, such as child support with only two years of payments remaining, may also be considered.

In addition, a property that meets energy efficiency guidelines can allow the borrower's ratios to be increased by 2 percent on housing and total debt ratios.

Q. *On which of the two ratios (housing or long-term debt) is the lender usually the more flexible?*

Lenders are usually more flexible on housing ratio. The rationale is that if the borrower's long-term debt ratio is 41 percent or less, the borrower could perhaps handle a larger house payment.

Documenting Income

Q. *What kind of income qualifications must the borrower prove to qualify for an FHA loan?*

As with all mortgages, the borrower must prove stability of income. While FHA does not mandate a minimum length of time a borrower must have held a position, the lender must verify the most recent two full years of employment. If part of this history included school or military time, the borrower must provide evidence supporting this, such as college transcripts or discharge papers. Allowances for seasonal employment, such are typical in the building trades, etc., may be made.

Changing jobs need not be viewed as negative if the changes were in the same line of work, advanced the borrower's position and were accompanied by income increases.

Q. *Are pay increases counted in qualifying income?*

Pay increases, such as performance raises, bonuses and cost-of-living adjustments, can be included as income if they will begin within 60 days of loan closing and can be verified by the employer.

Q. *Will overtime and bonus income count toward FHA qualifying?*

Overtime and bonus income may be used to qualify if the borrower has received it for the past two years and will in all likelihood continue to do so. The lender will use an average figure based on the past two-year history.

Q. *Does part-time income count?*

HUD recognizes that many low-income and moderate-income families rely on part-time and seasonal income. So FHA lenders may include part-time and seasonal income in qualifying if the borrower has worked the job uninterrupted for the past two years and will continue to do so. Seasonal employment is viewed the same way, focusing on the rehire for the next season. Other situations that do not meet the two-year history can be seen only as compensating factors by the lender.

Q. *How does the lender verify commission income?*

Commission income is averaged over the previous two years, and the borrower must provide his or her last two years' tax returns along with a recent pay stub to verify it. A borrower showing income decreases from year to year will need to show significant compensating factors to receive loan approval.

Q. *Do retirement and Social Security benefits count as income?*

Yes, but it needs to be verified from the source (usually the former employer or Social Security Administration) or through federal tax returns. If any benefits expire within approximately five years, it will be considered only as a compensating factor.

Q. *How is alimony or child support verified?*

Alimony and child support must be projected to consistently continue for at least the first five years of the mortgage. The borrower must provide a copy of the divorce decree and evidence that payments have been made for the past 12 months.

Self-Employed Borrowers

Q. *Are self-employed borrowers qualified for FHA in the same tedious way they are for conventional loans?*

More or less; but FHA may make an exception for self-employed borrowers who have been employed less than two years, but more than one year. The self-employed borrower may qualify for an FHA loan if he or she has at least two years' previous employment in the same line of work or a combination of one year employment and one year formal training.

Determining Debt for Loan Qualifying

Q. *How does the lender view debt for FHA loan qualifying?*

The borrower's liabilities included in the long-term debt ratio for qualifying include installment loans, revolving charge accounts, real estate loans, alimony, child support and all other continuing obligations. The basic guideline is that any debt that extends six months or more must be considered in the qualifying ratios. Debts lasting less than six months need not be counted unless they substantially affect the borrower's ability to repay the mortgage in the early months of the loan; an example of a loan that might be counted would be a substantial car payment with four payments remaining.

Q. *Didn't FHA previously count joint debts of spouses for qualifying even after the divorce occurred?*

The FHA has amended its stand on contingent liabilities between divorced parties. If a borrower's former spouse was awarded the home and the responsibility for loan payment as part of the divorce decree, then payment will not be counted as a debt for qualifying purposes. This is true even if the borrower's name still appears on the loan paperwork, and the lender has not released him or her from liability.

Q. *Does child care count as a borrower debt?*

The FHA requires that families with young children must provide information regarding child care expenses or satisfactory evidence that no expenses are or will be incurred; for example, a relative may have taken financial responsibility for the care of the minor child, costing the parents nothing. Any monthly child care expenses must be included in the long-term debt ratio.

Q. *Are cosigned loans counted as debt for qualifying?*

Cosigned loans will be considered against the long-term debt ratios unless all of the following are provided:

- A statement from both parties that the cosigner has never made any of the payments
- Copies of canceled checks proving that all payments are being made by the other person
- Documents showing that half of the total debt has been paid off
- Proof that all payments have been made on time
- If the cosignature is for a mortgage, one year's canceled checks are needed. Payment of half of the obligation will not be counted.

Q. *What are the other special guidelines that relate to debt for an FHA loan?*

If a borrower has a debt projected to begin within 12 months of mortgage closing, such as student loan repayment, the lender must include the anticipated monthly obligation in the underwriting analysis. Similarly, balloon notes that come due within one year of loan closing must be considered as debt.

Alternative Documentation

Q. *Is quick processing available with FHA, similar to TimeSaver on conventional loans?*

Lenders can use the alternative documentation method, which expedites processing. The borrower is required to provide the following to use this method:

- Bank statements for the most recent three months
- W-2 forms for the past two years
- Pay stubs covering the most recent 30-day period, which show the borrower's name and Social Security number

The lender will verify employment by phoning the employer prior to closing, confirming position and salary range.

If any of these cannot be obtained, standard processing is required.

Bankrupt Borrowers

Q. *Can borrowers who have previously declared bankruptcy purchase a home using an FHA loan?*

Yes. In fact, FHA's evaluation of previous bankrupt borrowers is one of the most liberal in the mortgage lending industry. A lender may allow a bankrupt borrower to secure a mortgage loan if the bankruptcy has been discharged for at least one year and credit has been satisfactorily reestablished.

Borrowers who have filed bankruptcy under Chapter 13 must be one year into the payout and have trustee approval to add the debt.

In either case, borrowers must provide detailed letters of explanation and supporting documentation to the lender.

Property Guidelines

Q. *What kinds of property certifications need to be done to secure an FHA loan?*

FHA will require termite inspections if applicable, testing of wells for bacteria and chemical analysis and other property certifications based on the borrower's geographic area.

Q. *Does FHA have to comply with the Energy Policy Act of 1992 on new construction?*

For both FHA and VA loans, new construction begun after October 24, 1993, must comply with the Council of American Building Officials' (CABO) 1992 Model Energy Code (MEC). A written certificate must be obtained from the builder stating that minimum energy standards have been met before the loan can be approved.

Leverage

Q. *Are coborrowers allowed on FHA loans?*

Coborrowers are allowed on FHA loans. By definition, coborrowers take title to the property and obligate themselves on the mortgage note, but do not live in the property. Loan-to-value ratio on coborrower transactions is limited to 75 percent of the appraised value of the property.

The only exception to this 75 percent loan-to-value rule would be if the coborrowers were related by blood (parent and child, siblings, aunts, uncles, nieces or nephews, etc.) or for unrelated individuals who can document evidence of a family-type long-standing relationship. Individuals proving these relationships can obtain a maximum loan-to-value loan.

Similar to a coborrower, a cosigner with no ownership interest in the property (who does not take title) will be permitted to become jointly liable for repayment of the obligation. The coborrower and cosigner's income, assets, liabilities and credit history will be used for qualifying.

MORTGAGE INSURANCE PREMIUMS

Q. *How is mortgage applied to the loan amount?*

There are two kinds of mortgage insurance premiums with FHA loans: initial premiums and renewal premiums. The borrower either must pay the initial premium in cash at closing or finance it into the loan. This amount is determined based on when the loan is originated (see Figure 7.3 for loan origination dates and payment amounts).

The renewal premium is also based on the date of loan origination, but also takes into account loan-to-value ratio on the loan.

To calculate MIP, consider the following example:

To finance the initial MIP on a $70,000 loan originated in January 1994, George Hoffmann would add 3 percent, or $2,100, to the loan amount. In addition, the annual renewal premium for a minimum down payment loan would add one-half of 1 percent annually to the payment ($350 annually) paid monthly, or $29.17 added on to the payment. This monthly premium would remain in effect for 30 years, the life of the loan.

The maximum area loan size can be exceeded by the amount of the MIP if it's added to the loan amount and financed into the loan. In addition, a third party (seller, relatives or employer) may pay part or all of the MIP in cash at closing.)

Q. *Can a portion of the MIP be refunded to the borrower?*

If the borrower satisfies the mortgage prior to the final payment and the mortgage is not in default, the borrower may be entitled to a refund of a portion of the mortgage insurance premium. The refund is calculated on a descending percentage basis, and is not returned dollar for dollar. The refund paperwork is usually processed by the lender who administrates the loan payoff, and the borrower is requested to sign several request documents. If a refund is not received within approximately 120 days after loan payoff, the borrower can write (including the FHA loan number) to the FHA at Mortgage Insurance Accounting, Insurance Operations Division, HUD, 451 Seventh St., SW, Washington, DC 20410.

Figure 7.3   Mortgage Insurance Premium Chart*

Fiscal Year	**Up-Front Mortgage Insurance Premiums**	Loan-to-Value Ratio	Annual Premium	Term of Annual Premium
	3.8%			
1991 and 1992		89.99% and under	.50	5 years
		90.00% to 95.00%	.50	8 years
		95.01% and over	.50	10 years
	3.00%			
1993 through 4/16/94		89.99% and under	.50	7 years
		90.00% to 95.00%	.50	12 years
		95.01% and over	.50	30 years
	2.25%			
4/17/94 and later		89.99% and under	.50	11 years
		90.00% to 95.00%	.50	30 years
		95.01% and over	.55	30 years

*Applicable to the following sections, regardless of loan term:

Sections 203 (b), (h), (i) and (n), 244 (coinsurance; subject to change in regs), 245 (excluding condominiums) and 251 (excluding condominiums).

CONCESSIONS

Q. *What are sales concessions, and why are they limited in an FHA loan?*

A sales concession is a cost paid by someone other than the buyer, such as the seller or another third party. It is viewed as an inducement to purchase and limits the buyer's investment in the property. For that reason, HUD requires that sales concessions paid or offered by the seller or other third party be deducted dollar for dollar from the sales price before the maximum mortgage amount is calculated. Sales concessions include prepaid items, personal property items, decorating allowances, moving costs, buyer-broker fees, condominium or homeowner association fees, excess rent credit or seller payment of borrower's sales commission on present residence.

Q. *What's the difference between sales concessions and financing concessions?*

Financially, quite a lot. While financing concessions include discount points, interest rate buydowns, mortgage interest payments or the borrower's up-front mortgage insurance premium paid for the borrower by the seller or other third party, they are treated differently than sales concessions for qualifying purposes. Financing concessions are not subtracted dollar for dollar from the sales price until they exceed 6 percent of the sales price. Then, they are subtracted dollar-for-dollar before figuring the maximum loan amount.

How does this affect the borrower's position? If possible, it's financially better for a seller or third party to contribute financing concessions rather than sales concessions if the borrower is in need of a maximum-allowable loan. It's best to spell out on the purchase agreement just what the concession is to apply to; otherwise, it would be determined by the lender, possibly not to the buyer's advantage.

ASSUMPTION GUIDELINES

Q. *What does the term simply assumable mean when referring to FHA loans originated before December 1, 1986?*

A simply asssumable FHA loan is one that can be assumed by a new borrower without qualifying through the lender. Should the assumptor default on the loan, however, the original borrower could be held responsible for satisfying the debt.

If the initial mortgagor wants to be released of all liability under an FHA loan written prior to December 1, 1986, the assumptor needs to qualify to assume the loan (called a "novation"). This includes providing the lender with information regarding monthly income and debt, as well as credit history and employment, and requesting the novation with the lender. If the borrower meets the lender's criteria, the original borrower may be released from further liability on the loan.

Q. *How can FHA loans originated after December 1, 1986, be assumed?*

With greater difficulty! Loans originated after December 1, 1986, and before December 15, 1989, are freely assumable unless assumption occurs during the first two years of ownership. If a person assumes the property for a principal residence during the first year, that new owner must meet FHA qualifying guidelines. If an investor assumes the property during the first two years, that person must also qualify. After the first two years of ownership, the loans are freely assumable.

Q. *What about loans originated after December 15, 1989?*

Borrowers must qualify and meet all FHA guidelines for assumptions on these types of loans. Only owner-occupants, not investors, may assume these loans.

PREPAYMENT PENALTIES

Q. *Is there a prepayment penalty on FHA mortgages?*

This question provokes several answers. The guidelines state that if an FHA loan was insured prior to August 2, 1985, the borrower must give a 30-day written notice to HUD stating that the loan will be paid in full. This notice can come from a real estate agent or loan officer and constitutes 30 days of interest. FHA, however, views this as an interest charge, not as a prepayment penalty.

For loans insured on or after August 2, 1985, FHA will no longer require a 30-day notice to prepay. Under this guideline, however, the lender can refuse to credit full prepayment without requiring interest to the next due date if the payment is not made *on* the monthly due date. The solution? Make sure the loan is repaid on the monthly due date!

DISCOUNT POINTS AND BUYDOWNS

Q. *Who can pay points on FHA loans?*

Anyone can pay points on FHA loans. Since many FHA buyers are short on cash, sellers often assist with points. A third party—such as a relative of the buyer, or someone in another real estate transaction who has an interest in seeing this sale close so that his or her home can be purchased—could also pay points. No matter who pays the points, they are tax deductible for the homebuyer.

Q. *Could a buyer use discount points and then reduce the interest rate using buydowns in the same transaction?*

There's no reason why not. The discount points are charged by the lender to help increase the overall yield and defray the cost of discounting the loan when it's sold to the secondary market. The buydown, on the other hand, uses points (actually prepaid interest) to buy down the note rate either temporarily (like a 3-2-1 buydown) or permanently for the life of the loan (for example, from 8 percent to 7 percent).

REFINANCING

Q. *What are the guidelines for refinancing an FHA loan?*

If the borrower is taking cash out of the property, the loan-to-value ratio cannot exceed 85 percent of the appraised value, and the borrower must occupy the property.

If the borrower takes no cash out of the property, the maximum loan is based on the lower of the FHA purchase formula (financing

97 percent of the first $25,000 and 95 percent of the remainder up to the area maximum) or costs and liens on the property.

Q. *Is there a streamlined program such as those available with other loan types?*

Yes. The FHA streamlined refinance program is designed to lower the monthly principal and interest payments on a current HUD-insured mortgage and involves no cash back to the borrower.

Streamline refinances can be completed with or without an appraisal but must meet the following guidelines:

- Refinances *without* an appraisal are limited to the unpaid principal balance (but no interest), minus any refund of mortgage insurance premium (MIP), plus the new up-front mortgage insurance premium if it's to be financed in the mortgage. Term of the refinanced mortgage is the lesser of 30 years or the unexpired term of the old mortgage plus 12 years.
- Refinances *with* appraisals allow the closing costs and reasonable discount points to be financed. Loan maximums are subject to FHA loan-to-value limits.

Refinancing is considered a pay-off of the old loan and releases the original seller on an assumed loan.

Borrowers could take advantage of this program to lower 30-year loan into a 15-year term (provided the new payment does not increase by more than $50), or to convert an FHA adjustable rate mortgage into a fixed rate loan.

OTHER FHA LOAN OPTIONS

The FHA/VA Tandem Loan

Q. *Is there an FHA loan for veterans?*

The loan is called FHA/VA 203 (v) and it is used to finance only single-family structures (duplexes and other multi-family units are not permitted). The loan is often used by veterans who have used their VA eligibility or who want to preserve their VA certificate for a later time. In other words, the FHA/VA loan does not involve the veteran's entitlement, and there are no limits restricting the amount of times it can be used.

Under the FHA/VA loan, the down payment is less than with the standard 203(b) program: zero down payment on the first $25,000 of FHA total value and 5 percent down payment on the remainder. The veteran must obtain a Certificate of Veteran Status form from the VA (and a Form DD208 from the commander if the veteran is still in service). Maximum loan amounts are the same as with the standard 203(b) program.

The FHA Adjustable Rate Mortgage

Q. *Are FHA ARMs competitive?*

The FHA ARM (FHA loan Section 251) is very competitive, combining the down payment guidelines of the standard (203)b program with the features of an ARM. Here are some of its characteristics:

- Maximum interest rate increases (caps) are limited to 1 percent per year and 5 percent over the life of the loan. In addition, the FHA ARM has no negative amortization.
- The loan is assumable (with borrower qualification) at the loan's current interest rate.
- The index is the treasury bill index, and the margin is determined by supply and demand for GNMA mortgage-backed securities.
- Qualifying guidelines and maximum loan amounts are the same as those found under the 203(b) program.
- The FHA ARM can be used to refinance any existing HUD loan.

The FHA Graduated Payment Mortgage

Q. *What other FHA programs could interest a borrower?*

The graduated payment mortgage (GPM) plan, a variation of the regular HUD mortgage insurance program, can allow a borrower to pay a lower initial monthly payment in the early years of the loan.

With a GPM, mortgage payments rise gradually for a set period, usually five to seven years, then level off and remain fixed for the balance of the mortgage. In other words, a GPM enables borrowers to "grow into" higher monthly payments as their income increases.

Negative amortization, or payment shortfall, was once a major part of early GPM mortgages. Today, however, most graduated payment programs require larger down payments in order to prevent payment shortfall being added back on to the loan's principal balance.

The FHA Growing Equity Mortgage

Q. *What is the growing equity mortgage (GEM) and how does it work?*

The GEM program was designed to allow a borrower to "grow" equity quicker than with the traditional 30-year mortgage, while keeping payments low in the early years of the loan.

In the GEM loan program, payments increase between 2 percent and 7.5 percent per year, depending on the plan chosen, with the annual increase being applied directly to reduce the principal balance. The affect is that the loan retires in a little over 15 years, dramatically reducing the total cost of the mortgage to the borrower.

Unlike a graduated payment mortgage, there is no negative amortization, because the initial interest rate is lowered through up-front interest buydowns.

The GEM loan is easier to qualify for than a shorter-term 15-year loan, since the monthly payments start out lower. By about the tenth year of the loan, however, the payment will be higher than that of the 15-year loan. This is attractive to borrowers who need the benefit of the lower payment qualification up-front, but could manage a higher payment later. Borrowers could include young professionals or buyers in their 50s who are making their last home purchase.

SPECIALIZED FHA MORTGAGE PROGRAMS

Q. *Which other FHA programs might be of interest to borrowers?*

Although many FHA programs are not widely used, here are some that have sparked interest lately:

Disaster Victim Housing Loans

● Section 203(h) mortgage programs provide mortgage insurance for loans financing the purchase of a single-family
dwelling by the victim of a disaster.

Loans To Rehabilitate Properties

● Section 203(k), rehabilitation home mortgage insurance,
insures loans used to rehabilitate an existing residential
dwelling that will be used primarily for residential purposes, or to refinance an outstanding indebtedness plus
rehabilitate such a structure. This program may also be
used to convert nonresidential buildings into residential
use or to change the number of family units in the dwelling.

● The 203(k) provides the investor/borrower with interim
and permanent financing in one loan. The loan amount,
which is based on the property's after-renovation value,
can't exceed the current FHA maximum mortgage in the
borrower's area. While the down payment is steeper, approximately 15 percent, the borrower can finance closing
costs and fees into the loan.

Even though it's called a rehab program, repairs can
include almost anything beyond minor or cosmetic adjustments. Replacing floors, tiles or carpets is considered
rehab work, as is new siding, roofing, gutters, plumbing,
heating/cooling or electrical systems.

● The 203(k) loan can also be used to finance repairs outside the structure such as major landscaping work, patios
or terraces.

While repairs are under way, borrowers don't have to make mortgage payments; however, tax or insurance may be due. The payment moratorium can last up to six months if repairs require and the property is unoccupied.

Coborrower Suggestions for College Students

Q. *Previously FHA had a coborrower shared appreciation/equity mortgage. Did anything take its place?*

It's true that FHA abolished its official shared appreciation mortgage. But as mentioned previously, they will lend to coborrowers.

One of the more exciting adaptations of coborrowing is a system for parents and their college students to purchase. This "kiddie condo" application (although the property can be detached single-family dwellings) will allow a student living at school (usually more than 80 miles from home) to purchase a property with his or her parents.

The program is underwritten using the same rates and terms as the standard 203(b) loan. Its purpose is to help parents provide affordable housing for a child attending college. For that reason, FHA prefers to make loans when the student is a freshman.

The student must occupy the property, and the property cannot have "excessive" room (like a five-bedroom house for a single student). In addition, the parents can't own any other income property.

The loan is based on the parents' income and qualifications, so they must have good credit. The student's good credit could be used as well; but the student couldn't have bad credit, although a nonexistent credit history for the student is acceptable.

Parents and the student take title as coborrowers. The student should keep this in mind, since the debt might be used later if he or she qualifies individually to purchase a house. The loan does not accelerate after the student graduates, since it is a standard loan purchased by coborrowers.

Economically, the "kiddie condo" purchase makes much more sense than renting, the student is establishing a purchase history and credit record and the parents get appreciation and tax benefits to boot!

Manufactured Housing Loans

Q. *Does FHA allow loans on mobile homes?*

FHA calls mobile homes "manufactured homes" and will lend money for their purchase under the FHA Title I program, similar to the residential guidelines under the 203(b) program. In fact, a borrower can receive a loan for purchase of a manufactured home, if he or she owns the land, to fund a combination purchase of home and land, or just for the land, if the borrower already owns the manufactured home.

Since state laws vary regarding manufactured housing as real property, the borrower should check with a local lender to determine program guidelines.

CHAPTER 8

VETERANS ADMINISTRATION LOAN PROGRAMS

This chapter offers an overview of VA single-family housing programs. Information in this chapter comes from standard VA guidelines and therefore may have different applications in your area.

In 1944, Congress passed the Serviceman's Readjustment Act. This legislation, more commonly known as the GI Bill of Rights, was developed to assist veterans in readjusting to civilian life by providing them with medical benefits, bonuses and low-interest loans. Title III, one of six sections of the bill, guaranteed home loans to eligible veterans. Although loans were to be a type of bonus for those who had served their country, credit standards and underwriting guidelines were strictly enforced so that veterans would not undertake a mortgage obligation they could not fulfill.

Local lenders make loans for up to 100 percent of appraised value with the Veterans Administration, indemnifying the lender against loss on a portion of the loan. Originally, the guarantee was for 50 percent of the mortgage balance, not to exceed $2,000. Today's guarantee is still a maximum of 50 percent of the loan balance, but the dollar amount over the years has increased to a maximum of $46,000.

Unlike FHA loans, with VA loans the veteran does not pay a premium for the loan guarantee. This factor, plus others discussed in this chapter, helps make VA loans some of the most successful and rate-competitive programs in the mortgage market today.

LEVELS OF VA LOANS

Borrowers who have spoken with someone from a different area about VA loans, sometimes find discrepancies in what they thought were firm guidelines or practices. Who was correct? Both

160

probably were! Similar to FHA, VA national loan underwriting guidelines establish basic guidelines for loan administration, regional VA offices as well as local lenders can choose to be more restrictive if they so desire.

For example, if a military base closing in a local lender's market had foreclosures edging up, that lender might choose to be more cautious about risks in order to help control the problem.

That's why it's important for the borrower to shop not only for the type of VA loan, but for the lender who will make it. In general, lenders who do a high volume of VA loans will be more in tune with little-known exceptions and underwriting nuances than a lender who does one or two VA loans per year.

PROS AND CONS

Q. *What are the advantages of using VA financing?*

- There is no down payment requirement unless the purchase price of the property is greater than the VA appraisal called the Certificate of Reasonable Value (CRV); or if, based on the borrower's qualifications, the lender requires a down payment to make the loan.
- There is no VA limitation on the size of the mortgage; however, the lender or the requirements of the secondary mortgage market may set one.
- Loan rates are typically below market rate when compared to conventional fixed-rate loans.
- A seller is allowed to pay all or part of the buyer's closing costs.
- A veteran can own more than one property secured by a VA loan.
- Loans originated prior to March 1, 1988, are simply assumable (assumable without qualification of the new purchaser). All VA loans are assumable (even by non-veterans) at the note rate under which they were originated (with the exception of VA ARMs, which would be assumed at their current rate of interest.)
- The veteran can pay discount points, making VA loans rate-competitive.

- VA loans have no prepayment penalty.
- Since a new VA loan pays off existing encumbrances, the seller receives all his or her equity, less costs of sale.
- Qualifying guidelines are designed to assist the veteran in financing a home; therefore, some guidelines may be more liberal than found in conventional financing.
- Although the VA doesn't lend money, it acts to guarantee the lender against default on a portion of the loan.
- No mortgage insurance is charged on VA loans (unlike FHA and some conventional mortgages).

Q. *What are the disadvantages in financing with a VA loan?*

- Loans originated on or after March 1, 1988, are no longer assumable under simple assumption guidelines. The VA must approve the new purchase, and an assumption fee must be paid.
- For loans originated prior to March 1, 1988, veterans who sell property with assumptions of the mortgage may not be relieved of liability should the subsequent purchaser default.
- In case of default, the veteran may be held liable for repaying the VA any guaranteed amount paid to the lender.
- Sellers and veterans may object to paying discount points or other closing costs.
- Loan-processing time is typically longer than conventional loans.
- Since the seller's costs of sale are higher than those attributable to conventional loans, the seller may accept only his or her full asking price.
- A funding fee based on the amount financed must be paid at closing.

PROFILE OF A VA BUYER

Q. *Who is the typical person who buys through VA programs?*

Although each buyer's qualification and profile are unique, the following are some typical characteristics: The VA borrower

- is a veteran who has never used his or her entitlement, or has purchased previously with partial entitlement remaining
- is looking for a zero–down payment loan
- requests that the seller pay all of the closing costs
- is looking for a loan that has no mortgage insurance premium
- wants a loan that can be assumed at the rate originated (with the exception of the VA ARM loan, which would be assumed at the loan's current rate)
- wants a loan that has no prepayment penalty

ELIGIBILITY

Q. *Who is eligible for a VA loan?*

The following list gives a breakdown of the amount of days of active duty that must have been served in order to be eligible for VA home loan benefits:

	Days of Active Duty
September 16, 1940, to July 25, 1947	90
July 26, 1947, to June 26, 1950	181
June 27, 1950, to January 31, 1955	90
February 1, 1955, to August 4, 1964	181
August 5, 1964, to May 7, 1975	90
May 8, 1975, to September 7, 1980	181
Persian Gulf: August 2, 1990, to present	90

In addition, the following guidelines apply:

- Twenty-four months of continuous active service is required for everyone beginning active duty on or after September 7, 1980 (except Persian Gulf/Desert Storm veterans).
- Persons serving in selective reserve/National Guard are eligible if they have six years' service in the reserves. Service must have been active: that is, one weekend per month and two-week annual training each year. Inactive reserve time does not count as qualifying service.

- Veterans who were discharged before they served the minimum amount of time may be eligible if they were discharged for the convenience of the government, for a service-connected disability or a hardship. These exceptions do not apply to persons serving in the Selective Reserves/National Guard.
- Spouses of service personnel missing in action or of prisoners of war may be eligible for one VA home loan if the veteran has been missing in action, captured or interned in the line of duty for more than 90 days.
- Unmarried surviving spouses (widow or widower of a veteran) may claim VA home loan benefits if the veteran's death was caused by a service-connected injury or ailment. The surviving spouse cannot have eligibility by virtue of his or her own military service. Any VA eligibility previously used by the veteran will not be subtracted from the full guarantee allowed the surviving spouse.
- Any U.S. citizen who served in the armed forces of a country allied with the United States in World War II is eligible.
- A veteran who meets the qualification guidelines is eligible for VA home loan benefits even if he or she is hospitalized pending final discharge.

Q. *How does one show proof of eligibility?*

The Certificate of Eligibility must be submitted at the time of loan application. This certificate is VA form 26-8320 and contains the following information: veteran's name, Social Security number, service serial number, entitlement code, branch of service, date of birth, date the certificate was issued, signature of an authorized agent and the issuing office. On the reverse side of the form is the amount of entitlement or guaranty used, as well as the amount of any guaranty available for real estate loans.

Q. *How does one obtain a Certificate of Eligibility?*

The applicant must complete VA form 26-1880, Request for Determination of Eligibility and Available Loan Guaranty Entitlement. This request must be accompanied either by a DD214 (a synopsis of the applicant's military record and the veteran's physical characteristics) issued to service personnel discharged after January 1, 1950; a form WDAGO, Notice of Separation (for veterans discharged before this date); or a computer-generated Certificate of Eligibility, which was issued to veterans who served for one period of service after approximately 1970.

Mortgage lenders who originate VA loans usually will have the necessary filing forms on hand and will assist in procuring the certificate.

Q. *What happens if the applicant has lost his or her form DD214, WDAGO, or other evidence of military service?*

The applicant could substitute GSA Form 6954, Certification of Military Service, available from the applicable service department concerned.

If the veteran has lost the DD214, a duplicate might be obtained from the War Records Department; county records; a civil service agency employing the veteran; the local draft board, if the veteran was drafted; or the branch of service from which the veteran was discharged.

Q. *What does an applicant currently on active duty use for eligibility documents?*

Form DD 13, Statement of Service, is acceptable; or the applicant can submit a statement in letter form on military letterhead from his or her personnel officer or commanding officer. Stated would be the applicant's name, service serial number, active duty dates, previous periods of service (if any), character of service and notation of any lost time.

Q. *Does the veteran have to be present for loan application or closing?*

No. The veteran's spouse or other member of his or her immediate family can apply on the veteran's behalf. In regard to signing papers, a power of attorney can be used; however, the VA has several guidelines that must be met. If a loan will be closed in the veteran's absence, the borrower should consult the lender for current VA requirements.

Q. *If a veteran had served in more than one conflict, would it be possible to apply for and receive two VA loans?*

When the first property is purchased (for example, using World War II eligibility), the dual eligibility would have no impact. However, if the home was later sold and loan payments were not delinquent, the veteran could apply for a second VA loan pertaining to benefits from a second conflict period (for example, the Korean War) regardless of release from the first loan or the amount of the outstanding guaranty. The VA has set specific time limits within which to apply for the second loan.

Q. *How long does a veteran have to use his or her eligibility?*

There are no specific time frames, other than the requirement for dual eligibility just discussed. Eligibility is good until used.

THE GUARANTY

Q. *What are the VA guaranty and veteran's entitlement and eligibility?*

The difference in the terms guaranty, entitlement and eligibility when referring to VA loans is more semantic than actual. *Guaranty* in VA loans refers to the amount of the loan the VA will indemnify, or guarantee, for repayment to the lender should the borrower default. The terms *entitlement* and *eligibility* are used more when referring to the VA's relationship with the veteran.

In 1944, the original maximum entitlement available for home loan purposes was $2,000. It was raised to $4,000 on December 28, 1945; to $7,500 on July 12, 1950; to $12,500 on May 7, 1968; to $17,500 on December 31, 1974; to $25,000 on October 1, 1978; to $27,500 (or 60 percent of the loan amount, whichever is less) on October 1, 1980; and to $37,500 on January 1, 1988. On December 18, 1989, the VA guaranty was increased to a maximum of $46,000 for home and condominium loans, but the guaranty is based on the size of the loan.

Guaranty Guidelines

The guidelines, amended December 18, 1989, are as follows:

- For loans of $45,000 or less, 50 percent of the loan is guaranteed.
- For loans from $45,001 to $56,250, the guaranty is $22,500.
- For loans from $56,251 to $90,000, 40 percent of the loan is guaranteed.
- For loans from $90,001 to $144,000, the guaranty is $36,000.
- For loans from $144,001 to $184,000, 25 percent of the loan is guaranteed.
- For loans from $184,001 and up, the guaranty is $46,000.

Changes in the guaranty were made when it was found that the size of the loan was related to the frequency of defaults.

Applying these guidelines to a loan in the amount of $150,000, the following calculation would apply:

$$\$150,000 \times .25 = \$37,500 \text{ (guaranty)}$$

Q. *What kind of home could someone buy for even the full guaranty amount of $46,000?*

Don't confuse the guaranty amount with the loan amount. Most lenders, as a rule of thumb, will loan four times the amount of the guaranty with no down payment. The rationale is twofold:

1. When VA loans are sold into GNMA in the secondary market, a ceiling prohibits the purchase of mortgages in excess of $184,000 into the regular pool of loans (they have to be sold separately). In other words, the maximum guaranty of $46,000 times four would equal the GNMA ceiling!
2. The GNMA criteria for accepting a loan into its pool of mortgages require that the amounts of the veteran's entitlement (plus additional cash if needed) must equal at least 25 percent of the sales price. The bottom line is that even though VA has no maximum loan amount, secondary market restrictions may insist that a lender making a loan exceeding $184,000 (without additional down payment) either hold it in portfolio as an investment or

market it outside of the traditional secondary market channels.

Q. *So a borrower could actually get a VA loan in excess of $184,000?*

Absolutely. He or she would just have to make a 25 percent down payment on the difference between the sales price and $184,000 (and qualify for the loan, of course).

For example, if a veteran needed to finance a $200,000 sales price as a veteran, the first $184,000 of the purchase would have no down payment. He or she would have only to put down 25 percent of the difference.

$$\$200,000 - \$184,000 = \$16,000 \times 25 \text{ percent,}$$
$$\text{or a } \$4,000 \text{ down payment!}$$

Q. *Does the government set the interest rates allowed for VA loans?*

No. Interest rates for VA loans are negotiated between the lender and the borrower. In essence, this means that if more discount points are paid, the borrower can receive a lower interest rate. These points must be paid in cash at the time of closing and cannot be financed into the loan.

Q. *If just a portion of the entire loan is guaranteed, what actually happens if there's a default?*

First, since the lender becomes the owner of the defaulted property after foreclosure, VA could accept the property from the lender by reimbursing the amount of the outstanding loan balance plus foreclosure expenses. Second, the VA could instruct the lender to keep title to the foreclosed property and accept a check equal to the remaining balance times the guaranty percentage originally issued when the loan was originated. Typical risk to the lender in the case of default is minimal. Even with a mere 25 percent guarantee from VA, the lender will generally recoup 100 percent of the potential loss.

Q. *When else could a veteran have more than one VA loan at a time?*

While the veteran must agree, and sign papers to the effect, that he or she will live on the property when purchased, the veteran could have more than one outstanding VA loan at a time. Obviously, he or she would have to have adequate eligibility, and any outstanding loans would need to be paid current.

Q. *If someone can use his or her remaining VA eligibility for additional purchases even though VA loans remain outstanding, how does one calculate the amount of the guaranty available?*

In calculating a veteran's partial entitlement, the older $36,000 guaranty remains in effect for loans of $144,000 or less.

The calculations are a little tricky, but here's an example for calculating leftover, or "partial entitlement":

Joan Koch previously used $12,500 entitlement not restored (paid off). She has $23,500 additional entitlement:

$$36,000 - 12,500 = 23,500$$

However, if her new loan is in excess of $144,000, Joan's remaining entitlement is the difference between $46,000 and the previously used guaranty amount. In other words, she would have an additional entitlement of $33,500.

Q. *So how large a loan could a veteran with a remaining entitlement of $23,500 receive?*

Remember the rule of "four times the amount of the guaranty"? If the veteran could qualify, the lender would probably make a loan of $94,000 with no down payment.

Q. *Although the veteran must reside on the property after the initial purchase, does it have to be a single-family residence?*

No, the veteran could purchase a duplex, triplex or four-unit building as his or her residence; however, no additional guaranty is available just because the number of units in the purchase increase.

QUALIFICATION GUIDELINES

Q. *What are the buyer's qualifications for new VA loans?*

The following is an overview of how a veteran qualifies based on income, residuals and long-term debt.

In 1986, the VA began using a debt-to-income ratio for loan qualification. It is calculated by taking the sum of PITI (principal, interest, property tax and insurance), any special assessments (such as condo fees or local improvement district levies) and long-term obligations (those with repayment in excess of six months). Divide that amount by the total income, which includes gross salary and other compensation. The resulting percent or ratio cannot exceed 41 percent. If it does, it is fairly unlikely that the application will be approved.

Residual income remains a secondary VA qualifier along with the ratio. Residual income is determined by subtracting PITI, heat, maintenance and other utilities from the net effective income (income after taxes, long-term monthly debts and any child care, child support or alimony) (see figure 8.1). Think of residual income as leftover income. For example, according to the chart, a family of four in the West applying for a $60,000 mortgage must have a minimum of $930 per month left over after the residual income calculation.

While each case will be decided on its own merits, these are fairly firm guidelines that most local lenders will use in accepting or rejecting a loan. A typical qualifying form is shown in Appendix A.

Q. *Can a borrower ever exceed the 41 percent ratio rule and still be acceptable?*

The borrower can exceed the 41 percent ratio rule if the residuals are 20 percent (or more) than the residual income amount required based on the number of family members, the veteran's geographical area and the loan amount requested.

Q. *Do in-service veterans get any concessions in qualifying for a VA loan?*

Figure 8.1   Veterans Administration's Table of Residual Incomes, by Region

Loan Amounts of $69,999 and Below*

Family Members	Northeast	Midwest	South	West
1	$375	$367	$367	$409
2	629	616	616	686
3	758	742	742	826
4	854	835	835	930
5	886	867	867	965

Loan Amounts of $70,000 and Above**

Family Members	Northeast	Midwest	South	West
1	$433	$424	$424	$472
2	726	710	710	791
3	874	855	855	952
4	986	964	964	1,074
5	1,021	999	999	1,113

*For families with more than five members, add $75 for each additional member up to a family of seven.

**For families with more than five members, add $80 for each additional member up to a family of seven.

Note: For active duty service persons, the residual income figures from both tables can be reduced by a minimum of 5 percent if military benefits will continue to be received.

Geographic Regions

Northeast   Connecticut, Maine, Massachusetts, New Hampshire, New Jersey, New York, Pennsylvania, Rhode Island and Vermont.

Midwest   Illinois, Indiana, Iowa, Kansas, Michigan, Minnesota, Missouri, Nebraska, North Dakota, Ohio, South Dakota and Wisconsin.

South   Alabama, Arkansas, Delaware, District of Columbia, Florida, Georgia, Kentucky, Louisiana, Maryland, Mississippi, North Carolina, Oklahoma, Puerto Rico, South Carolina, Tennessee, Texas, Virginia and West Virginia.

West   Alaska, Arizona, California, Colorado, Hawaii, Idaho, Montana, Nevada, New Mexico, Oregon, Utah, Washington and Wyoming.

They certainly do. In-service veteran applicants can qualify with 5 percent less residual income than other applicants. The only criterion is that it must be proven that their military benefits will be continuous.

Q. *Even though the long-term debts are considered those that can't be paid off within six months, what about substantial short-term payments?*

Good point. The lender must consider the impact of any "substantial" monthly payment, even though it is scheduled to last less than six months. It's also the lender's decision to include monthly repayment amount minimums for credit accounts that have no outstanding balance.

Employment History

Q. *Do VA loan applicants need a two-year employment history as required with other loans?*

Yes. Two years of employment history will be verified. In addition, the borrower is asked to supply an original pay stub from his or her current employment.

Q. *What about active duty applicants? What do they have to verify?*

Active duty military must provide the lender with a current, not more than 90 days old, Leave and Earnings Statement.

Service members within 12 months of release from active duty will require additional information. The veteran will need to provide reenlistment documentation, verification of civilian employment following release, or a statement from the service member that he or she intends to reenlist or extend the period of active duty. The latter alternative would need to be supported by a letter from the service member's commanding officer confirming that the veteran is eligible for reenlistment.

Other offsetting factors that would weigh heavily in favor of the veteran getting the loan would be a down payment of at least 10 percent, significant cash reserves at closing or both.

Recently Discharged Veterans

Q. *What about recently discharged veterans who are currently employed, but haven't held a civilian job for two years? Would they be able to qualify for a loan?*

Perhaps. Veterans who are recently discharged (including veterans who have retired after 20 years of active military duty) may be able to secure a loan without the two year's employment history. Consideration is made on a case-by-case basis, weighing how similar the current line of work is to the veteran's military duties.

For example, a veteran who was formerly an airplane mechanic in military service, currently successfully employed as a machinist would give good indication that the work could be performed and the employment steady. But a former airplane mechanic who is now selling insurance may not give the lender a strong indication of employment stability in the early stages of the new job.

Overtime and Part-Time Income

Q. *Could overtime and part-time income count for VA qualifying?*

Again, the guidelines are pretty much the same as with other loans. Unless there is a two-year work history and the income is projected to continue, it might be used as a compensating factor, but not as true qualifying income.

Q. *Can educational loan benefits be included in income qualification for a VA loan?*

No, just on-the-job training benefits and VA retirement or disability income can be included for qualifying.

Q. *If the veteran can't qualify on his or her own, could a coborrower be used?*

Yes, the VA will consider the income and credit of a comortgagor who resides on the property. The VA will only guarantee the portion for which the veteran has qualified. This may pose a problem from the lender's standpoint as a partial guaranty is usually unacceptable to their thinking.

One solution might be to use two veterans as joint mortgagors, thus allowing an extended guaranty amount. Any loan processing in coborrower situations must be done directly by VA, not through automatic approval by direct endorsement lenders. (These are lenders who have met approval guidelines of the VA, and can approve loans in-house, without first submitting them to their respective regional VA offices.)

Borrowers with Bankruptcies

Q. *Would a veteran who had declared bankruptcy ever be able to get a VA loan?*

Obviously, each situation is evaluated on its own merits; and since there are several chapter filings of bankruptcy, each may be handled differently.

In general, the VA will want to see that the bankruptcy has been discharged for at least 24 months, and that credit has been satisfactorily reestablished. In addition, the lender may require letters of explanation, especially if the bankruptcy was less than three years ago, stating the circumstances behind the bankruptcy, and an indication that it's unlikely to reoccur.

Compensating Factors

Q. *What compensating factors could a veteran use to get VA loan approval, even with marginal qualifications?*

As with other loans, the VA has its own set of compensating factors:

- Excellent long-term credit
- Conservative use of consumer credit
- Minimal consumer debt
- Long-term employment
- Significant liquid assets
- Down payment or the existence of equity in refinancing loans

- Little or no increase in shelter expense
- Military benefits
- Satisfactory home ownership record
- High residual income
- Low debt-to-income ratio

Q. *To what extent can a seller financially help a buyer purchase his or her home under VA guidelines?*

Possibly to a great degree. If the buyer has adequate eligibility, the lender can lend 100 percent of the CRV (VA appraisal), and the seller is allowed to pay all closing costs, including prepaid items (such as insurance impounds and property tax impounds). This is sometimes referred to as "zero down, zero closing."

Q. *Could the veteran borrow the down payment for a loan?*

It depends. It would be acceptable if the borrowed funds were used to pay closing costs, or the down payment, provided the total of the down payment and loan do not exceed the CRV. Loan terms would have to be included in the application, and therefore the repayment amounts would be included in the qualifying ratio.

This is one of the areas where a borrower may have to shop for a lender who will take on this type of increased risk.

Q. *Can a borrower have a second mortgage simultaneous to originating a new VA loan?*

It *is* possible to use secondary financing simultaneous to the origination of a VA first mortgage, within certain boundaries:

- The CRV must exceed the amount of the first mortgage. In this way, the second mortgage could be used to secure the monetary difference between the appraised value and the first mortgage.
- The lender will want to know the repayment terms on the second mortgage and will add the debt service payment into the veteran's debt ratios.
- The lender may ask that the interest rate on the second mortgage not exceed the rate of the first mortgage, and

that any second mortgage be assumable. The idea is to avoid putting undue stress on the borrower, and to keep both loans from defaulting.

Even though second mortgages initiated simultaneous to first mortgages are approved by the VA, many lenders shun the practice, as they feel it creates too much leverage and possible stress on the veteran, which may strain the loan and cause default. The key here is to shop for local lenders who won't be afraid to take the risk with an otherwise qualified buyer.

Q.   *When might someone use an initial second mortgage simultaneous to a new VA first mortgage?*

A veteran might consider initiating a second mortgage simultaneous to a first not only for down payment but for qualifying as well, as in the following example:

The lender's VA interest rate has just jumped to 11 percent, making it impossible for Joe Smith to financially qualify for a $50,000 loan. However, if his credit union would carry a second mortgage of $10,000 at 9 percent with the balance of $40,000 at the lender's 11 percent first mortgage rate, he could qualify. The melding of the two rates for qualifying was enough to make the difference between no loan and owning his or her dream home.

Q.   *Could someone other than the seller pay for the veteran's costs of sale?*

Yes. In addition to those charges enumerated before that could be paid by the seller, a third party might pay part of the closing costs, e.g., attorney fees, title company fees and escrow closing agent fees. In fact, it would not be considered an illegal kickback for a lender to pay any or all of those costs mentioned, particularly if the loan was made to a buyer who was short on closing costs! Remember, if you don't ask, you usually don't get!

Q.   *What closing costs can the borrower pay?*

Although allowable charges to the veteran vary by VA regional office, here is a list of some of the more typical allowable costs for the borrower:

- Credit report charge
- Appraisal fee
- Recording and tax fees
- Proration of taxes or assessments
- Survey charges
- Hazard insurance
- Title fees
- Loan origination fee (up to 1 percent of the loan amount)
- Funding fee charged by VA
- Any allowable discount points

(For cost estimate worksheets, see Appendix A.)

Q. *Does each regional office tell the veteran exactly what costs he or she can pay?*

Somewhat; however, they phrase it as "costs the veteran is *not allowed* to pay"! Don't forget that closing costs (except the ones specified for payment by a certain party) are negotiable between the buyer and seller. The VA loan is the most restrictive type of loan when it comes to mandating which party can pay which cost.

Q. *Does the buyer have to pay the funding fee charged by the VA?*

No; in fact *anyone* can pay the funding fee—the buyer, the seller or another third party; or the fee can be financed into the loan. Also, veterans with any degree of permanent disability do not have to pay the funding fee, nor do surviving spouses of veterans who died in service or from a service-related disability.

Q. *Are funding fees different based on whether a veteran was active duty military, reservist or National Guard status?*

Yes. Figure 8.2 compares funding fees, including a new category for veterans who are making a subsequent (repeat) purchase using a VA loan.

Figure 8.2   VA Funding Fees (October 1, 1993)

Served in Active Duty

Down Payment	Fees for First-Time Use	Fees for Subsequent Use
0-5%	2.0%	3.0%
5-10	1.5	1.5
10 or more	1.25	1.25

Served in Reservists/National Guards:

Down Payment	Fee for First-Time Use	Fee for Subsequent Use
0-5%	2.75%	3.0%
5-10	2.25	2.25
10+	2.0	2.00

Q.   *What are discount points, and how do they work with VA loans?*

Lenders use discount points to increase the yield of a loan. Since VA and FHA loans are usually made at below-market rates, what lender in his or her right mind would be excited about making a guaranteed or insured loan at a lesser rate of interest? They wouldn't. That's why points can help bridge the gap between what they could lend conventional money for compared to what they can receive on government programs.

By definition, a point is equal to 1 percent of the amount financed. As a general rule of thumb, it takes between six and eight points to increase the interest rate by 1 percent over a 12-year period (which, by the way, is the median time most 30-year loans exist before being paid off). Knowing this, the lender is now ready to evaluate where conventional rates are today, how many discount points need to be charged to equalize the two rates, how much of a discount investors buying this loan will charge (such as in the secondary market), and what competing lenders are charging for points.

Therefore, if conventional money is typically going for 8 percent, while VA/FHA funds are at 7.5 percent, the lender would probably be looking at between three to four points to equalize the rates.

Q. *Do lenders ever negotiate points?*

It depends on the lender. Many times, in an effort to be competitive, a lender will negotiate or even waive part or all of the potential points to make the loan. This might occur if someone had been a good customer of a lending institution or had the potential to be a good customer. Lenders will sometimes loosen up on points when there's a glut of money in the marketplace and demand is down, or if they're in an expansion mode, vying for a heftier share of loans in the marketplace.

Q. *Who can pay points on a VA loan?*

Anyone! Points are negotiated between the parties in the purchase agreement. VA loans are getting more competitive; allowing veterans to pay points makes them even more so.

Q. *Are there times when the veteran is most likely to pay VA points?*

Yes, when he or she is building a home on his or her own property, refinancing an existing loan or purchasing a property from a legal entity that cannot or will not pay points, such as the executor of an estate, trustee or sheriff at a sheriff's sale.

Q. *Could the veteran ever pay more for the property than the value shown on the CRV?*

Yes, if the difference was paid in cash and did not come from a borrowed source. Note the amendatory language clause (Figure 8.3), which must accompany each VA purchase and sales agreement.

Q. *Would it be wise for a seller who would consider selling a home with VA financing to get a CRV before putting it on the market?*

It depends. Although the CRV does give a reasonable estimate of value, it may sometimes lean towards the more conservative end of the price range. This is particularly true when a VA appraisal is ordered prior to having an offer on the property. It puts more strain on the appraiser to determine valuation when there is no

Figure 8.3   VA Amendatory Language Clause

The purchase agreement entered into _____ ,
                                                           (date)
between the undersigned seller and purchaser, is hereby amended to include the
following statement:

"It is expressly agreed that, notwithstanding any other provision of this contract, the
purchaser shall not incur any penalty by forfeiture or earnest money or otherwise
be obligated to complete the purchase of the property described herein, if the
contract purchase price or cost exceeds the reasonable value of the property
established by the Veterans Administration. The purchaser shall, however, have
the privilege and option of proceeding with the consummation of this contract
without regard to the amount of reasonable value established by the Veterans
Administration."

_____   _____
(Date)   (Seller)

                                  _____
                                  (Seller)

                                  _____
                                  (Purchaser)

                                  _____
                                  (Purchaser)

offer setting the stage for what someone is ready, willing and able
to pay for a property. And if the appraisal is low, the damage has
been done since it is very difficult to massage the price up to where
it should or could be. Unless a particular buyer demands a VA
appraisal prior to making an offer, the borrower should use a
well-prepared comparative market analysis done by a real estate
agent to estimate value.

An appropriate time to secure a CRV prior to placing a property
on the market could be in the case of a specialty property, where
the approximate market value might be difficult to determine.

Q. *For what period is a CRV good?*

A CRV is generally good for six months on existing construction and up to one year on proposed new construction.

Q. *Are there any other points one should know regarding CRVs?*

Here are several additional tips for dealing with VA appraisals:

- The VA accepts FHA appraisals.
- Proposed construction should be preapproved by submission of plans and specifications to VA so that it can then make periodic inspections. Exceptions to this rule might include any dwelling with previous approval by FHA, a new dwelling that has been substantially completed for more than 12 months or a house located in a rural area, making routine inspections impossible.
- A veteran cannot be charged for a CRV unless the appraisal is ordered in his or her name.
- VA uses only VA-designated fee appraisers. Some private individuals who have met certain VA criteria are authorized to make VA appraisals.
- A particular VA regional office may change or adjust the value or conditions specified by a particular VA appraiser.

LOAN TYPES

Q. *What types of VA guaranteed loans are there?*

There are far more varieties of VA loans than we tend to think of! Even though VA loans must have a fixed rate of interest, payment amounts can vary according to the needs of the veteran. If, for example, a young couple wants to begin with a moderate payment to suit their budget, and then increase the amount paid monthly at the end of five years, they have several VA alternatives from which to choose, as described in this chapter.

VA Adjustable Rate Mortgages

Q. *What is the VA ARM?*

The VA ARM is a competitive ARM, using the same format as the FHA adjustable program. Using an annual payment cap of 1 percent and a lifetime payment cap of 5 percent, the program uses the treasury securities index and allows no negative amortization. The loan is assumable, with qualifying, at the loan's interest rate at the time of assumption.

The only negative factor is that, because of its typically lower rates, veterans must qualify at 1 percent above the loan's initial rate.

VA Graduated Payment Mortgage

Q.   What is the VA GPM?

The VA GPM is a great loan for using a minimal down payment while "graduating" the payment typically over the first five years by approximately 7.5 percent. The starting interest rate for the loan is usually approximately 2 to 3 percent below the standard VA rate.

VA Growing Equity Mortgage

Q.   Does VA have a GEM?

The VA permits a growing equity mortgage (GEM). Basically, the GEM grows equity more rapidly since, based on a 30-year amortized amount, payments increase 3 percent, 5 percent or 7.5 percent per year (based on the plan), with the additional monthly payment being applied directly to the principal. Under this program, loan payoffs usually occur in a little less than 17 years!

The GEM is a relatively new program for VA. The lender must be proactive in requesting this program, which includes submitting his or her GEM loan guidelines to the regional VA office for approval.

As mentioned previously, not all lenders may be interested in working with "creative" VA programs, which differ in underwriting guidelines from the regular VA programs. Borrowers may need to shop for the right lender just as fervently as they shop for the right program.

Q.   Is it possible for a VA loan to have a late charge?

A late charge may be levied if any installment is more than 15 days late. The amount charged cannot exceed 4 percent of the installment due.

Q. *Does VA insist that all tax and insurance payments be collected monthly along with the regular principal and interest payment?*

Interestingly enough, the VA does not mandate that impounds be held. However, the VA feels that it is a sound matter of practice and therefore allows the individual investors to hold escrow accounts if they so desire. In other words, this is more of a lender request and criterion than it is of the VA. The buyer may be able to use this as a bargaining point when applying for a VA loan; for example, the veteran may be willing to hold taxes and insurance fees in escrow monthly with the lender in return for lower points!

Q. *Does the VA require fire insurance as well as title insurance?*

The VA does require fire insurance to protect its collateral; however, the amount of the policy could exclude the value of the land.

Q. *Is there a prepayment penalty on a VA loan?*

VA loans can be paid at any time without penalty. In fact, any partial prepayment will apply directly to reducing the outstanding principal balance. And, unlike FHA loans that need at least one month's notice before prepaying (otherwise there will be a payment penalty), VA loans can be paid in full without notice.

Q. *What is a Certificate of Commitment?*

That's what this chapter has been about—getting the loan! The Certificate of Commitment, or loan approval, is valid for six months for existing and proposed dwellings. Although it cannot be extended for an existing dwelling, there is an extension period of six months if a proposed dwelling is involved.

ASSUMPTION GUIDELINES

Q. *What about selling a home encumbered by a VA loan? Would the loan have to be assumed by another veteran?*

A veteran or nonveteran can assume an existing VA loan. Loans written prior to March 1, 1988, can be simply assumed, meaning that there is no mandatory qualification process by anyone assuming an existing VA loan unless the veteran wanted either a total release of liability or a substitution of certificate. A total release of liability means that the veteran would not be held liable for any delinquencies or deficiency judgments should the loan default. Substitution of certificate goes one step further and releases the veteran from all liability on the loan, plus reinstates that amount on his or her Certificate of Eligibility. The latter can be accomplished only if the assumptor is a veteran who substitutes his or her Certificate of Eligibility for that of the selling veteran.

Q. *What are the assumption rules governing loans written on or after March 1, 1988?*

All VA loans originated after March 1, 1988, require prior approval by the loan holder (as trustee for the VA) before transfer of the property. Mandated by Public Law 100–198, the mortgage or deed of trust must clearly state the following in large letters on its first page: "This loan is not assumable without the approval of the Veterans Administration or its authorized agent." If the veteran fails to notify the lender before transferring the property or if the property is transferred to a buyer who has failed the credit-worthiness test, the lender could accelerate the loan, with the outstanding balance becoming immediately due and payable. The selling veteran has 30 days to appeal to the VA if a lender determines that a buyer is not creditworthy. If the VA overrides the lender's determination, the lender would then approve the assumption.

The assumption clause, which should be placed in all purchase and sales agreements of VA loan properties, is shown in Figure 8.4.

Q. *Will there be a charge for this new assumption policy?*

An assumption fee equal to one-half of 1 percent of the loan balance as of the date of transfer shall be payable to the VA at the time of transfer. If the assumptor fails to pay this fee, it will constitute an additional debt, and will be added to the face

---

Figure 8.4   VA Assumption Clause

Subject to a mortgage dated _____, 19____, in favor of _____, which mortgage grantee hereby assumes and agrees to pay according to its terms and also hereby assumes the obligation of _____ (Name of Veteran Mortgagor) ____, under the terms of the instruments creating the loan to indemnify the VA to the extent of any claim payment arising from the guaranty or insurance of the indebtedness above mentioned, and consents to his release from his obligations under the loan instruments.

The inclusion of the assumption clause will not, of course, ensure that a release from the VA can be obtained. This will depend upon the deed being recorded, loan being current and the purchaser's income and credit being acceptable.

Such inclusion will, however, permit releases in many cases that could not otherwise be approved. Also, the inclusion of the assumption clause will afford the veteran a right of action against the transferee and thus give the veteran some measure of protection even though VA may decline to release the veteran because the loan is in default or the transferee's income and credit are not acceptable.

---

amount of the mortgage. In addition, the loan holder may charge a processing fee to determine the assumer's creditworthiness.

Q. *If the selling veteran wanted to be free of liability plus have his or her eligibility reinstated on a particular loan, is it correct that the new buyer would either have to pay off the loan, or be a veteran willing to substitute his or her Certificate of Eligibility?*

That's correct. Although it may seem to be a minor point, it's easy to see the possible conundrum created after the veteran sells the property and wants to use his or her entire VA eligibility to buy a new property with a VA loan—only to find that part of his or her eligibility is still tied up on the property just sold!

Q. *If the veteran who initiates a mortgage under the old guidelines sells without obtaining a release of liability, could he or she ever obtain a release?*

Yes, if a subsequent purchaser down the line applied to the VA for the release of liability. The following conditions must be met to qualify: the loan must be current; income and credit of the purchaser must be acceptable to VA; and the purchaser must assume the loan and the indemnity obligation (owner occupancy is not required).

Remember, too, that unless that subsequent purchaser was also a veteran and substituted his or her Certificate of Eligibility, the original purchaser's Certificate of Eligibility (pertaining to that property) would not be released.

Q. *Is there any way the veteran could avoid liability from the VA when the property is sold outside of release of liability?*

No, but there is one measure the veteran could take to keep apprised of the condition of the existing loan:

The veteran can write the lender using certified mail, with return receipt requested, asking that the veteran be notified of any pending default on the loan. It would be important to keep the veteran's address updated with the lender as well. It may also be a good idea to record this letter at the courthouse. Even though this does not affect the title or the real estate, it does serve as notice should a default arise. It would be quite difficult for the lender to state that he or she was not aware that the veteran desired notification, especially if the buyer were requested to pay a deficiency judgment in the assumptor's behalf.

Q. *But doesn't the lender have to notify the veteran of any possible default?*

There is no VA regulation or law that requires that the initial mortgagor be notified. This has become a misconception by the public due to the fact that sometimes the lender searches out the veteran to step back in and take over payments in lieu of foreclosure (especially given the high cost of foreclosure to the lender). The VA generally attempts to contact the original veteran borrower, since courts in some states have ruled that VA may not collect an indebtedness from a veteran who did not receive notice of the foreclosure proceedings.

Nevertheless, should the loan default, the original obligor would still be secondarily liable. And remember, that original veteran was the one who pledged that he or she would repay the obligation, along with his or her VA eligibility entitlement.

The *VA Home Loan Guaranty Informational Issue* looks at foreclosure in this manner:

> Under the governing law, a veteran who obtains from a private lender a loan which is guaranteed or insured by the Veterans Administration is legally obligated to indemnify the United States government for the net amount of any guaranty or insurance claim the VA may hereafter be required to pay to the holder of the loan. This right of indemnity has been upheld by the Supreme Court of the United States, notwithstanding that a deficiency judgment was not obtained or was not obtainable by the mortgage holder under local state law. (U.S. v. Shimer, 367 U.S. 374, 1961)

Q. *In a default, could the original veteran purchaser ever be responsible for paying the guaranty amount back to the VA?*

Yes. The VA is entitled to receive indemnification from the veteran, which includes judicial action within our court system. Through this channel, the VA could attach the veteran's pension or Social Security income, and also withhold any subsequent VA benefits until the defaulted guarantee amount is paid in full.

Q. *Besides obtaining a release of liability, what other precautions should a veteran take when selling a property encumbered by a VA loan originated before March 1, 1988?*

Although there are no guarantees, here are some steps that may help:

- Know as much about the buyer as possible. Is he or she creditworthy? Ask that the buyer provide a credit report (if necessary, ask a credit counselor for help).
- How has the buyer managed his or her rent or mortgage payments in the past? Check with references provided, or ask to see canceled checks to landlords or to mortgage companies. Make these requirements conditions of sale and specify them in the purchase and sale agreement. In

other words, if the veteran is not satisfied with the answers provided, there won't be a sale.

- As a condition of sale, require that a performance guaranty be executed by the buyer, secured by a second mortgage on the property or any other real property they might have. This is a possible insurance policy in case of default, since the veteran would be notified of any pending default as a holder of a second mortgage (and therefore could step back into an equity position in the property).

  In addition, if a first or second mortgage was taken on an additional piece of property owned by the buyer, the veteran could foreclose on it to recoup any monies lost by the default of his own loan. In reality, most buyers are going to think long and hard before defaulting on a loan that could potentially take a large sum of money or assets out of their pockets.

- Ask that the assumptor give you a sizable down payment of your equity. Foreclosures on VA properties in recent years show that buyers with substantial down payments are far less likely to default.

REFINANCING

Q. *Can a veteran refinance an existing loan with a new VA loan?*

Yes. Up to 91 percent loan-to-value of the appraisal amount could be refinanced using a VA loan if equity is being pulled out. (This is equal to 90 percent loan-to-value plus the 1 percent funding fee.)

The Veterans Administration encourages interest rate reduction refinancing loans (IRRRL). The loan must be a VA loan, and the new rate must be lower than the previous rate. No appraisal or credit check is required, and the veteran does not have to currently occupy the property.

The refinanced loan amount may include the outstanding balance on the existing loan, allowable fees and closing costs including discount points and funding fees.

The lender can agree to pay all closing costs for the borrower and set an interest rate high enough to recover the advance of costs (but the rate must be lower than the loan being refinanced).

A VA fixed-rate loan can be refinanced with an adjustable rate loan as long as the initial ARM rate is lower than the fixed rate.

Q. *Is the Certificate of Eligibility automatically released to the veteran if the home is refinanced out of the VA program?*

No. It's a little-known fact that if one refinances an existing VA loan with a non-VA loan and does not sell the property, VA eligibility (pertaining to that property) will not be reinstated until the property is sold. The rationale is that VA housing programs are to benefit the owner/occupant, not to allow someone to amass income property units. At the time the property was sold or otherwise disposed of, the outstanding eligibility from that property would be reinstated.

Q. *Does an owner have to live in a property in order to refinance it with a VA loan?*

No, the property does not have to be owner-occupied. This is good to know if the original VA residence was purchased with the high interest rates of the early 1980s and is currently being used as a rental. Refinancing may be a chance to bring the rate down, lower the monthly payment and increase rental cash flow.

WORK-OUT PROGRAMS

Q. *It sounds as though the VA really wants to work with veterans to secure home loans. Do they ever help borrowers out if they get behind in their payments, rather than forcing foreclosure?*

The VA understands that base closures, layoffs and the like not only have adverse affects on borrowers, but can add incredible costs to guaranteeing VA loans in general. That's why they've introduced a VA preforeclosure program to eliminate formal foreclosure and work out loans in trouble.

Here's how it works. A veteran behind in payments contacts the lender. As discussed earlier, any borrower should not hesitate to contact the lender once he or she has trouble making any monthly payment. The lender will evaluate the situation, and if it appears that time, effort and money can be saved by doing a work-out program, the regional VA office will be contacted. If the regional office agrees and is willing to front any shortfall, the work-out is done.

If the veteran's property has $100,000 worth of liens against it and the fair market value of the property is only $95,000, that's a $5,000 shortfall. The work-out program would allow the real estate agent to bring in (and receive a commission for) a new buyer to step into the $95,000 loan, the $5,000 shortfall would be advanced to the lender from the regional VA office, and the seller (veteran) would be responsible for repaying the shortfall over time. Guidelines require that the veteran start repaying the shortage within 12 months of closing, plus a nominal rate of interest (approximately 7 percent).

While the veteran's loan eligibility is frozen until the shortfall is repaid in full, at least formal foreclosure has been sidestepped and the veteran may be able to qualify for another loan in the future. In fact, the lien that the veteran pays back is no longer secured by the property, merely by a promissory note to the VA regional office. Should the veteran fail to repay the note, however, the VA would be able to take action to enforce payment, including attachment of the veteran's assets. The VA and lender both win because they have a new, stronger buyer in the property and have not spent the time or expense in a formal foreclosure action. The veteran can then get back on track to use his or her VA eligibility on another home in the future.

It's encouraging to see that the VA and lenders are agreeing that foreclosure is not always the only way to satisfy a potential loan default, and that they are willing to work with borrowers to find alternative remedies.

VA regional offices are listed in Appendix B.

CHAPTER 9

LOAN PROGRAMS WITH LEVERAGE

As the saying goes, "money talks." But for many real estate purchasers today, there is barely enough in their pockets to whisper. That's why many loan programs employ the concept of leverage. By definition, real estate leverage is the use of a small amount of asset to purchase a larger asset (something like robbing Peter to pay Paul). Just like anything else, leverage is an excellent tool when used in moderation. When taken to the extreme, robbing Peter to pay Paul makes Peter a "Paul-bearer."

Lenders offer special programs, usually identified with acronyms such as GEM, RAM, GPM and PAM, tailor-made to assist a targeted market segment of mortgage buyers. Many of the programs discussed in this chapter are based on leveraging concepts introduced in Chapter 9.

GROWING EQUITY MORTGAGES

Q. *What is the GEM and how does it work?*

The growing equity mortgage, or GEM, is a fixed-rate, 20-year or 30-year amortizing loan, with annual payment increases of 3 percent, 5 percent or 7.5 percent annually, depending on the lender's individual plan. These characteristics alone may not sound unique; the difference, however, is that the monthly payment increases are applied directly to reduce the principal. This will cause most loans to be paid in full between years 13 and 15.

Most lenders will qualify GEM borrowers at the initial payment amount and ask for a minimum of 10 percent down. A bonus GEM program even allows the borrower to qualify at a discounted introductory rate, sometimes as low as 2 to 3 percent below the standard rate. This is done by using an up-front temporary buydown of the interest rate.

It's clear to see what type of buyer can benefit from the GEM—one who needs up-front leverage today, but will be able to meet the payment increases of the future: young professionals, M & Ms (married and mortgaged) and first-time buyers who need help in qualifying.

Q. *How about buyers making a final home purchase? Is the GEM good for them?*

It certainly is. As stated earlier, depending on the GEM plan chosen, the loan will be retired between 13 and 15 years. This is great for a final home purchase for people in their early 50s, since they are usually building into their highest income years. Many middle-aged buyers have trimmed their family expenses since their kids are grown, and want their new loan to retire by the time they do!

Q. *Are there any special types of GEM programs?*

Both VA and FHA allow GEM mortgages. In the fall of 1988, the VA began allowing lenders to write their own VA GEM programs. Once the individual lender's plan is approved by VA, the lender is free to add the program to his or her other guaranteed VA program offerings. Although many lenders are unaware of this expansion, VA lenders who do have their GEM programs approved are finding them a welcome source of funding.

Q. *What are the qualifying guidelines for the FHA GEM?*

The qualifying guidelines for the FHA GEM are the same as those for the standard FHA 203(b) program. Since there is no negative amortization and all payment increases are applied directly to reduce the principal balance, FHA does not see this as a high-risk loan.

Q. *Is it easy to find lenders who do special programs for FHA and VA?*

It may take some looking to find a lender who does enough of them to really know how to do them, and who wants to take them on. If a lender is doing a small volume of these specialty loans, it may cost him or her more when they are sold into the secondary market because of the deeper discount that may be taken. It may help to refer back to some of the tips offered in chapter 7 regarding how to develop a working relationship with a progressive lender.

REVERSE ANNUITY MORTGAGES

Q. *How do reverse annuity mortgages, available to older home owners, work?*

The reverse annuity mortgage (RAM) allows persons over the age of 55 to release equity in their primary residences without having to sell and move from their homes. Although the concept has been around for quite some time, it has only been in practice by several large insurance companies since the late 1970s. One of the best ways to explain it is through the following example.

> Mr. and Mrs. Barker are retired. He's 73 years old, she's 71. They have few financial assets with the exception of their home, which is worth approximately $100,000 and is free and clear. Mrs. Barker falls ill, requiring an extended hospital stay. Their meager health plans are not enough to cover all the medical expenses, present or anticipated. In searching for a way to pull money out of their home, the only source they find is a high-rate, relatively short-term mortgage. Even if they take this option, the prospect of having to repay the debt on a monthly basis terrifies them. (Note the fixed rate comparison in Figure 9.1.) It seems that the only solution is to sell the property to free up their cash.
>
> One of their friends suggests that they investigate the RAM, which she had read about in a newsletter from the American Association of Retired Persons (AARP). She said that lenders who use the RAM would base the loan amount on a percent of the owner's equity in the property, without the owners having to sell the property or repay the loan in their lifetime.
>
> The Barkers found a lender, a mortgage company subsidiary of a large insurance conglomerate, that was willing to loan them up to 80 percent of the equity in their home through monthly

---

Figure 9.1   Comparison of Standard Mortgage with Term Reverse Mortgage

---

	Standard Mortgage at 10% Interest for 30 Years	**Term Reverse Mortgage at 10% Interest for 7 Years**
When Loan Is Made		
Home Value	$70,000	$70,000
Homeowner's Equity*	$5,000	$70,000
Loan Terms		
Principal Advanced to Borrower	$65,000 at loan origination	$459.17 per month for seven years (= $38,570)
Repayment by Borrower	$570.42 per month for 30 years (= $205,351)	$56,000 at end of loan term
Total Interest Paid by Borrower	$140,351	$17,430
At End of Loan Term		
Homeowner's Equity	$70,000 plus 30 years of appreciation	$14,000 plus seven years of appreciation

---

*This comparison assumes that the standard mortgage borrower makes a $5,000 down payment, and that the reverse mortgage borrower owns the home free and clear of any other debt.
©1991, American Association of Retired Persons. Reprinted with permission.

payments over the next five years (thus the term *reverse annuity* mortgage). This payout schedule was based on the Barkers' remaining actuarial years as shown from life insurance statistics. (Several types of RAM plans are compared in Figure 9.2.)

What about paying the money back? Their particular program specified no mandatory payback until neither of the spouses had use of the property and were to sell or the heirs desired to dispose of the property to settle the Barkers' estate. If Mr. and Mrs. Barker outlived the annuity period, the sum advanced would accrue simple interest until either of these occurred.

Figure 9.2   Comparison of Reverse Annuity Mortgages

**Four Different Term Reverse Mortgages
on an
$80,000 Home at 10 Percent Interest**

	Loan A	Loan B	Loan C	Loan D
Loan Term	4 years	4 years	8 years	8 years
Monthly Advance	$300	$1,000	$300	$400
Total of Monthly Advances	$14,400	$48,000	$28,800	$38,400
Total Interest	3,364	11,212	15,420	20,560
Maximum Loan Balance at Term	17,764	59,212	44,200	58,960
Remaining Equity at Term with				
0% Appreciation	$62,236	$20,788	$35,780	$21,040
3% Appreciation	72,277	30,829	57,122	42,382
6% Appreciation	83,234	41,786	83,288	68,548

©1991, American Association of Retired Persons. Reprinted with permission.

The Barkers got the funds they needed, were able to remain in their home and felt as though they had settled the situation on their own without burdening their family.

Q. *What are the tax implications of the RAM?*

As shown in Figure 9.1, a good portion of the sum advanced is attributed to interest. Early on, there was some controversy as to whether the RAM generates taxable income or not. Some proponents claim that it's not taxable, much like refinancing your home. Prior to recommending this type of financing, one is best advised to consult a CPA or tax adviser.

Q. *How many lenders are making RAMs, and who are they?*

Large insurance companies and their subsidiaries continue to be a logical source of funding, since they would also benefit by writing life insurance for applicants as well.

To find out more about RAM programs and general guidelines, write to AARP at 1909 K Street, NW, Washington, DC 20049.

Since insurance companies must be licensed by each state in which they do business, the state insurance commissioner could probably provide a list of companies and may even have them earmarked as to the type of business they do.

Q. *Weren't the first RAMs tied to some bad publicity?*

That's putting it mildly. The first RAMs in the late 1970s created much controversy, as they required that repayment to the mortgagee begin once the entire annuity had been paid out. This was exactly what the retired person was trying to avoid—thus an initial "black eye" was given to the early RAM programs. Today the program guidelines are monitored not only by consumer groups such as the AARP, but by federal guidelines as well.

GRADUATED PAYMENT MORTGAGES

Q. *It seems as though GPMs fall in and out of favor with homebuyers. Are they a good idea?*

Graduated payment mortgages were very popular in the late 1970s before the general economy (including the real estate market) lost steam. Many homeowners holding GPMs could not keep pace with the increasing payments during tight economic times, and foreclosures skyrocketed. In addition, many of the programs contained negative amortization—a payment shortfall that fails not only to cover any principal reduction, but also to cover interest charges. This shortfall is added back onto the principal. GPM-financed property in some cases had far more owing on it than it could conceivably bring at sale, creating a nightmare for sellers and lenders alike.

As FHA GPM programs are still available, they are described in greater detail in Chapter 7.

Q. *When do GPMs make sense?*

Underwriting guidelines and buyer protections have improved since those early years, and today make GPMs less of a frightful commodity. Graduated payment mortgages are actually a good idea when buyers' needs meet the following criteria:

- Income will increase (predictable increases).
- The property value is expected to rise (preferably at least keeping pace with the payment increase).
- Ownership of the property is not short-term (this prevents any negative amortization from overleveraging the real estate into a "zero-net" position, meaning no proceeds are received from the sale).

Q. *If the interest rate is fixed but the payments increase, what happens to the shortfall in the early years of the loan?*

The shortfall, or negative amortization that occurs, is added back onto the principal balance. Here is the way FHA (in consumer circular 60332) describes how the GPM works:

> Under the GPM program, the homebuyer will, in effect, be borrowing additional money during the early years of the mortgage, which will be used to reduce the monthly payments. The additional loan is added to the outstanding mortgage payments in later years.

In other words, the shortfall is tacked back onto the loan. And should one sell before falling even with the board, the seller may be faced with owing more than was originally contracted for—and heaven forbid, more than the property is worth.

The payments on this particular GPM do not exceed the regular amortization schedule until year five, not to mention the shortfall created up to that point. Even though the GPM can be an excellent leverage tool for the first-time buyer when used correctly, it's definitely a loan to approach carefully, and with strategies set. As seen by the figures, it's not a financing vehicle for short-term owners.

Q. *Does FHA insure GPMs?*

Yes; in fact, they currently have five plans that vary in annual payment increases and number of years over which the payments can increase. The greater the rate of increase or the longer the period of increase, the lower the mortgage payments are in the early years. After a period of five or ten years, depending on which plan is selected, the mortgage payments level off and stay at that level for the remainder of the loan.

BIWEEKLY MORTGAGES

Q. *Can a borrower save money by paying one-half of the regular monthly mortgage payment every two weeks?*

Yes. In fact considerable interest can be saved over the life of a 30-year loan with payments via the biweekly mortgage.

Instead of making 12 monthly payments per year, the borrower makes 26 half-payments (52 weeks in the year give that extra boost!). By attacking the principal balance with a reduction every two weeks, the borrower saves substantially on interest, and the loan's payoff period is reduced. Take a look at the example below.

A 30-year $100,000 fixed-rate loan with interest at 12.5 percent pays off 12 years faster with biweekly payments than it does with monthly payments—and with almost $127,000 less interest! And when the biweekly payment mortgage is paid off, there would still be over $78,000 worth of principal remaining on the monthly payment loan!

Q. *Why aren't more biweekly mortgage plans available?*

Initially, the secondary market did not purchase the loans after they were made. It also takes a total reworking of the lender's automated bookkeeping systems (converting from 30-day periods to 14-day time frames). Besides being very costly, this change is also very time-consuming and labor-intensive. And last, many lenders say they are concerned that if a buyer misses just one payment in a two-week period, technically he or she would be in default. So many lenders would prefer that borrowers go with the conventional 30-day payment and make additional payments if they so desire.

Regardless of whether these concerns are well founded, lenders using the program are finding that it does serve and benefit a certain segment of buyers. People who get paid every two weeks find that it helps them budget, since most payments are set up as automatic withdrawals from checking accounts. In this way, the check is deposited, say on Thursday evening, and on Friday, one-half of the mortgage payment is made. (The negative, of course, is that the lender gets use of the buyer's cash flow!)

Biweekly mortgaging is not new. Canadians have been using it for many years. Most lenders will be glad to run a computer printout showing how this program compares to the monthly payment mortgage.

One last point. After hearing about the biweekly mortgage, many people ask if they can convert their existing program to biweekly payments. Most lenders will not allow this, since the loan has already been set up for amortization, as well as sold into the secondary market. However, lenders encourage borrowers to make additional payments to apply strictly to principal reduction if they so desire.

PLEDGED ACCOUNT MORTGAGES

Q. *Who would use a pledged account mortgage and how does it work?*

The pledged account mortgage (PAM) has pretty well gone the way of the dinosaur, particularly with low interest rates on savings accounts. The concept is fairly simple, however. A sum of money is placed in an insured account (thus the term *pledged account*). The account draws interest, and there may be periodic withdrawals from the account to offset the payments on a first mortgage or second obligation, as in the following example.

Jim and Maria Donner have $50,000 to cash out and assume an existing $50,000 loan on a $100,000 property. Instead, they decide that they will close the sale initially with only $20,000, allowing the remaining $30,000 to accumulate interest. (They might also use a portion of the money to purchase CDs or other secure investments, if it were approved by the seller and placed in their contract.) At a predetermined time, the Donners take the balance of the cash-out sum out of the account and pay off the obligation to the seller.

This may seem like a fairly abstract example, but really it's no different than a seller setting aside a temporary 3-2-1 buydown account to assist the buyer in lowering the interest rate 3 percent the first year, 2 percent the second and 1 percent the third year. Builders many times will set aside a pledged account to offset the buyer's new payments in very much the same way.

BRIDGE LOANS

Q. *Are bridge loans a good idea, and when might one be used?*

A bridge loan is really an equity loan used for a specific purpose—usually to financially "bridge" the cash flow gap from one property into the purchase of another, as shown in the following example.

> Nalda Negri has $20,000 worth of equity in her home, and wants to purchase and close a loan on a second property because it's such a great buy! Small problem: Her first home has not yet sold. A lender might loan a percent (usually not more than 75 to 80 percent, which would be between $15,000 and $16,000 in this case) of the current equity in the home to bridge the transactions.

The bridge loan can be an effective acquisition tool, but not before answering the following questions:

- What are the terms of repayment for the bridge loan? (Many lenders may accept "interest only," with balloon payments within six to eight months.)
- What would happen if the first property does not sell within an estimated period of time? Are additional mortgage payments financially possible?
- What are the costs of borrowing bridge loan funds? Does it counter any anticipated savings on the second property?
- How will the bridge loan affect the financing possibilities on the sale of the first property? (This is particularly

important to consider if there's an underlying assumable first mortgage at a low interest rate.)

SAFE AND SANE LEVERAGE THAT WORKS

Q. *Using leverage to purchase sounds great. Is there a way that a prospective buyer can start thinking about all the options, particularly what costs to negotiate when purchasing?*

Conventional lender procedures have taken away a great deal of creativity in real estate finance. The sad part is that since many borrowers don't fit into a "conventional lender" mold, they feel that can't purchase a home! Whatever happened to the good old days when down payments were bartered, and a clod of dirt passing from the seller to the buyer constituted a sale?

This is not to suggest a return to these old ways; however, buyers can approach their purchases creatively when they understand how debits and credits come together on the closing statement.

Here's a question to get the creative wheels turning: Who must pay for standard title insurance in a sale? The buyer? The seller? Someone! Answers may be based on area custom or on what lenders typically do or real estate agents suggest; the bottom line is that title insurance, like most closing costs, is negotiable among the parties! Unless the loan program or lender specifies who can pay what, it's open season for negotiating those costs.

Q. *How does someone who doesn't know a lot about real estate finance find these options?*

It's a good idea to consult real estate professionals. Agents, appraisers, lenders and real estate educators are usually happy to help buyers and sellers uncover creative finance options.

CHAPTER 10

LEVERAGE FROM THE SELLER

Very few purchasers of real property today have the financial capability to pay cash for their purchases. In reality, any time someone finances all or part of a property purchase, he or she is using leverage. A 5 percent down payment may be considered a highly leveraged purchase when using seller financing; whereas that amount of down payment may be the norm for a conventional loan from an institutional lender.

This chapter will show the positive and negative effects of leverage and ways it can be used to assist in purchasing real estate. The focus will be on seller financing, including its use along with conventional programs. Two other techniques involving the seller will be discussed—lease purchases and loan assumptions. Seller financing is often an option in a buyer's market. Depending on the circumstances of the seller, it can work well for everyone no matter what the market.

THE POWER OF LEVERAGE

Here's a simple example to show the power of real estate leverage:

If the Patels had $50,000 to use as a down payment, they could use it in a variety of ways. They could put the entire sum down on a $100,000 piece of property called property A; or they could put $10,000 down on each of five separate $100,000 properties, A, B, C, D and E. If appreciation were estimated at 10 percent per annum, should the Patels decide to sell in one year, they would have made $10,000 on property A. But look at the increase in property value with properties A through E—a whopping $50,000! By using leverage, the Patels have been able to double their investment in one year!

The foregoing example shows how leverage can be positive. When does it become negative? Possibly when any combination of the following are present in extreme amounts: low equity, low appreciation or low inflation.

Consider the following example regarding how these three items may interact to create a leverage nightmare:

The Carpenters have purchased their first home, using a land sales contract/seller finance agreement. They felt that this was the best way to purchase the property, because they had less than the typical 10 percent down payment required by local lenders in their area, and were marginally qualified for the $820 per month principal and interest payment. Their offer to the seller contained a provision that they would refinance the property at the end of their fifth year of ownership. This was agreeable to the seller, as she would soon be retiring and would need her equity out of the property at that time to supplement her Social Security.

The Carpenters closed the sale and all appeared fine—until the balloon payment due date neared. A preliminary loan qualification appointment with the lender revealed that not only were the Carpenters not qualified to receive a loan the size of the one needed, but the property would not appraise for anywhere near the amount of the balloon promised to the seller. What could be done? The seller needed her equity to retire and the Carpenters' financial hands were tied, not to mention that they felt that they had purchased a property that might be capable of wagging its tail and barking! The alternative, to not fulfill the balloon payment, could mean foreclosure, with the Carpenters forfeiting their down payment and any potential equity in the property, plus blemishing their credit rating.

But luck was with the Carpenters. The seller was willing to extend the period on the balloon, which not only helped the Carpenters build equity, but gave inflation a chance to bring the appraisal price up.

Is seller financing negative because it creates too much leverage? Absolutely not. Seller financing can serve as one of the most beneficial ways to finance a property, not to mention one of the best sources of higher return on seller investment. To create a win-win situation, however, reality, desires and financial capabilities of the parties must be addressed.

PROS AND CONS OF SELLER FINANCING

Q. *Who is the typical purchaser who uses seller financing?*

As stated earlier, it is difficult to generalize about types of buyers; however, many purchasers who use seller leverage fall into the following categories:

- He or she is creditworthy but has only a limited amount of funds for down payment and closing costs.
- The buyer has only enough for a down payment, but not closing costs.

Q. *What are the advantages to the buyer in having the seller finance all or part of a real estate purchase?*

Depending on the circumstances, there can be quite a few. Here are some of the more common positive points the buyer would want to consider:

- There are no constraints on what the seller can and cannot pay to assist the buyer, such as may be found with bank financing programs.
- The buyer could negotiate the interest rate and the repayment schedule, and might even request that payments be made biweekly (½ payment twice monthly) in order to save interest during the life of the loan. The buyer could also negotiate a partial amortization of the loan. For example, a $50,000 obligation might have monthly payments on only $25,000 for the first five years. The remaining $25,000 would sit idle, waiting to be amortized at a predetermined date. Balloon payments could also be used to satisfy the balance.
- The buyer could request special conditions of purchase, such as having a portion of the property released free and clear upon the repayment of a certain sum of the principal.

- The buyer could include personal property in the purchase, such as household appliances and vehicles.
- The buyer can save on closing costs, since loan processing fees and points are eliminated and therefore make a larger down payment or buy a more expensive home.
- The buyer would only have to pass the scrutiny of the seller, not a loan committee or loan underwriter, such as with bank programs. In addition, he or she could stretch to a more expensive property than customarily could be afforded if qualifying through conventional mortgage lenders.
- He or she could sidestep the cost of PMI by using seller financing.
- The buyer could purchase a property that does not meet the appraisal guidelines of most bank lenders. The property might vary from the norm in condition, age, amount of land included or style of architectural structure for the area.
- He or she can purchase the property without the constraints of an appraisal. Sometimes buyers may want to offer a price at the top of market value to compensate the seller for carrying the financing.
- The buyer could have input as to what type of security document is used to secure the sale, such as mortgage, deed of trust or land sales contract. For example, if the buyer desired that title not transfer until the obligation was paid in full, an unrecorded land sales contract might be used (depending on the statutes of the state). On the other hand, if the buyer were making a large down payment and desired that title pass at closing, the mortgage or deed of trust might be more appropriate. Obviously, the seller and his or her attorney would have an equal, if not greater amount of input here.

Q. *Seller financing sounds very flexible and positive for the buyer; but what are the negative factors of seller financing for the buyer?*

Although the negative factors will vary based on the situation, here are a few of the more common problems. It's interesting to note that the advantages can also become disadvantages depending on the circumstances.

- The buyer could pay the loan in full and still not receive title to the property. Although fairly uncommon, it could occur when a land sales contract is used and title does not pass until the obligation is paid in full. In rare cases, the seller may not have title vested in his or her name, or there may be liens or other encumbrances against the property about which the buyer or seller did not know. The buyer might have to sue the seller to gain title.
- The purchaser could make payments to the seller, but the seller might not make payments on senior loans that could result in property foreclosure. Placing the documents with, and making the payments through, a third-party escrow holder is advisable for buyer and seller.
- The buyer might be paying too much for the property, since appraisals are not always done in seller-financed transactions.
- He or she might buy a property with severe physical deficiencies that go uncovered, since a technical property inspection or appraisal generally is not part of seller-financed transactions.
- The buyer may be using only a small down payment and may therefore not be strongly committed to withstand tough financial times with the property should they occur.
- The buyer might get in over his or her head as far as size of monthly payment is concerned. If very creative terms such as "interest only" are used, payments will not be decreasing the principal balance. This could be dangerous, particularly if appreciation is low and the property will be held only for a short period.
- The buyer could finance personal property into the loan, causing depreciated property to actually cost the buyer many times worth its value.
- The buyer would have no mortgage insurance to protect any loss he or she might incur. Depending on state statutes, a deficiency judgment could attach to all property owned by the buyer, real and personal, if the property were foreclosed.

- The buyer would not necessarily have the property in his or her name until paid in full (depending on the type of security document used). Therefore, additional loans secured by the equity in the property could not be made to the buyer until the property was paid in full.

Q. *What are the benefits to the seller in carrying financing for a buyer?*

The following are several of the more common advantages to the seller who carries financing for the buyer:

- The seller could increase his or her yield on investment in the property due to the return of equity plus interest. For example, a $30,000 seller-carried 15-year second mortgage with interest at 9 percent per annum would give the seller $24,774 in additional proceeds on the sale. This is an 83 percent increase over what would have been received without the use of seller financing.
- The seller could possibly negotiate a higher interest rate than could be received on many other types of investments. (Rates are typically on a par with those of commercial real estate funds.)
- The seller could ask for full price, since he or she is assisting the buyer with financing.
- The seller could negotiate the terms and conditions of the sale, including remedies for default, maintenance of property condition and repayment schedule (biweekly, etc.).
- He or she can open up the property to a larger field of buyers by offering seller financing.
- The seller can trim closing costs, especially the payment of points and other fees typical to mortgage lenders.
- The seller could sell the property "as is" without costly repairs required by conventional lending institutions.
- He or she could screen the buyer for creditworthiness, ability to pay, and verification of employment.
- He or she could ask the buyer to provide a PMI policy to protect the seller against default on the financing.
- The seller could choose (with legal counsel) which security document is best to secure his or her interest until the loan is paid in full.

- The seller could defer payment of tax on gain, since tax would only be paid as proceeds are received.

Q. *What is the downside of seller financing for the seller?*

Obviously, many of the buyer advantages, reversed, could become the seller disadvantages. Here's how they stack up.

- The seller could accommodate the buyer by taking a small down payment or paying closing costs, only to discover later that the buyer walked away from the property because his or her investment was minimal.
- The seller may not have gotten the true credit picture of the buyer; or the financial strength of the buyer may have changed after the sale was closed. Since a loan officer is usually not qualifying the buyer based on ratios or debts, the buyer may also have taken on too much of a payment obligation.
- The seller may have to foreclose to regain ownership of the property. Depending on the type of security document used, as well as where the property is located, this could take between 30 days up to more than a year before complete.
- The seller may find the foreclosed property in a different condition than when it was sold; repairs may be needed to restore it to proper condition.
- The owner could sell personal property with the real estate, only to find it destroyed or missing should default occur.
- The seller could use creative terms in the loan, such as "interest only" or balloon payments, only to find that there has not been sufficient appreciation to increase the property value, making any subsequent buyer refinancing impossible.
- The seller might use a security document that transfers title to the borrower, such as a mortgage or deed of trust, only to find that the buyer secured a junior lien against the property to pull out equity, and then abandoned the property.

- Judgments or liens may attach to the property, clouding the title and making it impossible to transfer it free and clear to the buyer, even though the loan has been satisfied.
- Tax liens for unpaid taxes may attach to the property, causing it to be sold at tax sale.
- The seller might not use a competent real estate attorney in the preparation of a land sales contract; therefore, the seller's interests may be ill protected in a weak, loophole-laden agreement should it ever be tested in court.

Q. *Although seller financing seems to have many strong points, what are some steps both buyer and seller could take in order to protect against mishaps?*

A seller-financed sale won't be good for either party unless it's good for both parties. Besides having a meeting of the minds between buyer and seller, there are several questions that need to be answered thoroughly and satisfactorily:

- Is the seller aware of the buyer's credit status? Has the buyer's employment been checked? What assets does the buyer have in addition to the property? Remember, the seller is serving the same capacity as a bank and should ask many of the same qualifying questions.
- Is the payment structure feasible and plausible for the buyer?
- Is the down payment coming from a borrowed source? Repayment of the down payment may create extra leverage, causing financial strain on the buyer.
- If creative terms or a balloon are part of the transaction, how much stress do they place on the sale? It's amazing how time flies when a balloon payment is due in five years!
- Are both parties' interests spoken to in the contract drafted between the parties? Even though one party's attorney may be drawing the document, it's wise for the second party's attorney to at least review the paperwork before closing.

- Will a third-party escrow holder keep the documents in safekeeping for the parties, as well as receive and disburse payments between the parties?
- Is the remedy feasible for curing a default should it occur? Is the time frame for doing so a standard one based on the security document and applicable legal statutes?
- What are the provisions for insurance coverage? Will the seller continue to carry any coverage? This is particularly important if there are senior lien holders. Will funds be impounded monthly for payment of taxes and insurance, or will the seller merely require that the buyer deposit paid receipts annually with the escrow holder?

As with any type of real estate transaction, emphasis should be placed on making the sale an equitable, positive experience. This is particularly important in seller financing, however, since the business relationship between the parties extends until the loan is paid in full. In this way, the success or demise of the transaction is directly proportionate to the terms and conditions negotiated between the parties.

USING SELLER FINANCING

Q. *In what ways could seller financing be used to put sales together?*

As Second Mortgage

Seller financing typically has been used as a method of bridging the difference for the buyer between an existing loan and the down payment he or she has available, as illustrated in the following example.

The purchase price of the Carlsons' house is $80,000. The Carlsons have an assumable loan of $55,000. Therefore, it would take $25,000 for the Buxtons to cash out all of the Carlson's equity. But if the Carlsons would take the Buxtons' $10,000 down payment and agree to carry the remaining $15,000 in seller financing, the sale could be made.

Q. *With so many mortgage loans today containing the due-on-sale clause, isn't it difficult to assume an underlying loan and use a seller-carried second loan without disturbing the terms of the first mortgage?*

Yes. Since the alienation, or due-on-sale clause began receiving renewed interest in the early 1980s, it has been more difficult to simply assume existing mortgage loans without the lender altering the interest rate, charging assumption fees and qualifying the new buyer. In fact, some lenders will not allow loans with a due-on-sale clause to be assumed at all! It should be stressed here that seller financing is not a method to sidestep the due-on-sale clause in loans. The potential downstream effects of trying to hide a sale from a lender are not worth the benefits a seller or buyer might glean from making the sale.

As Wraparound Financing

Q. *I've heard of people trying to sidestep the due-on-sale clause by using wraparound seller financing. This isn't a good idea, is it?*

No, it isn't. Wraparound financing, whether financed by a seller or an institution, is exactly what its name implies—it's new financing that "wraps around" existing financing. The best way to explain it is through an example.

In the previous example, the Carlsons had an existing $55,000 mortgage, at an interest rate of 9 percent, on their $80,000 house. Since the Buxtons had only a $10,000 down payment ($15,000 short of cashing out all of the seller's equity), the Carlsons agreed to carry the $15,000 on a second mortgage for 15 years including interest at 11 percent per annum. The monthly payment on the second mortgage will be $170.50, plus, of course, the payment on the first mortgage, which was assumed by the Buxtons. This situation would be an assumption, with a seller carryback.

The party in control in the earlier example is the lender on the first mortgage. Based on what he or she would require, the new buyer might have to fully qualify to assume the loan, withstand an interest rate increase on the loan (perhaps raised to current market-rate interest) and pay an assumption fee to the lender. Sometimes the buyer is capable of satisfying the lender's requirements; sometimes not. As mentioned previously, the lender might disallow any assumption of the loan, causing the buyer to find new financing, often at a higher rate of interest.

This is where the wraparound comes in. Prior to test cases in courts of law concerning the due-on-sale clause, it was thought that if the first mortgage remained untouched, and a new loan was wrapped around the old loan, the lender wouldn't be the wiser, and ownership of property could transfer without intervention (and fees charged) by the pesky lender.

The configuration of the wraparound is different than that of the assumption and second mortgage. With the wraparound, the sales price minus the down payment gives a new principal balance to amortize, as in the following example:

Going back to the Carlsons and the Buxtons, if the Buxtons' $10,000 down payment were subtracted from the $80,000 purchase price it would create a new loan to amortize of $70,000, including interest at 11 percent, payable at $795.66 per month for 15 years. These terms could be anything negotiated between the parties, but should at least match the term of years remaining on the first mortgage. This is so title on the underlying loan could be released upon satisfaction of the obligation.

The Buxtons would ideally make their monthly payment to an impartial third-party escrow holder, who would subtract the payment on the underlying first mortgage, mail it to that lender, and send the balance to the seller, or to any other depository the seller had designated. This system has some definite benefits for both buyer and seller.

Court cases came hard and fast during the early 1980s, ruling in favor of the lender in virtually all cases (except in California). In other words, the lender said that since he or she had loaned money to one party who was approved of and trusted, and only to that party, any subsequent transfer or assignment of interest in that property was only to be accomplished under the lender's approval and scrutiny.

Even though it was presumed that the lender wouldn't discover the wraparound sale, since no documents were recorded at the court house, the lender did know. Most times the sale was discovered when the lender received an insurance rider amendment, showing a new party as the policy holder.

Q. *If a first mortgage didn't have a due-on-sale clause, and could be assumed, why might the buyer and seller choose to use a wraparound mortgage to secure a secondary loan?*

Wraparound financing might be attractive to both buyer and seller for several reasons:

- Higher yield on the seller's investment
- Perhaps a lower interest to the buyer than with financing through a lending institution
- Careful accounting of all payments, since they are best made through an escrow holder
- Knowledge that the payment on the underlying mortgage is being made in a timely fashion (best to have the escrow holder disburse it)
- Costs saved by the new buyer in not having to pay new loan fees
- Seller does not have costs customary to lending institution loans
- Loan documents held in safekeeping by the escrow holder

Seller Financing in First Mortgages

Q. *Can seller financing also be used as a first mortgage?*

Absolutely. In fact, in many rural areas in the United States, seller financing has been and continues to be a primary source of real estate finance. This is due in part to qualifying guidelines coupled with the fact that much of the real property contains large parcels of bare land that traditionally are not financed by mortgage lenders.

Seller financing is also considered by many to be the wave of the future. The graying of America finds more than 50 percent of those over the age of 65 years old owning property that is free and clear of debt. If these citizens have saved well and have funds available for living expenses, it is a golden opportunity for them to sell their real estate through installment sales, thus creating a retirement annuity.

Q. *It sounds as though carrying seller financing could be a good financial move for the seller.*

That's correct. A strong major advantage to the seller in carrying financing is that many times he or she can receive a higher return on investment than with other investment vehicles. It goes without saying, however, that the seller must be doubly sure that several vital points of the sale are covered:

- Sufficient down payment from the buyer
- Creditworthiness of the buyer
- Strong security document written by a competent real estate attorney
- Capacity of the buyer to repay the debt in a timely fashion

Q. *What techniques could be used to negotiate seller financing?*

The following could be major negotiating points between the buyer and seller:

- Interest rate
- Term of the loan
- Balloon payments allowed or disallowed
- Type of security document used (contract for deed, deed of trust or mortgage?)
- Prepayment privileges or penalties
- Time allowed for curing defaults
- Payment of taxes inside or outside of the monthly payment
- Allowing a quitclaim deed (that quits all interest the buyer has in the property) to be placed with the escrow holder to be recorded should the buyer default

- Personal property financed with the real estate
- Collateral in addition to the property secured in the case of default and foreclosure
- The right of the seller to assign or sell the contract to another party (the buyer might be considered a potential purchaser of the contract—maybe even with a discount on the principal balance)

FINANCING DOWN PAYMENTS

Using Personal Property and Services as Down Payment

Q. *I heard that someone once used a pickup truck as a part of her down payment on a seller-financed property.*

That's being creative, and there's certainly nothing wrong with that. One of the advantages of using seller financing is that whatever the buyer and seller agree upon (within the law, of course) can create a sale. The buyer might try a combination of cash, personal property, collectibles (such as coins, guns and antiques) or even services in trade as a down payment. As a real estate broker, I once took three head of cattle as earnest money and down payment on a piece of property. Unfortunately, they were still eating, and nearly broke us in hay until the sale closed! We negotiated with the seller (at his request) that the cattle become part of our commission. So at closing, Curly, Larry and Moe became guests in my freezer and the freezers of two of my salespeople! (Needless to say, we were much too attached to the little fellows to enjoy them as food, and ended up giving the meat to Goodwill!)

The premise is that anything of value can potentially serve as "boot" in a sale. But one word of caution: Be sure there is a definite value placed on the item being offered. It's best to get an outside opinion or appraisal of value (especially if the buyer and seller can't agree) or when the item has fluctuating value. Examples here would include gold, jewelry, coin collections, vehicles, even beef! And heaven forbid the collateral should "pass on" before closing! For a checklist for exploring financing options between seller and buyer, see Figure 10.1.

Figure 10.1   Seller Financing Checklist

Exploring Financing Options with the Seller

	YES	NO
1. Carry seller financing?	___	___
If so, at what interest rate?	___%	
For what term? / What LTV?	___yrs. /	___LTV
Are balloons acceptable?	___	___
In how many years?	___yrs.	
2. Participate in seller financing on a partnership basis (low buyer down payment and seller share in equity)?	___	___
3. In lieu of a seller buydown, give the buyer a cash rebate (or seller price discount) that would assist in securing institutional financing?	___	___
4. Consider a lease option?	___	___
5. Consider a lease purchase, with a portion of the monthly lease payment applied to closing costs or to reduce the purchase price?	___	___
6. Purchase a buydown mortgage for buyer (for all or part of the purchase price)?	___	___
7. Consider borrower if strengthened by a coborrower?	___	___
8. Consider liening buyer's other real estate or personal property for collateral? Or take lien positions in same until the property is liquidated?	___	___
9. Have buyer purchase term life insurance with seller as beneficiary?	___	___
10. Seller take out second mortgage, and buyer assume same?	___	___
11. Allow buyer to assume seller's personal debts (using an "assignment of debt" contract)?	___	___
12. Consider a property exchange?	___	___
13. Accept chattel (personal property) as all or part of down payment?	___	___
14. Accept notes held by buyer as partial down payment?	___	___
15. If rental property, take a portion of rents in addition to monthly payments for a period of time?	___	___

Q. *How are services used as a down payment?*

It's really not as difficult as it sounds. Suppose a husband and wife are just shy of having enough down payment to satisfy the seller; but since the wife provides professional child care, buyer and seller strike a bargain. The buyers' attorney drafts a personal service contract as part of the down payment, stating that within a specific period the buyers will provide X dollars worth of service in child care to the sellers. Obviously, if the buyers do not fulfill their obligation, the sellers would have no other recourse than to sue them. But in most cases the services are rendered, and all are happy.

A second area of down payment negotiation in seller financing can occur in the area of sweat equity. If the seller agrees to repair certain aspects of the property, but doesn't have the time or money, why not let the buyer do physical labor as part of the down payment? The seller might retain the right to inspect the improvements and it would probably be smart to have a specific time frame for completion of the work. The concept of sweat equity is also acceptable (with guidelines, of course) on conventional loans as well as FHA and VA financing.

Using Seller Debits as Down Payment

Q. *Is it possible to transfer a property with outstanding debts against it when selling with seller financing?*

Yes, it is. Although this method is sometimes overlooked, it can prove to be one of the very best methods of leverage, working positively for both buyer and seller.

The following is a real-life example of a property I purchased in the early 1980s using this technique.

I was the principal broker and owner of a northwestern real estate company. One of my salespersons had listed a six-unit building with a market value at that time of approximately $50,000. (Yes, it's true—it was in pretty sad shape, even for studio apartments.) The agent had decided to follow his wife to the Seattle area since she had "a real job," so I took over the listing. Times were tough, the property had not sold, and one evening the owner called me to say, "I'm two months behind on my contract payments to the seller, one year behind on my taxes, and I want to give the property to you!" At first I thought it was a bad connection, but she assured me that my hearing was not impaired and that she couldn't go on mismanaging the apartment building any longer.

It's easy to see a potential conflict of interest here—I was the broker, the listing agent and could potentially be the buyer. To separate myself from the negotiations, I had her contact her attorney to bargain for her. In addition, I insisted that an appraisal be secured before we proceeded.

I was buying a new home for myself at the time, so I had very little money to put into a purchase. The only offer I could make the seller was that I take over her debits (including back payments and delinquent taxes) and use them as my down payment. In real estate, debits are those items that have been used up or are owing; credits, on the other hand, are items that are paid in advance.

As shown in Figure 10.2, debits totaled $8,000 (including a $4,000 charge for a commission since I had, in essence, sold the property); credits totaled $220. The debits minus the credits left a balance of −$7,780, which I used as my down payment. Obviously, this down payment was merely on paper, since I was assuming the obligation to pay these amounts in the future.

There were some "hard" costs to pay totaling $445. These included title insurance, attorney fees, recordation and water, sewer and garbage charges. This was the only cash I brought to the closing table. So for less than $500 cash, I had leveraged into a $50,000 asset! (Currently worth in excess of $70,000.)

As shown in Figure 10.2, I assumed a land sales contract at 7.5 percent interest and gave the seller a second contract for her equity, including interest at 9 percent.

But what about the delinquent amounts I assumed? I went to the holder of the first contract (with credit report and letters of reference in hand) and asked him if I could pay the delinquent $520 owing him at $100 per month over the next six months. He was most happy to not have to foreclose and signed an agreement to the fact that he would give me the extra time requested to retire the delinquent debt.

████████████

Figure 10.2   Example of Using Seller's Debits as Buyer's Credits

Leverage with Expenses, Costs and Prorations

Items	Debit	Credit
Closing November 1 Purchase Price $50,000		
Seller's Expenses		
Current year's taxes at $100/month	$1,000	
Prior year's delinquent taxes	600	
Utilities		
Water, Sewer, Garbage	50	
(LIDs) Local Improvement Districts		
Current Month's Rent Due		200
Delinquent Rents	500	
Transfer of Rental Deposits	500	
Personal Property (plus coin ops, etc.)		20
Title Insurance Costs	225	
Attorney Fees and Recording	170	
Discount Fees		
Commissions at 8%	4,000	
Interest on Current Loan(s)	175	
Current Month's Loan Payment	260	
Delinquent Loan Payments	520	
Other: _____		
Totals	-8,000	+ 220

Buyer's Costs ("Hard" Costs To Pay)
   Title Insurance, Attorney, Recording (W,S,G) = $445

Debit	Credit		
-8,000	+220	=	$-7,780

Costs Assumed by Buyer (Total Down Payment) $7,780
                             Cash To Close   **445**

Payment Calculations

     $50,000
     <u>- 7,780</u> Down
     $42,220
     <u>- 18,000</u> Assume 7 1/2% Contract
     $24,220 at 9% = Second Contract

In addition, over the next six months I made additional payments toward the delinquent taxes to bring them current. (Even though penalty and interest charges were accruing, it made sense to catch the taxes up gradually as the cash flow from the property improved.)

What had been the problem with the property? It appeared to be a classic case of mismanagement. The owner was spending the gross rents as fast as they were paid to her, not enforcing timely payment from the tenants and ignoring deferred maintenance. An on-site manager remedied most of the problems, and giving the tenants a rent reduction for rents paid by the semester helped, too, since the building is across the street from a college. I even sold my old washer and dryer to the building, converting them to coin-op and therefore creating a new source of revenue (and depreciation).

The moral of this example is that many debits owed by the seller in seller-financed property transactions do not necessarily have to be paid in cash at closing. Letters of debt assumption can be written by attorneys, with negotiations between sellers and buyers setting the stage.

The seller was happy because she protected her credit rating while being able to receive her equity, plus interest, over a period of time. I was pleased because I had been able to turn a negative situation into a positive one.

OPTIONS FOR SELLERS HOLDING FINANCING

Q. *When a seller takes a second mortgage on a property, isn't he or she pretty well "stuck" with it until it is paid off?*

It's true that many times the seller thinks in terms of collecting the principal (and of course, the great interest) over the life of the second mortgage. And it's generally thought that should that seller want to convert that second to cash, he or she will have to deeply discount the face of the mortgage in order to provide a good yield to an investor purchasing it.

Here's a solution to both concerns. I call it "half now, half later." Why not find an investor to purchase all or part of the payment cash flow in lieu of selling the second mortgage outright? Here's how it works. This example is illustrated in Figure 10.3.

Charlene Morgan is willing to sell her home at the $60,000 sales price with the buyer, the Schmidts, assuming the first mortgage. In addition, Charlene will take a $22,000 second mortgage at 10 percent ("interest only" with a balloon in seven years). The only problem is that the Schmidts' $6,000 down payment will leave only $2,000 remaining after the costs of sale, which is not enough for Charlene to relocate.

Here's the solution. Simultaneous to closing the sale, an investor is brought in, who gives Charlene one-half of the second mortgage ($22,000), or $11,000. (These investors are found in the form of bank officers, relatives, retirees or most anyone!) This, less approximately $1,400 to cover attorney fees and extra title insurance fees (10 percent of the amount invested paid as a finder's fee to a mortgage broker) leaves $9,600—plus the $2,000 net from the sale, for a total of $11,600. This is much more palatable to Charlene than the initial $2,000 from the sale.

What does the investor get for the $11,000? He or she gets the assignment of the "interest only" proceeds from the $22,000 (based on the fact that only $11,000 has been advanced, $2,200 per year equals a 20 percent yield!)

But it's not over yet! Charlene still has $11,000 principal due at the payment of the balloon; or she could buy the note back at any time for the $11,000 advanced (depending on the minimum time the investor wants to stay in the picture). Thus the term, "half now, half later."

While the seller is actually sacrificing valuable interest on the principal, the face of the note is not being discounted. This can work well when the seller needs cash for a short period of time and can later step back into the position of receiving interest on the loan.

Seller Financing and 75/10/15 Mortgages

Q. *Seller financing could be used in addition to a new conventional loan, couldn't it?*

Figure 10.3   Converting Second Mortgage to Cash Without
Discounting

Cash for Second Mortgages with No Discount
"Half Now, Half Later" Plan

$60,000	Sales Price
-32,000	Assume the First
- 6,000	Cash from Buyer (10%)
-22,000	Second Mortgage to Seller at 10% Interest
	with Seven-Year Balloon (Interest Only)
$ 6,000	Down
- 4,000	Less Cost of Sale
$ 2,000	Net to Seller—Not Enough Cash

Solution:
Investor Gives Seller

Half of Second	$11,000	(Half Now)
Less Costs	- 1,400	
	$ 9,600	
Plus Down Payment	+ 2,000	
	$11,600	to Seller

Seller still has $11,000 due at
payment of balloon (half later), or can
buy note back at any time for $11,000.

Yes. The secondary market will allow a buyer to originate a new
conventional loan with a loan-to-value ratio not to exceed 75
percent of appraised value to be placed with a seller-carried
second mortgage. Of course, if the lender's conventional loan is
not going to be sold into the secondary market, the loan-to-value
ratio allowed would be determined by the individual lender. This
loan is often described as 75/10/15—75 percent conventional
loan, 10 percent down payment, 15 percent seller carried second
(see Figure 10.4).

Figure 10.4   75/10/15 Flexible Conventional Financing

Sales Price	$85,000
75% Lender Loan	$63,750
10% Down Payment	$ 8,500
15% Seller Financing	$12,750

Advantages

• Seller gets some cash
• Buyer may secure a good rate on the second
• No origination fee on the second
• No PMI insurance

Note: Lender will count the debt-service for both loans.

In qualifying for this type of financing, the lender will include the repayment of the second mortgage in the qualifying ratios for the first mortgage loan. But the advantages to both parties are great. The seller gets some cash (from the proceeds of the first mortgage, less costs of sale) plus interest on the second mortgage. The buyer sidesteps any origination fee on the second mortgage since it's financed by the seller. In addition, the buyer may negotiate a good interest rate and good terms on the second mortgage, as well as avoid paying PMI, since the first mortgage is less than 80 percent loan-to-value.

What circumstances might be best for using the 75/10/15 approach? Perhaps a borrower who wants the lower costs and interest rate of a 75 percent loan and has cash coming in several years to pay off the second mortgage.

Or a borrower might use this approach to avoid the higher rates of a "jumbo" mortgage (a loan amount exceeding the traditional secondary market guidelines). The borrower would secure a first mortgage less than jumbo, make a 10 percent down payment, and the seller would carry the balance.

The 75/10/15 option could also be used by a relocating buyer who only has a 10 percent down payment now, but has the monthly cash flow to qualify for both payments, and could later use proceeds from another home to pay off the second mortgage. The possibilities (and flexibilities) are endless!

One caution: As a condition of making that loan, the lender of the first mortgage may require a copy of the second mortgage's terms and conditions in order to approve them. The rationale is that the lender's first mortgage, although superior to a second mortgage, could be at greater risk if the second mortgage has highly leveraged terms, for example, with a balloon in two years. Some lenders will require that balloons not occur before five years, that regular monthly payments be made on the second mortgage, and that the terms exceed "interest only" to the seller.

Q. *Can a second mortgage be used with an existing FHA loan?*

Yes. If the first FHA loan was written prior to December 1, 1986, and the property is being sold on a simple assumption (without qualification), there would be no lender to review and approve of the terms of the second mortgage. If the first mortgage was originated after December 1, 1986, and is being sold instead under a *novation* (formal assumption with qualification), the lender approving the assumption will include the debt service on the second mortgage in approving the buyer's new ratios, and may ask to see a copy of the second mortgage to review the terms and make sure it's not too restrictive, putting undue strain on the buyer.

Q. *Can a second mortgage be originated simultaneous with that of an FHA first mortgage?*

Yes, with restrictions. Remember the three levels of the FHA system discussed in Chapter 7? Allowing second mortgages with FHA first mortgages is a prime example of the varying practices and degrees of acceptability between national, regional and local lenders. The FHA national guidelines state that a buyer can have an initial FHA second mortgage at the time of originating an FHA first mortgage under the following circumstances:

- The standard loan-to-value ratio for the program is not exceeded. A copy of the second mortgage is reviewed and approved by the loan officer originating the first.
- Repayment method is similar to that of the first (meaning that "interest only" payments are discouraged).

- No balloon is due prior to ten years after closing.
- The second mortgagee is not a party to the transaction (e.g., seller, real estate agent, etc.).

While these are the national FHA guidelines, regional or lender guidelines may impose more strict requirements; and, if they are more restrictive, would take priority over the national underwriting guidelines.

Q. *Is it possible to place a second mortgage behind an existing VA first mortgage?*

The overview given for FHA second mortgages applies here as well. If it's merely a simple assumption, neither it nor the second mortgage will be approved by a lender. If the second mortgage is initiated in tandem to a formal assumption or novation, then the lender will include the debt service on the second in the qualifying ratios for the assumption of the first VA loan. In addition, he or she will want to approve of the language on the second mortgage so that the repayment doesn't create a financial hardship for the buyer.

Q. *Can a second mortgage be originated with a new VA first mortgage?*

Yes, under certain guidelines. The tier system as shown in the previous question applies to VA. Again, VA national underwriting guidelines state that second mortgages can originate simultaneous to VA firsts under the following circumstances:

- The loans do not exceed the CRV on the property.
- The mortgagee is not a party to the transaction (e.g., seller or real estate agent).
- The payments of the first and second mortgages are comparable (e.g., no "interest only" payments).
- Unlike FHA seconds, there can be a balloon prior to ten years with VA.

Again, if the regional or local lender underwriting guidelines are more restrictive, those guidelines prevail.

DISCOUNT POINTS AND BUYDOWNS

Q. *Is it true that borrowers who use discount points, interest rate buydowns, and pay extra to lock in an interest rate are using leverage to help them purchase?*

That's correct. All those techniques are a form of leverage, no matter who pays them. (For more information about points, buydowns and lock-ins review Chapter 3.)

Discounting the Purchase Price

Q. *Is it better to have the seller discount the purchase price than to pay a buydown?*

It depends.

Figure 10.5 shows a comparison of buydown and discount situations, and is based on the following example:

Mr. Frye is a builder who prefers to pay $3,600 to a buyer in either a buydown or price discount arrangement than to pay another month's worth of interest on his construction loan.

If Frye pays the $3,600 in increments of $100 per month for three years toward the buyer's payment (temporary buydown), his total cost is a little less than $3,600, since the money is coming from an escrow account that is collecting some additional interest. If, however, the buyers decide they would prefer to have the up-front price of the home discounted by the $3,600, the numbers change. Not only will the buyer's 20 percent down payment be figured on a lesser purchase price, but so will the other costs of borrowing—including origination fees, title insurance and PMI. In fact, should they hold the loan for the entire term, the $3,600 savings will more than double—into more than $7,600 using the discounted sales price.

What about builder Frye? Are there any additional benefits for him in using the price discount? The most obvious drawback is that he may not want to discount the price of the home for fear that it will impact future comparable sales. (Many times not wanting to discount a price is more of a mental roadblock than a financial one.) Nevertheless, if he does discount the price,

---

Figure 10.5   Buydown Compared with Price Discounts

Which Is Best: Buydown or Discount?

A builder will contribute $3,600 to pay for
a buyer's temporary (three-year) interest rate buydown,
or will discount the purchase price by the same amount.
Here's the comparison:

	Buydown	**Discounted Sales Price**
Sales Price	$ 100,000	$ 96,400
Loan Size (20% down)	80,000	77,120
Monthly Buydown	100	
Effective Interest Rate		
Years 1-3	6%	9%
Years 4-30	9%	9%
Buyer's Monthly Payments		
Years 1-3	480	620.82
Years 4-30	632	620.82
Projected Interest Cost	142,266	146,268
Projected Buyer Savings	3,600	7,602
Qualifying Income (for PITI)	20,472	26,580

---

he also discounts the price of those closing costs predicated on
sales price, including title insurance, loan origination fees, loan
closing fees and real estate commissions.

In comparing buydowns to price discounts, short-term buydowns usually work best with short-term ownership; price discounts work best with long-term ownership. As we've seen with
most types of creative financing techniques, unless both parties

realize some advantage, the parties may not want to make the concessions it takes to put the sale together.

Q. *What are blended rates, and how do they work?*

Blended rates are exactly that—two or more rates "blended" together to yield a more preferential rate to the borrower. They usually make the most sense when the gap between the old and the new interest rate is great, and new mortgage money rates are high. The following example shows how they work.

> The Martins have a home worth approximately $60,000, with an outstanding $25,000 mortgage at 8 percent. They want to pull an additional $15,000 out of the property to add on a family room, but are not excited about refinancing with new first mortgage money, since rates are at 11 percent. The other option of second mortgage money at 12 percent is also not enticing, so they propose the following to the holder of their mortgage: Knowing that the lender would like to move the 8 percent loan off the books, the Martins ask that the lender make them a new first mortgage, based on a blended rate of the 8 percent old money and the 11 percent new money. The new loan will be $40,000 for 30 years, at a rate of 10 percent. This moves the 8 percent loan off the books, while giving the Martins a much more attractive overall rate of interest.

Obviously the lender has to win, too, so he or she may require some new origination and processing fees.

Also, as with most types of lending, to the degree that the borrower can show other options for borrowing the money, that will be the degree of motivation the lender will have in making this type of concession. In other words, if the borrower doesn't need the money, he or she can probably get it! For example, if the existing loan can be assumed, that's in the borrower's favor. If the interest rate on the underlying loan is at a rate much lower than current market interest, that's a plus for the borrower, too. And if the borrower has cash on hand, letters of credit from other banks or second mortgage alternatives with competing lenders, it all contributes to the borrower's favor.

Q. *Could a new purchaser use a blended rate loan rather than using a second mortgage or a wraparound?*

As seen with the prior question, the answer here is yes, by working with the right mix of circumstances. It's a little more difficult to convince a lender to use a blended rate with a new purchaser, however, since the recycling of funds is a primary base of profit vehicle for the lender, through charging origination fees, exercising the due-on-sale clause, and so on. But remember, if you don't ask, you don't get!

Q. *When a buyer uses a second mortgage simultaneous to a first, isn't that similar to blending the rates?*

Effectively, yes. Even though the rates may differ on the two separate loans, overall one could say that the rates are blended. The effect of this blended rate could be seen if a lender were qualifying the buyer on ratios from the standpoint of the two interest rates and the loans' repayment. The lender would use the debt service on both loans in determining whether the buyer could qualify to pay both obligations.

LEASE PURCHASE

Q. *Is there a difference between lease option and lease purchase?*

Most definitely yes. A lease option is a lease with an option to buy, which the optionee is not obligated to exercise. If he or she does exercise the option to purchase, then a sales contract results.

A lease purchase is already a purchase. It is drafted on a purchase and sales agreement and is merely awaiting the fulfillment of a term or condition before it culminates in a closing (the date of which is predetermined).

Joan Cohn, who is short of the total down payment to purchase, might ask that the seller, Walter Jones, to enter into a lease purchase arrangement. The terms of the contract would set a future closing date, as well as spell out the balance of the terms, such as financial arrangements and payment of closing costs. The buyer usually takes possession of the property, and terms and conditions are spelled out as to the occupancy.

In addition, Joan might ask that a portion of her monthly lease payment apply to reducing either the purchase price or closing costs. Note the difference here: If on a $1,000 per month lease payment $100 per month will be attributed to her closing costs when the sale closes in six months, someone should be impounding the $100 monthly for a total of $600 actual cash available to her at closing. On the other hand, it would not be quite so important to impound the $100 monthly if the total amount were merely to be subtracted from the sales price (unless, of course, Walter had virtually no net proceeds coming from the sale).

It's important to note that most lenders will only allow a credit to the buyer if it exceeds the fair market rent paid. With our previous example of $1,000 per month lease payment, monthly credit would have to exceed the fair market rent to be counted. So if $1,000 was truly fair market rent, usually as determined by an appraiser or other market expert, the buyer would have to pay $1,100 in order to receive a $100 per month credit toward the purchase price or closing costs.

The Seller's Advantage

Q. When could a lease purchase be an advantage to a seller?

A lease purchase could make sense for a seller if the real estate market is slow and the property hasn't sold, or if the seller needed to move quickly. In addition, the seller might feel that a prospective buyer in the property would take better care of it than a renter would, and might add improvements.

The Buyer's Advantage

Q. When could a lease purchase be an advantage to a buyer?

A lease purchase could allow a buyer time to accumulate the balance of a down payment, establish a two-year work history, or meet some other lending requirement such as pay off debts.

Q. *It sounds as though a lease purchase could be quite tricky to put together. What questions can be asked to make it a positive choice?*

It's true that lease purchases, particularly if engineered incorrectly, can result in a nightmare situation. That's why they should be utilized only for the right reasons.

First, the buyer needs to be a strong buyer, merely needing extra time to fulfill his or her obligation because of special circumstances. For example, the buyer's prior home may be in the final closing process, the balance of the down payment may be coming from a verifiable estate or the buyer may be waiting until his or her CDs mature to avoid penalty for early withdrawal. It's sometimes difficult to tell how "legit" the lease purchase buyer is, but there are some questions to pose:

- Is the down payment source valid, timely and logical?
- Is there sufficient "safe" earnest money? Depending on the area and property price, minimums may range from $1,000 to 5 percent of the sales price. Also, what happens to the earnest money should the sale fall? Is it returned to the buyer or defaulted pursuant to the language in the purchase and sales agreement? Most contracts go with the latter.
- Has the buyer had a preliminary financing prequalification for the type of loan he or she is seeking? Also, what will be the seller's costs, if any, for the buyer to secure this financing?

Q. *What are the lease purchase guidelines?*

Either in the purchase and sales agreement, or as a lease purchase addendum to the sales agreement, the following questions should be answered:

- Who pays what and when in regard to the lease? (For example, when are utilities prorated? When are deposits transferred?)
- Are improvements allowed on the property prior to closing? (This is one area the seller should consider carefully

since mechanics' liens for unpaid materials or labor could attach to the property and become the sellers' debt.)

- Who has insurance coverage? (It's usually a good idea if the seller keeps his or her existing coverage until closing, with the buyer adding any additional liability insurance deemed necessary.)
- What are the provisions for default, and the remedies? (Usually they are the same provisions for default as under the purchase and sales agreement.)
- What monthly lease amount credit will apply (if applicable) to closing costs or to reducing the purchase price?

Additionally, it may be wise to have a preliminary title report drawn prior to the buyer taking occupancy. This will reflect any possible defects on the title, as well as show any liens and other costs of which the parties were unaware against the property, seller and buyer.

By using these guidelines, there should be less havoc should the buyer and seller choose to take this course of sale.

ASSUMPTIONS

Q. *Is loan assumption a form of leverage?*

Yes it is, because it means less loan that the borrower has to arrange or less cash that the borrower needs to bring to closing. When the borrower assumes a seller's debt, that amount is subtracted from the purchase price. For example, a buyer assuming a $40,000 loan as part of a $90,000 purchase price would only have to make up a $50,000 difference, either in cash or in another type of financing.

Q. *Why don't borrowers hear more about loan assumption if it's a form of leverage?*

It's because many of the previously assumable types of loans have gone the way of the dinosaur! Lenders realized that buyers assuming loans were not always as good a risk as the first borrower, not to mention the fact that the lender wanted the ability to make new loans with new fees and possibly higher interest rates.

While some loan types (such as FHA, VA and ARMs) originated today are assumable with qualifying, most others are not. And a majority of the simply assumble (without qualifying) loans are those originated before the mid 1980s, many of which bore high interest rates and were either refinanced or paid off.

Q. *If a borrower did get a loan that allows an assumption, would he or she automatically be off the hook for the loan if someone assumed it?*

Not necessarily. It's a little-known fact that there are three different types (or levels) of assumptions, each with different sets of obligations and liabilities attached to them. They are assignment, "subject to" and novation.

Q. *What is a mortgage assignment?*

An assignment of mortgage is the first level of loan assumption. Assignment transfers the responsibility to pay an obligation from one party to the other. In essence, the assumptor actually steps into the shoes of the first mortgagor, assuming the repayment of the debt. Should the second party default, however, the first party is secondarily liable for paying the remaining balance on the note. (In other words, a co-stuckee!) Note that the first borrower is responsible only for repaying the note balance should the assumptor default—for example, there could be no deficiency judgments against the first borrower for other liens if the property did not sell for enough to satisfy the debts.

This is a common type of assumption, but it is used by lenders to a lesser degree than the second type of assumption, the "subject to."

Q. *What is assuming a "subject to" mortgage?*

A "subject to" mortgage assumption is one that is subject to the terms and conditions of the existing loan. This rather dangerous type of assumability is very much like the assignment in that it transfers the obligation to pay the debt from one party to another. But the "subject to" assumption takes it one step further. In addition to being secondarily liable for repayment of the debt should the second borrower default, the original borrower is also responsible for any deficiency (shortfall at foreclosure sale) against the property. This excess of debt can actually attach to the first mortgagor in the form of a judgment against him or her, depending on the state and the type of security document used, e.g., mortgage or deed of trust.

In other words, on a sale subject to the loan, the assumptor of the loan is liable only for the loss of his or her equity in the property should default occur. Here's an example. An assumptor of a "subject to" loan hires a contractor to build a carport on the property. The owner does not pay for the improvements, and mechanics' liens subsequently attach to the property. Simultaneously, the property falls into default, causing the lender to foreclose. Should the property not bring enough at sale to satisfy both the outstanding mortgage plus the mechanics' liens, the original obligor could be held responsible for satisfying the deficiency to the lender! Not only would the original borrower be stuck with the mortgage obligation, but he or she could be faced with other debts secured by the property as well. Since each state's statutes vary regarding deficiency judgments, the consumer could check with local lenders, title company representatives or legal counsel.

If a loan written today is assumable, it usually will contain either assignment or "subject to" language.

Q. *What is it called when a seller is relieved of both the mortgage payment and the liability when he or she sells on an assumption?*

That's called a novation, coming from the root word *nova,* meaning new. A novation is an entirely new obligation, releasing the original obligor from all further liability on the loan. The buyer steps into the loan and the seller steps out.

One of the reasons that many erroneously feel that they are receiving a novation when they sell is that the lender asks the new buyer "to qualify to assume" the existing mortgage. This process includes employment verification, a credit check and research to ensure that the qualifying ratios are within standard guidelines. The seller, however, may not be receiving a novation, but is merely transferring ownership, since the lender goes through virtually the same qualifying process for all types of assumptions.

Depending on the loan type, additional paperwork and assumption charges may be involved with the novation, but in most cases the biggest difference comes in asking. Many lenders will not grant or process a novation unless one is requested. The rationale here is that the lender has made the loan to one borrower based on that party's qualifying strength, and until the second borrower can provide the information needed to prove that he or she is equally strong, the lender will not relieve the original mortgagor of secondary liability.

Q. *What can happen when a lender is asked for a novation?*

Responses can vary. First, it will depend on the type of loan being assumed. With VA and FHA loans (Chapters 7 and 8), some cannot be assumed without qualification (depending on the date of origination).

With adjustable rate mortgages, it depends on the plan used and what the individual mortgage documents allow. The Estoppel Letter, (Figure 1.4), is used to request loan payoff information from the lender, including whether the loan is assumable and under what conditions (qualifying, etc.).

Q. *When is the best time to ask the lender about assumption options?*

The very best time to inquire about assumption policies regarding a specific loan is not when the property is put up for resale, but before the loan is originated. This certainly is not a widespread practice, since the buyer is focused on getting the loan, sometimes at most any cost. If the initial borrower takes the time prior to loan closing to ask questions concerning the assumption guidelines of a particular loan, he or she may be able to negotiate to change the loan language and assumption guidelines (depending on the lender and the loan type). The borrower may even ask the lender to hold the loan in portfolio, so as to later allow a novation.

It may not always be possible to get a definite answer from the lender. The lender may state that it depends on how well the borrower repays and to whom the loan is sold, as well as policies of the institution's board of directors at the time of the assumption. What the borrower can do, however, is to ask what the current assumption procedures are for this type of loan. Assumption policies rarely get easier, so if the borrower can live with the current guidelines, chances are they will set the stage for future policies. The downstream effect of this action may more than compensate for the time and effort it takes the borrower to clarify the situation.

Q. *If the seller is still liable in an assignment and "subject-to" sale, would that debt still show up on his or her credit report?*

This is one last reason why a seller may want to request a novation on an outstanding loan. Since an original obligor is not totally released from liability on the loan in an assignment or "subject-to" situation, a lender may still report the first borrower as having a contingent liability in his or her name for credit reporting purposes. While this is not a widespread practice, it's easy to see the potential conundrum created when the seller attempts to qualify for a second loan, only to find that his or her credit report shows an outstanding mortgage.

If this occurs, the original obligor should request that the lender remove this posting from the credit report, citing the strengths of the second borrower and his or her positive loan repayment history. The original obligor should then check back with the credit bureau in approximately 30 days to make sure it has been removed from the record. The best protection against this is to ultimately obtain a novation when the property is sold.

Q. *If the seller can't get a novation, doesn't the lender have to notify the seller in case of any pending default by the assumptor?*

It's very much a misconception that the lender has to notify the original obligor in case of an assumptor's default. Realistically, most lenders do notify the original obligor so that a financial arrangement might be worked out prior to foreclosure proceedings. This is particularly true today in areas where property values have not increased or have decreased, where selling the property at a loss only compounds the situation. And since foreclosure is expensive for the lender, taking steps to avoid it saves time and money.

If the original mortgagor had carried back seller financing, and notice of it was recorded, he or she would be formally notified prior to sale of the property.

The prudent thing for the original mortgagor to do, however, is to send a written request by certified mail to the lender, asking that he or she be notified of any potential default on the outstanding loan. In addition, this notice should be recorded at the county courthouse. Even though it creates no lien or other encumbrance on the property, it is on record. If these steps are taken when the sale to the assumptor occurs, a lender would later find it difficult to deny that he or she was not aware that the original mortgagor wanted notification in advance of any pending default.

In addition, some sellers even request that the buyer purchasing with an assumption give the seller a small second mortgage (say $100), payable at some time in the future (say the year 2030) with no payment due until that time. Once this mortgage is recorded, it makes the seller a lienholder of record and he or she would be notified in the case of any default of the second owner. The downside is that the seller would later have to release the lien or the title wouldn't be clear when the purchaser tried to sell.

CHAPTER 11

AFTER THE CLOSE:
Managing the Mortgage

The buyers and sellers have made it through the close, perhaps with some sweaty palms, but it's behind them. The buyers don't need to be reminded that the mortgage is a significant financial obligation. The mortgage is also a financial opportunity, and buyers should give it attention as they plan their families' financial futures.

This chapter answers some common questions borrowers have after the mortgage is closed. The focus is on two significant choices to make in mortgage management: to prepay the mortgage, thus building equity faster, or to refinance with a new mortgage. And, given that we live in uncertain times, also included is advice on working with lenders for borrowers who are concerned about possibly defaulting on their mortgages.

WHEN THE MORTGAGE IS SOLD

Q. *Some people who get one loan through one lender are advised after closing to send their payments to a different company in a different state. Why?*

In cases such as these, the loans or their servicing (payment collection) have been purchased by another company. The terms and conditions of the original loan stay the same; just the company and the location to which payments are sent change.

By law, the original lender must send the borrower a "good-bye" letter at least 15 days before the date of the next payment. This letter should state the name of the new company, its location, and the name and number of a contact person or department in case the borrower has questions.

Under the same time guidelines, the new company is also required to send the borrower a "welcome" letter outlining the same information.

It is very important that the borrower receive both letters, and that they are on both companies' letterheads. If a letter is received only from the supposed new servicer, the borrower should call the original lender to verify that the loan was sold. Several bogus operations have recently attempted to intercept mortgage checks by claiming to be the new servicing company.

If the borrower's monthly payment is made each month through automatic checking withdrawal or electronic transfers, the borrower will need to cancel the present arrangement and fill out new forms. Since this often creates a time lag, the borrower may need to send a check directly to the new company before the new servicer receives the withdrawal. The welcome letter (or a call to the new company) can help determine this.

A free booklet entitled *When Your Loan Is Transferred to Another Lender* is available from the Mortgage Bankers Association of America. It can be requested by writing to them at 1125 Fifteenth St., NW, Washington, D.C., 20005.

PREPAYING A MORTGAGE

Benefits of Prepaying

Q. *What are the benefits to a borrower of prepaying a mortgage?*

Prepaying a loan offers a borrower many advantages:

- A borrower would pay thousands of dollars less in interest than he or she would in a 30-year loan. For example, a $100,000 30-year loan with interest at 8 percent would end up costing the borrower $264,240 if the loan ran to maturity. But the same loan amount for just 15 years would cost the borrower only $172,080, or $92,160 less. Even though mortgage interest is tax deductible, more interest is seldom better than less!
- Owning a home free and clear can be a liberating feeling. If monthly cash flow were to shrink, owners would not be plagued with worry over making monthly mortgage pay-

ments and potentially losing their homes. And their equity could always be a potential source of cash through refinancing or equity lines of credit.

Detriments To Prepaying a Mortgage

Q. *Are there any detriments to prepaying a mortgage?*

Every positive can have a negative. In addition to a borrower losing some interest deductions, he or she is parting with cash that could potentially be used for other investments or financial padding. In other words, using funds to prepay a loan could hinder the borrower's liquidity and other investment options.

Questions To Ask Before Prepaying a Mortgage

Q. *What questions should a borrower be able to answer before launching into a big mortgage prepayment campaign?*

Here are a few potential questions a borrower should explore:

- Is the current mortgage payment a burden? Have some payments been late or even missed? Paying off the mortgage may make sense, since erratic payments may put the loan in jeopardy and damage the borrower's credit.
- What impact will the lack of interest deductibility have on the borrower's overall tax picture? Consulting a tax adviser for preplanning is always a wise move.
- What are the long-term cash needs for the borrower's future and are current savings sufficient to weather them? If savings are minimal or nonexistant, it may be financially premature to use extra funds to prepay a mortgage.
- Is a change pending in the borrower's financial future that would make it prudent to save more money instead of using cash to pay off the loan? Financing a child through college or aiding an elderly parent might be better paid in cash, rather than borrowing through a nondeductible consumer interest loan.
- Where could the extra cash be invested that would generate a greater return?

- How long does the borrower plan on keeping the property and the loan? Retiring a 9 percent mortgage may not be a wise financial move if the borrower is going to sell quickly or replace the loan with another one soon.

The Best Time To Start Prepaying a Mortgage

Q. *Should a loan be prepaid when it has just a few more years to run?*

While there's never a bad time in a loan's history to start making prepayments, a look at a loan amortization schedule (Figure 11.1) can help answer this question. Considering how much of the monthly payment goes to principal and interest, it's easy to see that a larger portion goes to interest in the early years of the loan. The best time to make extra principal reductions, then, is actually in the early stages of the loan where the funds have a bigger impact!

A Structured Prepayment System

Q. *What logical, systematic plan might a borrower follow to reduce the loan balance without going bankrupt?*

Before the borrower begins any prepayment program, structured or not, it's advisable to make sure the loan has no prepayment penalties. If mortgage documents are silent on the issue, prepayment is usually allowed, but it's best to contact the lender for verification.

If possible, the lender should be asked to put prepayment terms in writing and send the information to the borrower. At the very least, the borrower should document on the mortgage payment book the date called and the name of the person who gave the prepayment information. Putting the lender on notice of the intention to make loan prepayments also alerts him or her to make sure advanced payments are posted correctly.

The following program is a favorite of many savvy real estate purchasers, since it's simple to calculate, methodical and won't financially break the borrower.

1. The borrower should obtain an amortization schedule of the loan, showing each payment's principal and interest

Figure 11.1   Loan Amortization Chart and Prepayment Schedule
($100,000, 30-Year Loan at 10 percent Interest)

Month of Loan	Principal and Interest Payments	Interest Portion of Payment	Principal Portion of Payment	Loan Balance at End of Month
1	878.00	833.00	45.00	99,955.00
2	878.00	832.96	45.04	99,909.96
3	878.00	832.58	45.42	99,864.54
4	878.00	832.20	45.80	99,818.74
5	878.00	831.82	46.18	99,772.56
6	878.00	831.44	46.56	99,726.00
7	878.00	831.05	46.95	99,679.05
8	878.00	830.66	47.34	99,631.71
9	878.00	830.26	47.74	99,583.97
10	878.00	829.87	48.13	99,535.84
11	878.00	829.47	48.53	99,487.31
12	878.00	829.06	48.94	99,438.37

distribution for the life of the loan. A computer printout can be secured from the lender (or any financial institution), real estate professional or financial adviser.

2. The borrower should look at the next payment, say January. When the January payment is made, the borrower should make an additional payment to include February's principal reduction (Figure 11.1).

    The borrower, in essence, eliminates one full payment from the 30-year loan schedule because the loan balance after that payment would correspond to the loan balance shown at the end of February.

    In February, the borrower should send in March's principal reduction payment in addition to the February payment, and so on, every month thereafter.

If this procedure is followed religiously every month, a 30-year loan will basically be cut in half! How's that for savings?

Don't forget that just because a principal prepayment has been made, it doesn't allow the borrower to skip a payment! Missing payments would put the loan in default, since prepayments have no bearing on scheduled payments.

Documenting Prepayments Is Vital! Imagine the myriad terror stories from borrowers who thought they had made prepayments, only to later discover that the amounts had been erroneously applied to late fees, advanced interest, insurance premiums or taxes.

Following are some precautions borrowers can take.

- If using payment coupons, be sure to mark "principal prepayment" and the amount on the face of the coupon.
- Make the prepayment in a separate check so it can be tracked and shown as evidence if prepayments are later disputed.
- If making prepayments on a separate check, borrowers should be sure to mark the loan number and the words "principal prepayment" on the face of the check.
- If possible, the borrower should request an annual accounting of payments. While many lenders don't do this as normal procedure, many will accomodate a borrower who requests it. The borrower can compare the lender's balance with canceled checks to make sure the prepayments were applied correctly.

Having prepayment options with a loan can add incredible payment and financial flexibility to the borrower's situation, while not saddling him or her with higher payments typical of shorter-term loans.

REFINANCING

Q. *Does it pay to refinance a mortgage? Is there any quick rule of thumb?*

Yes and no! A very broad rule of thumb is that it will probably pay to refinance if the borrower can lower the interest rate by 2 to 3 percent and intends to keep the loan long enough to recoup the costs of refinancing. To get the true picture of whether refinancing makes sense, borrowers should work it out based on each scenario.

Figure 11.2 includes a refinancing worksheet. Basically, borrowers tally up the total amount of payments they would make for the remaining time they would own the property, subtract the lower payments they would make under the lesser interest rate, then add back the costs of refinancing, plus any additional income taxes they would pay because of the reduced interest deductions. What is saved in payments, less what is paid in refinancing and taxes, should give a net gain or loss figures.

When Not To Refinance

Q. *Could refinancing actually cost more money than it saves?*

Unfortunately, not all homeowners consider this question. The following example shows how refinancing can be an imprudent choice.

The Johnsons own a home worth approximately $100,000. They wish to refinance to reduce their 11 percent interest rate to 9 percent, and won't be taking any cash out.

The lender informs them that she will loan up to a maximum of $85,000 (including points and closing costs). With out-of-pocket expenses (such as title work, etc.) plus two discount points to obtain the lowest possible rate, the Johnsons finance $3,926 in costs into their loan. At the time of closing, the Johnsons' new loan total is $84,926.

It's now one year since refinancing, and the Johnsons decide they need a larger home. The market has shown little appreciation in real estate values, so the Johnsons list their home for $100,000 (the previous appraisal figure). After four months of marketing the property, a buyer, Jim Judge, offers them $94,000, contingent on his obtaining a 100 percent VA loan.

Jim asks the Johnsons to pay the two discount points needed to get the loan ($1,880). With the other costs the Johnsons need to pay, $5,640 for the real estate commission and miscellaneous

---

Figure 11.2   Refinancing Worksheet

Would It Pay To Refinance?

A general rule of thumb is that if a borrower can shave 2 percent to 3 percent annually off interest costs, and will hold the property long enough to recoup the cost of refinancing, it may pay to refinance. Following is a chart to use in analyzing each individual situation:

Refinance Worksheet

Present Monthly Payments - - - - - - - - - - - $ _____
*Number of Months To Pay - - - - - - - - - - -   x _____
    Total Payments .... $ _____ A

Payments at the Lower Rate - - - - - - - - - - $ _____
*Number of Months To Pay - - - - - - - - - - -   x _____
    Total Payments .... $ _____ B
    Difference in Total Payments
    (A Minus B) .... $ _____ C

Refinancing Costs:
    Prepayment Penalty (if applicable) $ _____ D

    Closing Costs for New Mortgage,
    including Points $ _____ E

    Added Income Taxes over Loan
    Term Since Reduced Deduction
    from Lower Interest $ _____ F

Total (D plus E plus F) $ _____ G

Net Savings over Life of Mortgage (C minus G) = $ _____

*Be sure that the number of months to pay is for the period of time the borrower expects to own the property, *not* the number of months remaining on the loan.

closing costs of $840 (plus pay off the remaining loan, reduced now to $84,331), guess how much the Johnsons will net from the sale to purchase their new home? A whopping $1,309, not even enough to pay first and last month's rent, let alone to make another purchase.

If they accept the sale, they will have used $12,286 worth of their equity in one year's time on refinancing and sales costs, and still will be unable to achieve their goal of a larger home.

What should the Johnsons have done? They should have thought ahead to their future housing needs and purchased a new home instead of refinancing their old one. Their mistake was using precious equity to buy a lower interest rate while forgetting how long it would take to recoup the cost of refinancing (32 months, based on their $124 per month payment savings.) Come April 15th, they may find that they actually owe income tax, since they now have less mortgage interest to deduct.

As with the Johnsons, the issue of short-term ownership after refinancing could cause a low-equity, or no-equity position should the homeowner need to sell in a short period of time. In fact, good lenders counsel and caution homeowners to carefully evaluate refinancing if they do not plan to own the property for a minimum of three to five additional years. (Lenders will be glad to do break-even projections based on a homeowner's individual circumstances.)

One last way the Johnsons could have radically improved their equity position was to shop for lower refinancing costs in the first place. Since fees and points can vary widely from lender to lender, taking the time to check out what's available from several lenders may make the difference between preserving equity or losing money.

Cautions When Refinancing

Q. *Are there any other cautions to consider when refinancing?*

Since lenders estimate that between 20 and 30 percent of borrowers take cash out of the property when they refinance, it goes without saying that prudent use of this cash is important. If the cash is used to add a hot tub, pool, or other improvement to the real estate that may not add dollar-for-dollar resale value to the property, is that a prudent decision? Paying off nondeductible high interest consumer loans is good, but using equity to pay cash for a lessening value asset such as a car or new refrigerator may not be prudent based on the individual's financial circumstances.

It's also wise to consider the type of loan being retired. A simply assumable, no-qualifying low interest rate loan may be more enticing when the borrower sells than one that is not assumable. And remember, too, that if the borrower obtains a new loan of greater than 80 percent of the appraised value, he or she may be faced with PMI. This could add approximately $23 per month to an $80,000 loan.

Should A Borrower Pay Points When Refinancing?

Q. *Is it a good idea to pay higher points to get a lower interest rate?*

Paying higher points to secure a lower rate of interest depends on several things. First, how long will the borrower keep the loan on the property? Obviously, paying hefty points up front to secure a lower-than-market interest rate loan won't be as valuable if the loan and the property will be held for only a short period of time. This can be illustrated through the following example.

A lender gives Gus Wellington a choice of an $85,000 loan at 9 percent with two points ($1,700 paid at closing) or at 9.5 percent with no points. Which is better? It depends on what Gus wants to accomplish.

While the difference between an interest rate of 9 percent and 9.5 percent is just $30.79 per month principal and interest for 30 years ($683.95 payment versus $714.74), it would take almost 56 months to retrieve the $1,700 in points at the rate of $30.79 per month payment difference. So if Gus is not planning to hold the property for at least five years, paying the higher points up front wouldn't make economic sense.

Paying points at settlement also means the borrower has lost the use of that money, plus any possible interest or investment potential.

Refinancing into Shorter-Term Loans

Q. *What are the pros and cons of going to a shorter-term loan when refinancing?*

It may be helpful to review the basic differences of payment terms in Chapter 3.

The following example shows some of the benefits and problems of short-term loans.

> Mr. and Mrs. Russell are in their late 40s and are thinking of refinancing their 10 percent, 15-year mortgage. They have ten years remaining on a $51,000 loan, with monthly principal and interest payments of $645. Their question is, should they refinance for another 15 years or go with a higher payment for only ten years?
>
> When the total costs are analyzed, the Russells find that keeping their current loan for ten years would cost them $77,400. And, while they would pay less if they went with a new 7 percent ten-year mortgage ($71,040), they would not save money if they went with a new 15-year mortgage ($82,440).
>
> Here's why: With a 7 percent, ten-year loan, the monthly principal and interest payment would drop to $592. And with the 15-year loan, the monthly payments would drop even more, to $458 per month. But when five additional years of payments are added with the 15-year loan, it adds $11,400 to the cost!
>
> Since the Russells have paid five years on their existing loan, they've whittled down a fair amount of interest. That's why the new ten-year loan makes the best economic sense.

Remember, when making this decision, the borrower should consider the time he or she wishes to keep the home and the amount of monthly payment he or she can afford to make.

Closing Costs

Q. *When would the borrower find out exactly what the closing costs would be if he or she were refinancing?*

Lenders do the same up-front disclosure of costs for a refinance as they would do for a new purchase loan. Therefore lenders should make certain disclosures to a borrower at application or within three days after application. The disclosures describe the settlement costs of the loan, the effective interest rate and the possibility that the lender will transfer the servicing rights.

But as many lenders take refinance applications over the phone, disclosure may be verbally minimized. Broad quotes on costs and discount points may change drastically by the time closing rolls around.

If the refinanced loan were for an ARM, the lender should disclose a worst-case scenario on the loan. This should be disclosed at time of application or before any nonrefundable loan fees are paid.

If a borrower feels he or she can't go through with closing on a loan that was misrepresented, there is an escape through the three-day right of rescision law that applies to refinances. This federal law allows a borrower to cancel a loan if he or she does so in writing within three days of loan settlement, provided the lender is different than the one holding the old loan.

Since there are no maximum ceilings on costs of refinancing, the term *standard costs,* used by some lenders, means little. A lender not willing to update cost estimates for the borrower may have something to hide and may not be worth the borrower's time and effort. Avoiding these lenders is the consumer's best protection.

When Refinancing Makes Sense

Q. *When does it make sense to refinance?*

The answer lies in what it can achieve for the borrower. Depending on the borrower's circumstances, good reasons could include lowering the interest rate, lowering the monthly payments, reducing the term of the loan (e.g., from 30 to 15 years) and pulling out cash to pay off high, nondeductible consumer debt, like credit cards.

The bottom line is to look at the total picture of refinancing. How can this be done? The borrower can ask the lender to prepare an analysis in order to evaluate the options. The home-owner should also answer the following questions before refinancing:

1. How long will the homeowner keep the property? (If this period is not long enough to recoup the costs of refinancing, the homeowner should not refinance.)
2. What types of situations are anticipated in the homeowner's personal and economic future? (Will equity be needed in three years to send a child to college or pay possible expenses for personal health care or nursing home care for an elderly relative?)
3. Will cash pulled out now be used for a sound reason that makes economic sense (such as adding a second bath in lieu of moving to a more expensive home)?
4. What are the benefits in keeping the existing loan on the property (such as easy loan assumability or flexibility by adding seller financing if the property is sold)? Do they outweight the tradeoffs?
5. Would a new loan require additional costs of PMI or impound accounts for taxes and insurance that weren't previously required?
6. How does the proposed loan compare to others based on interest rate, points, closing costs and fluff fees (unregulated, extra fees for services like tax checking, courier service, and so on)? In the previous refinancing example, the Russells' high loan fees were a big part of their problem!
7. How would a lower interest rate affect the homeowner's tax picture?
8. If the homeowner wants cash out, which is better for his or her situation: a new refinanced loan or an equity line of credit?

The reality is that a home (and its equity) are for most people their largest personal asset and savings account. The homeowner should make changes with the right loan, the right lender and for the right reasons.

EQUITY LOANS

Q. *How do equity loans differ from refinancing?*

Equity loans (also called equity lines of credit) don't disturb the existing first mortgage and do not require the strongest of personal profiles, since they are underwritten primarily based on the strength of the property. Since these loans don't have to be sold to the secondary market, lenders may be likely to accept higher-risk borrowers. They do have some negatives, however:

- Some lenders may make equity line of credit loans up to 80 percent loan-to-value based solely on a "drive-by" appraisal. This could result in overleveraging, especially if the owner needs to sell in a short period of time.
- Equity lines of credit can bear higher-than-market interest rates, and can overleverage borrowers who make "interest only" repayments.
- While borrowers access only the amount needed (up to a predetermined ceiling) and interest accrues only on the amount borrowed, the loan may include balloon payments or other negatives. If not complied with, the borrower could risk losing the property.
- If the borrower tries to refinance a first mortgage and not disturb the equity line, the equity line holder probably won't allow it. This means that a new refinance would have to pay off both loans, causing a higher payment on the combined loans.

WHEN THE BORROWER FALLS BEHIND IN PAYMENTS

Q. *If a borrower's financial position changes after getting the loan, and he or she falls behind in the payments, what can be done?*

Contrary to popular belief, lenders really do want to work with delinquent and potentially defaulting borrowers. The cost of foreclosure for the lender can be as high as 20 percent of the remaining principal balance. And a delinquent loan on the books as a nonperforming asset continues to cost the lender money. That's why most lenders see foreclosure as a last, and many times unattractive, resort.

It's important that the borrower who is behind on payments does not take a wait-and-see approach. Being proactive and immediately contacting the lender to discuss the situation is imperative, since some of the most attractive alternatives are those exercised in the early stages of default.

The lender will want to know what caused payments to fall behind, whether that cause has been remedied, and how the situation can be reversed. For example, a borrower with delinquent payments caused by temporary job loss, who is once again employed, may need just a few additional months to catch up payments. Conversely, a borrower with a severe long-term illness might need other options.

Lenders could assist the borrower by accepting "interest only" payments, partial payments or deferring payments entirely for several months (these amounts would be added to the end of the loan). In fact, for loans purchased by Freddie Mac (FHLMC) in the secondary market there is a system in place to help borrowers catch up or refinance a delinquent loan.

The borrower should ask the lender under what circumstances someone else could assume the loan. This may be a solution, since it could bypass formal foreclosure, get the current owner out of the picture and supply the lender with a potentially stronger buyer.

Q. *Does a delinquent borrower have any other recourse if the lender is not willing to work with him or her?*

If the loan has PMI, or is an FHA or VA loan, there may be other options.

Private mortgage insurance companies insure the conventional lenders' loans against loss. So when the borrower can no longer make the mortgage payments, the PMI company stands to lose as well.

Many PMI companies are focusing their efforts on preforeclosure work-out programs, designed to intercept the defaulting loan and "work it out" before formal foreclosure occurs. Their rationale is that if they can find a way to help a new, stronger buyer get into the property by merely paying the lender some of the defaulting owner's back payments, they stand to lose less than if they paid an entire claim for loss. (For a breakdown of these costs, see Chapter 5).

A work-out program might create a more equitable solution than foreclosure for all parties.

Q. *If it's a conventional loan, how does the borrower find out which PMI company insures the loan?*

Lenders are usually willing to contact the PMI company to see if a work-out program can be done (especially if the property owner requests this). If not, however, the borrower might check his or her loan settlement papers from the purchase to see which company the initial PMI premiums were paid to. (All of the PMI companies have toll-free 800 numbers, and are listed in Chapter 5).

FHA and VA Work-out Programs

Foreclosure can be expensive not only in terms of payments lost, but also in preforeclosure property maintenance fees until foreclosure and other costs of property repair. Understanding this, FHA and VA have initiated preforeclosure work-out programs for their loans.

Initiated only when circumstances warrant, these programs have helped defray the number of foreclosures under these two government plans.

Deed-in-Lieu of Foreclosure

Q. *What is the worst that could happen if a borrower gives the property back to the lender?*

I don't know about "worst," but something adverse could certainly happen!

This situation is called a deed-in-lieu of foreclosure, also called a friendly foreclosure. This means that the lender agrees to take the property back and the borrower forgoes any equity in the property. But that may not be all that happens.

While the borrower could negotiate with the lender to waive negative information from being posted to the borrower's credit report (and may even put this agreement in writing), other parties to the default, such as the PMI company, might make a negative posting to the borrower's credit.

Since a deed in lieu of foreclosure can carry major impact for the borrower, giving the property back to the lender, or agreeing to a work-out program should only be done after consulting with an attorney.

Q. *Are there any tax consequences if a borrower gives the property back to the lender?*

Potentially, yes. Since the IRS may consider deeding the property back to the lender to be debt relief or a taxable sale, an accountant or tax adviser should be consulted before the borrower agrees to transfer the property.

WE'VE COME FULL CIRCLE

There you have it—financing facts to bring you full circle from loan qualifying to mortgage maintenance.

We trust that *All About Mortgages* has provided both the quantity and quality of information necessary to make the home financing experience a pleasant one.

APPENDIX A: WORKSHEETS

Loan Comparison Worksheet

	Loan Type		
	Conventional	FHA	V A
Sales Price .... $_____			
Interest Rate .... $_____			
Down Payment .... $_____			
Total Loan To Be Amortized .... $_____			

Estimated Loan Costs

MIP (Unless FHA Included Above) .... $_____			
Loan Origination Fee .... $_____			
Assumption Fee .... $_____			
Credit Report .... $_____			
Appraisal Fee .... $_____			
Recording Fee .... $_____			
Title (ALTA) Policy (Use Loan Amount) .... $_____			
Attorney Fee .... $_____			
Escrow Closing Fee .... $_____			
Interest Proration .... $_____			
Tax Proration .... $_____			
Fire and Hazard Insurance 1st year .... $_____			
Lender's Application Fee .... $_____			
Purchaser's Buydown Points .... $_____			
Long-Term Escrow Set-Up Fee .... $_____			
Tax Service Fee .... $_____			
Misc., LID, City Code, Reserves .... $_____			
Home Inspection Fee .... $_____			
Total Estimated Closing Costs .... $_____			

Reserves and Prorates

Property Taxes (Minimum 2 Months) .... $_____			
Fire and Hazard Insurance (Minimum 2 Months) $_____			
Mortgage Insurance .... $_____			
Total Reserves and Prorates .... $_____			
Total Cash Outlay .... $_____			

Estimated Monthly Payment

Principal and Interest .... $_____			
Tax Reserves .... $_____			
Insurance Reserves .... $_____			
MIP Insurance (Unless FHA Included Above) ... $_____			
Total Estimated Monthly Payment .... $_____			

The undersigned hereby acknowledges receipt of a copy of this estimation.

By _____ Signed _____ Date _____

████████████

Adjustable Rate Mortgage Checklist

	Mortgage A	Mortgage B

Ask your lender to help fill out this checklist.

Mortgage Amount $ _____ $ _____

Basic Features for Comparison

	Mortgage A	Mortgage B
Fixed Rate Annual Percentage Rate (This is the cost of your credit as a yearly rate, which includes both interest and other charges.)	_____	_____
ARM Annual Percentage Rate	_____	_____
Adjustment Period	_____	_____
Index Used and Current Rate	_____	_____
Margin	_____	_____
Initial Payment Without Discount	_____	_____
Initial Payment With Discount (If Any)	_____	_____
How long will discount last?	_____	_____
Interest Rate Caps: Periodic	_____	_____
Overall	_____	_____
Payment Caps	_____	_____
Negative Amorization	_____	_____
Convertibility or Prepayment Privilege	_____	_____
Initial Fees and Charges	_____	_____

Monthly Payment Amounts

What will my monthly payment be after
12 months if the index rate:

	Mortgage A	Mortgage B
stays the same?	_____	_____
goes up 2 percent?	_____	_____
goes down 2 percent?	_____	_____

What will my monthly payment be after
three years if the index rate:

	Mortgage A	Mortgage B
stays the same?	_____	_____
goes up 2 percent per year?	_____	_____
goes down 2 percent per year?	_____	_____

Take into account any caps on your mortgage
and remember it may run 30 years.

FRB 2-300000-0585

████████████

Conventional Loan Qualification Form

Sales Price (1)_____
   Less Loan Amount (2)_____ Equals Required Down Payment $_____

Estimated Closing Costs *Plus* Estimated Prepaid Escrow   +_____
   Total Closing Cost $_____
Less Cash on Deposit   –_____
Required Cash To Close $_____

  (2) _____ Divided by (1) _____ Equals LTV _____%

Gross Income (Mortgagor)_____ and (Comortgagor)_____ = $_____ (A)

Proposed Housing Expense

     Principal and Interest $_____

     Other Financing   _____

     Hazard Insurance   _____

     Taxes   _____

     Mortgage Insurance   _____

     Homeowner Association Fees   _____

     Other:_____   _____

Total Housing Payment   _____ (B)

Total Obligations (Beyond Ten Months)   _____ (C)

Total Housing Payment (B), *Plus* Monthly Obligations (C) = _____ (D)

  (B) _____ Divided by (A) _____ = _____ %   Housing Ratio

  (D) _____ Divided by (A) _____ = _____ %   Total Debt Ratio

▰▰▰▰▰▰▰

Adjustable Rate Mortgage Qualification Form

Sales Price   (1)_____
   Less Loan Amount (2)_____ Equals Required Down Payment $_____

Estimated Closing Costs *Plus* Estimated Prepaid Escrow   +_____
   Total Closing Cost $_____
Less Cash on Deposit   –_____
Required Cash To Close $_____

   (2) _____ Divided by (1) _____ Equals LTV _____%

Gross Income (Mortgagor)_____ and (Comortgagor)_____ = $_____ (A)

Proposed Housing Expense

      Principal and Interest $_____

      Other Financing   _____

      Hazard Insurance   _____

      Taxes   _____

      Mortgage Insurance   _____

      Homeowner Association Fees   _____

      Other:_____   _____

Total Housing Payment   _____ (B)

Total Obligations (Beyond Ten Months)   _____ (C)

Total Housing Payment (B), *Plus* Monthly Obligations (C) = _____ (D)

   (B) _____ Divided by (A) _____ = _____ %   Housing Ratio

   (D) _____ Divided by (A) _____ = _____ %   Total Debt Ratio

Federal Housing Administration Qualifying Guidelines

	Borrower	Coborrower	Total
Monthly Income	$_____	$_____	$_____

Housing Ratio

Principal and Interest	$_____
Real Estate Taxes	+_____
Hazard Insurance	+_____
FHA MIP (if financed)	+_____
Other (Homeowner, Association Fees, Condo Fees, LIDs)	+_____
Total Housing Expense	$_____
Ratio (Divide Housing Expense by Income)	_____%

Fixed Payment Ratio

Total Housing Expense	$_____
Monthly Installment	+_____
Revolving Accounts	+_____
Child Care/Support	+_____
Other Recurring Charges	+_____
Total Fixed Payments	$_____
Ratio (Divide Fixed Payment by Income)	_____%

Acceptable Ratio: 29%   **Acceptable Ratio: 41%**

Note: Ratios can be exceeded when compensating factors such as the following are present:

–Large down payment
–Substantial cash reserves
–Low overall debt
–Excellent job history
–History of managing high housing expense
–Purchasing an energy efficient house

███████████

Veterans Administration Buyer Income Qualification Form

Loan Amount $_____

Gross Income Per Month (Veteran or Spouse) $_____ (A)
(Including pension compensation or other *net* income)

Less: Federal Income Tax $_____
          State Income Tax   _____

          Social Security Tax   _____
          Other   _____

Net Take-Home Pay $_____ (B)

Housing Expense:

          House Payment $_____
          (Principal and Interest)
          Taxes   +_____

          Insurance   +_____
          HOA/Assessments +_____

             Subtotal $_____ (C)

          Utilities $_____

          Other (pool, air conditioning, etc.) +_____
          Maintenance   +_____

             Total Housing Expense $_____ (D)

Fixed Obligations:
          Total of all monthly debt payments
          which will last six months or longer
          including "job related expenses." $_____ (E)

Balance Remaining for Family Support (B less D and E) $_____

                               Family Support
          Number of Family Members _____ Balance Required $_____
                               (refer to table Figure 8.1)

Ratio: (C plus E)   Divided by (A) $_____ = Ratio _____%*
                                         (round down to two digits)

*A statement that lists all compensating factors that justify approval must be
provided if ratio exceeds 41 percent unless the residual income exceeds the
required amount by at least 20 percent.

Buyer's Estimation Sheet

Buyer_____

Property Address_____

Sale Price .... $_____
1st Mortgage Balance To Be Assumed .... $_____
2nd Mortgage or Contract To Be Assumed .... $_____
Contract .... $_____
Down Payment .... $_____

Estimated Loan Costs:
Service Charge/Origination Fee .... $_____
Assumption Fee .... $_____
Credit Report .... $_____
Appraisal Fee.. $_____
Recording Fees .... $_____
ATA Policy (Title Insurance) .... $_____
Escrow Fee .... $_____
Escrow Preparation Fee .... $_____
Interest Proration... $_____
Tax Preparation Fee .... $_____
Fire Insurance .... $_____
Home Inspection Fee.. $_____
Discount Points (If Applicable) .... $_____
Initial Mortgage Insurance Premium* .... $_____
Total Estimated Closing Costs .... $_____

Reserves and Prorates:
Property Taxes .... $_____
Fire Insurance .... $_____
Mortgage Insurance† .... $_____
Total Reserves and Prorates .... $_____
Total Estimated Cash Outlay... $_____

Type of Loan _____ for _____ years
Rate of Interest _____ % (Approximately)
Principal, Interest .... $_____
Taxes Reserves... $_____
Insurance Reserves .... $_____
Total Monthly Payment... $_____

The undersigned purchaser hereby acknowledges receipt of a copy of this estimate and it is hereby understood that it is an *estimate only.*

Buyer _____

Buyer _____   Date _____

*VA loans do not incur this cost. For FHA loans, use FHA one-time premium (if not financed).
† FHA and VA loans do not incur this cost.

Seller's Estimation Sheet

Prepared for: _____ Address: _____

Prepared by: _____ Estimated Closing Date:_____

Selling Price... $_____

Approximate Indebtedness
    First Loan.............................. @_____% $_____
    Second Loan.......................... @_____% $_____
    Other .... @_____% $_____

Gross Equity... $_____

Seller's Estimated Costs:
    Brokerage Fee .... $_____
    Title Insurance Policy (Sales Price)...................... $_____
    Long-Term Escrow Set-Up Fee .... $_____
    Escrow Closing Fee... $_____
    Mortgage Discount .... $_____
    Contract Preparation .... $_____
    Attorney Fees .... $_____
    Appraisal Fee .... $_____
    Interest to Closing .... $_____
    Property Tax Proration.. $_____
    Payoff Penalty .... $_____
    Recording Fees .... $_____
    Reconveyance Fee .... $_____
    Required Repairs .... $_____
    City Inspection... $_____
    Local Improvement Districts (LIDs) Assessment .... $_____
    Misc. .... $_____
    _____ .... $_____

If Income Property:
    Prorated Rents .... $_____
    Security or Cleaning Deposits .... $_____

Less Total Estimated Costs .... $_____

Subtotal .... $_____

Estimated Credits
    Reserve Account... $_____
    _____ .... $_____

Plus Total Credits .... $_____
Estimated Seller's Proceeds... $_____
Less Loan Carried by Seller... $_____
Estimated Net Cash Proceeds .... $_____

Seller _____ Date _____

APPENDIX B: FIELD OFFICE RESOURCES

FEDERAL NATIONAL MORTGAGE ASSOCIATION OFFICES

FNMA Home Office
3900 Wisconsin Avenue, NW
Washington, DC 20016-2899
(202) 752-7000
Customer Education Group
(202) 752-2837

Northeastern Regional Office
1900 Market Street, 8th Floor
Philadelphia, PA 19103
(215) 575-1400
Serving lenders in Connecticut,
Delaware, Maine, Massachusetts,
New Hampshire, New Jersey, New
York, Pennsylvania, Puerto Rico,
Rhode Island, Vermont and the
Virgin Islands

Southeastern Regional Office
950 East Paces Ferry Road, Suite
1900
Atlanta, GA 30326-1161
(404) 365-6000
Serving lenders in Alabama, District
of Columbia, Florida, Georgia,
Kentucky, Maryland, Mississippi,
North Carolina, South Carolina,
Tennessee, Virgina and West
Virginia

Midwestern Regional Office
One South Wacker Drive, Suite 3100
Chicago, IL 60606-4667
(312) 368-6200
Serving lenders in Illinois, Indiana,
Iowa, Michigan, Minnesota,
Nebraska, North Dakota, Ohio,
South Dakota and Wisconsin

Southwestern Regional Office
Two Galleria Tower
13455 Noel Road, Suite 600
Dallas, TX 75265-5003
(214) 991-7771
Serving lenders in Arizona,
Arkansas, Colorado, Kansas,
Louisiana, Missouri, New Mexico,
Oklahoma, Texas and Utah

Western Regional Office
135 North Los Robles Avenue,
Suite 300
Pasadena, CA 91101-1707
(818) 568-5000
Serving lenders in Alaska, California,
Guam, Hawaii, Idaho, Montana,
Nevada, Oregon, Washington and
Wyoming

FEDERAL HOME LOAN MORTGAGE CORPORATION OFFICES

Corporate Headquarters
1759 Business Center Drive
Reston, Virginia 22090
(703) 759-8000

North Central Regional Office
Federal Home Loan Mortgage
Corporation
333 West Wacker Drive, Suite 3100
Chicago, Illinois 60606-1287
(312) 407-7400
Serving lenders in: Illinois, Indiana,
Iowa, Michigan, Minnesota, North
Dakota, Ohio, South Dakota,
Wisconsin

Northeast Regional Office
Federal Home Loan Mortgage
Corporation
2231 Crystal Drive, Suite 900
P.O. Box 2408
Arlington, Virginia 22202-3798
(703) 685-4500
Serving lenders in Connecticut,
Delaware, District of Columbia,
Maine, Maryland, Massachusetts,
New Hampshire, New Jersey, New
York, Pennsylvania, Puerto Rico,
Rhode Island, Vermont, Virginia,
Virgin Islands, West Virginia

Western Regional Office
Federal Home Loan Mortgage
Corporation
15303 Ventura Boulevard, Suite 500
Sherman Oaks, California 91403
(818) 905-0070

Serving lenders in Alaska, Arizona,
California, Guam, Hawaii, Idaho,
Montana, Nevada, Oregon, Utah,
Washington

Seattle Branch
Federal Home Loan Mortgage
Corporation
600 Stewart Street, Suite 720
Seattle, Washington 98101
(206) 622-9904

Southwest Regional Office
Federal Home Loan Mortgage
Corporation
12222 Merit Drive, Suite 700
Dallas, Texas 75251
(214) 702-2000
Serving lenders in Arkansas,
Colorado, Kansas, Louisiana,
Missouri, Nebraska, New Mexico,
Oklahoma, Texas, Wyoming

Southeast Regional Office
Federal Home Loan Mortgage
Corporation
2839 Paces Ferry Road, NW,
Suite 700
Post Office Box 723788
Atlanta, Georgia 30339
(404) 438-3800
Serving lenders in: Alabama, Florida,
Georgia, Kentucky, Mississippi,
North Carolina, South Carolina,
Tennessee

DEPARTMENT OF HOUSING AND URBAN DEVELOPMENT OFFICES

Boston Area Office
Bulfinch Building
15 New Chardon St.
Boston, MA 02114
(617) 223-4182

Hartford Area Office
One Hartford Square West
Suite 204
Hartford, CT 06106
(203) 244-2317

Manchester MF Service Office
Norris Cotton Federal Building
275 Chestnut St.
Manchester, NH 03103
(603) 666-7684

Providence MF Service Office
Rm. 330
John O. Pastore Federal Building
Providence, RI 02903
(401) 528-4835

Buffalo Area Office
Statler Building Mezzanine
107 Delaware Avenue
Buffalo, NY 11202
(716) 846-5710

Caribbean Area Office
Federico Deoptau Federal Building
U.S. Court House, Room 428
Carlos E. Chardon Ave.
Hato Rey, Puerto Rico 00918
(809) 753-4351

Newark Area Office
Gateway Building No. 1
Raymond Plaza
Newark, NJ 07102
(201) 645-3230

New York Area Office
26 Federal Plaza
New York, NY 10278
(212) 264-4975

Baltimore Area Office
Equitable Building
10 N. Calvert St.
Baltimore, MD 21202
(301) 962-2144

Charleston MF Service Office
Kanawha Valley Building
Captitol and Lee Streets
Charleston, WV 25301
(304) 347-7064

Philadelphia Area Office
625 Walnut St.
Philadelphia, PA 19106
(215) 597-3409

Pittsburgh Area Office
Fort Pitt Commons
455 Fort Pitt Blvd.
Pittsburgh, PA 15219
(412) 644-3431

Richmond Area Office
701 E. Franklin St.
Richmond, VA 23219
(804) 771-2001

Washington D.C. Area Office
Universal North Building
1875 Connecticut Ave.
Washington, D.C. 20009
(202) 673-5839

Atlanta Area Office
Richard B. Russell Federal Building
75 Spring St., S.W.
Atlanta, GA 30303
(404) 221-4017

Birmingham Area Office
Daniel Building
15 S. 20th. St.
Birmingham, AL 35322
(202) 254-1611

Columbia Area Office
Strom Thurmond Federal Building
1835-45 Assembly St.
Columbia, SC 29201
(803) 765-5826

Greensboro Area Office
415 N. Edgeworth St.
Greensboro, NC 27401
(919) 378-5673

Jacksonville Area Office
Peninsular Plaza, 661
Riverside Ave.
Jacksonville, FL 32202
(904) 791-2953

Jackson Area Office
U.S. Federal Building
100 W. Capital St., Room 1016
Jackson, MS 39201
(601) 960-4719

Knoxville Area Office
1 Northshire Building
1111 Northshire Dr.
Knoxville, TN 37919
(615) 558-1477

Louisville Area Office
539 River City Mall
P.O. Box 1044
Louisville, KY 40202
(502) 582-6467

Nashville MF Service Office
1 Commerce Place, Suite 1600
Nashville, TN 37219
(615) 251-5069

Chicago Area Office
One North Dearborn
Chicago, IL 60602
(312) 353-9174

Cincinnati MF Service Office
550 Main St.
Cincinnati, OH 45202
(513) 684-2884

Cleveland MF Service Office
770 Rockwell Ave.
2nd Floor
Cleveland, OH 44114
(216) 522-4032

Columbus Area Office
200 N. High St.
Columbus, OH 43215
(614) 469-5704

Detroit Area Office
McNamara Federal Building
477 Michigan Ave.
Detroit, MI 48226
(313) 226-4817

Grand Rapids Service Office
2922 Fuller Ave., N.E.
Grand Rapids, MI 49505
(616) 456-2214

Indianapolis Area Office
151 N. Delaware St.
P.O. Box 7047
Indianapolis, IN 46207
(317) 269-2087

Milwaukee Area Office
744 N. Fourth St.
Milwaukee, WI 53203
(414) 291-1028

Minneapolis St. Paul Area Office
220 South Second St.
Bridge Place Building
Minneapolis, MN 55803
(612) 349-3095

Springfield Valuation and
Endorsement Station
Lincoln Towers Plaza
524 S. Second St.,
Room 600
Springfield, IL 62701
(217) 492-4174

Albuquerque Service Office
625 Truman St., N.E.
Albuquerque, NM 87110
(505) 766-3249

Dallas Area Office
2001 Bryan Tower
4th Floor
Dallas, TX 75201
(214) 767-8394

Houston MF Service Office
Two Greenway Plaza East
Suite 200
Houston, TX 77046
(713) 226-4352

Lubbock Service Office
Federal Building
1205 Texas Ave.
Lubbock, TX 79408
(806) 762-7275

Little Rock Area Office
One Union North Plaza
Suite 1400
Little Rock, AR 72201
(501) 378-6148

Oklahoma City Area Office
Murrah Federal Building
200 N.W. 5th St.
Oklahoma City, OK 73102
(405) 231-4582

New Orleans Area Office
1001 Howard Plaza Tower
New Orleans, LA 70113
(504) 589-6635

San Antonio Area Office
Washington Square Building
800 Dolorosa, P.O. Box 9163
San Antonio, TX 78285
(512) 229-6830

Shreveport Service Office
50 Fannin St.
New Federal Building, 6th Floor
Shreveport, LA 71101
(318) 226-5405

Tulsa Service Office
State Office Building
440 S. Houston Ave.
Tulsa, OK 74127
(405) 231-4582

Des Moines MF Service Station
210 Walnut St.
Room 259
Des Moines, IA 50309
(515) 284-4770

Kansas City Area Office
Professional Building
1103 Grand St.
Kansas City, MO 64106
(816) 374-6125

St. Louis Area Office
270 N. Tucker Blvd.
St. Louis, MO 63101
(314) 425-4777

Omaha Area Office
Univac Building
7100 West Center Rd
Omaha, NE 68106
(402) 229-9428

Denver Regional/Area Office
Executive Tower Building
1405 Curtis St.
Denver, CO 80202
(303) 837-4721

Honolulu Area Office
300 Ala Moana Blvd.
Honolulu, HI 94830
(808) 546-2137

Los Angeles Area Office
2500 Wilshire Blvd.
Los Angeles, CA 90057
(213) 688-5978

Phonenix Service Office
Arizona Bank Building
101 N. First Avenue
Suite 1800
Phoenix, AZ 85002
(602) 261-4497

Sacramento MF Service Office
545 Downtown Plaza
P.O. Box 1978, Suite 250
Sacramento, CA 95809
(916) 440-2334

San Francisco Area Office
One Embarcadero Center
Suite 1600
San Francisco, CA 94111
(415) 556-6781

Anchorage Area Office
334 West Fifth Ave.
Anchorage, AK 99501
(907) 271-4175

Portland Area Office
Cascade Building
520 S.W. Sixth Ave.
Portland, OR 97204
(503) 326-3107

Seattle Area Office
403 Arcade Plaza Building
1321 Second Ave.
Seattle, WA 98101
(206) 442-0334

Tucson Service Office
33 N. Stone Ave.
Arizona Bank Building
Suite 1400
Tucson, AZ 85701
(602) 792-6779

Boise Service Office
800 Park Blvd.
Boise, ID 83705
(208) 334-1338

Spokane Service Office
746 U.S. Courthouse
West 920 Riverside Ave.
Spokane, WA 99201
(509) 456-4571

VETERANS ADMINISTRATION REGIONAL OFFICES

ALABAMA
VA Regional Office
474 South Court St.
Montgomery, AL 36104

ALASKA
VA Regional Office
2925 DeBarr Rd
Anchorage, AK 99508

ARIZONA
VA Regional Office
3225 North Central Ave.
Phoenix, AZ 85012

ARKANSAS
VA Regional Office
P.O. Box 1280
Building 65, Fort Roots
North Little Rock, AR 72115

CALIFORNIA
VA Regional Office
Federal Building
11000 Wilshire Blvd
Los Angeles, CA 90024

VA Regional Office
Oakland Federal Building
1301 Clay Street, Room 1300
North Oakland, CA 94612

COLORADO
VA Regional Office
P.O. Box 25126
44 Union Boulevard
Denver, CO 80225

CONNECTICUT
VA Medical and Regional Office
Center
450 Main St.
Hartford, CT 06103
*Note: Loan guaranty consolidated
with Manchester.*

DELAWARE
VA Medical and Regional Office
Center
1601 Kirkwood Highway
Wilmington, DE 19805
*Note: Loan guaranty consolidated
with Philadelphia.*

DISTRICT OF COMUMBIA
VA Regional Office
941 North Capitol St., NE
Washington, D.C. 20421

FLORIDA
VA Regional Office
144 First Ave., South
St. Petersburg, FL 33701

GEORGIA
VA Regional Office
730 Peachtree St., NE
Atlanta, GA 30365

HAWAII
VA Medical and Regional Office
Center
P.O. Box 50188, 96850
PJKK Federal Building
300 Ala Moana Boulevard
Honolulu, HI 96813

IDAHO
VA Regional Office
Federal Building and U.S.
Courthouse
550 West Fort St.
Box 044
Boise, ID 83724

ILLINOIS
VA Regional Office
536 S. Clark St.
P.O. Box 8136
Chicago, IL 60680

INDIANA
VA Regional Office
575 North Pennsylvania St.
Indianapolis, IN 46204

IOWA
VA Regional Office
210 Walnut St.
Des Moines, IA 50309

KANSAS
VA Medical and Regional Office
Center
5500 E. Kellogg
Wichita, KS 67218

KENTUCKY
VA Regional Office
545 S. 3rd St.
Louisville, KY 40202

LOUISIANA
VA Regional Office
701 Loyola Ave.
New Orleans, LA 70113

MAINE
VA Medical and Regional Office
Center
Route 17 East
Togus, ME 04330
Note: Loan guaranty consolidated
with Manchester.

MARYLAND
VA Regional Office
Federal Building
31 Hopkins Plaza
Baltimore, MD 21201
Note: Montgomery and Prince
Georges counties are under the
jurisdiction of VARO, Washington,
D.C.

MASSACHUSETTS
VA Regional Office
John Fitzgerald Kennedy
Federal Building
Boston, MA 02203
Note: Loan guaranty consolidated
with Manchester.

MICHIGAN
VA Regional Office
477 Michigan Ave.
Detroit, MI 48226

MINNESOTA
VA Regional Office and Insurance
Center
Bishop Henry Whipple
Federal Building
Fort Snelling
St. Paul, MN 55111

MISSISSIPPI
VA Regional Office
100 W. Capitol St.
Jackson, MS 39269

MISSOURI
VA Regional Office
1520 Market St.
St. Louis, MO 63103

MONTANA
VA Medical and Regional Office
Center
William Street off of Highway 12
West
Fort Harrison, MT 59636

NEBRASKA
VA Regional Office
5631 South 48th St.
Lincoln, NE 68516

NEVADA
VA Regional Office
1201 Terminal Way
Reno, NV 89520
Note: Loan guaranty consolidated with San Francisco. Loan Guaranty activities for Clark and Lincoln counties, Nevada consolidated with Los Angeles.

NEW HAMPSHIRE
VA Regional Office
275 Chestnut St.
Manchester, NH 03101

NEW JERSEY
VA Regional Office
20 Washington Place
Newark, NJ 07102

NEW MEXICO
VA Regional Office
500 Gold Ave., SW
Albuquerque, NM 87102

NEW YORK
VA Regional Office
Federal Building
111 West Huron St.
Buffalo, NY 14202

VA Regional Office
252 Seventh Avenue at 24th St.
New York, NY 10001

NORTH CAROLINA
VA Regional Office
251 North Main St.
Winston-Salem, NC 27155

NORTH DAKOTA
VA Medical and Regional Office
Center
2101 North Elm St.
Fargo, ND 58102-2498
Note: Loan guaranty consolidated with St. Paul.

OHIO
VA Regional Office
1240 East Ninth St.
Cleveland, OH 44199

OKLAHOMA
VA Regional Office
125 South Main St.
Muskogee, OK 74401

OREGON
VA Regional Office
Federal Building
1220 Southwest Third Ave.
Portland, OR 97204

PENNSYLVANIA
VA Regional Office and Insurance
Center
P.O. Box 8079
5000 Wissahickon Ave.
Philadelphia, PA 19101

VA Regional Office
1000 Liberty Avenue
Pittsburgh, PA 15222

PUERTO RICO
VA Regional Office
GPO Box 4867
San Juan, PR 00936

RHODE ISLAND
VA Regional Office
380 Westminster Mall
Providence, RI 02903
Note: Loan guaranty consolidated with Manchester.

SOUTH CAROLINA
VA Regional Office
1801 Assembly St.
Columbia, SC 29201

SOUTH DAKOTA
VA Medical and Regional Office
Center
P.O. Box 5046
2501 West 22nd St.
Sioux Falls, SD 57117
*Note: Loan gauranty consolidated
with St. Paul.*

TENNESSEE
VA Regional Office
110 Ninth Ave., South
Nashville, TN 37203

TEXAS
VA Regional Office
2515 Murworth Dr.
Houston, TX 77054

VA Regional Office
1400 North Valley Mills Dr.
Waco, TX 76799

UTAH
VA Regional Office
P.O. Box 11500
125 South State St.
Salt Lake City, UT 84147

VERMONT
VA Medical and Regional Office
Center
N. Hartland Rd
White River Junction, VT 05001
*Note: Loan guaranty consolidated
with Manchester.*

VIRGINIA
VA Regional Office
210 Franklin Rd, SW
Roanoke, VA 24011
*Note: Arlington, Fairfax, Loudoun,
Prince William, Spotsylvania and
Stafford Counties and the cities of
Alexandria, Fairfax, Falls Church and
Fredericksburg are under the
jurisdiction of VARO, Washington,
D.C.*

WASHINGTON
VA Regional Office
Federal Building
915 Second Ave.
Seattle, WA 98174
*Note: Clark, Klickitat and Skamania
counties are under the jurisdiction of
VARO, Portland, Oregon.*

WEST VIRGINIA
VA Regional Office
640 4th Ave.
Huntington, WV 25701
*Note: Brooke, Hancock, Marshall and
Ohio counties are under the
jurisdiction of VARO, Pittsburgh, PA.*

WISCONSIN
VA Regional Office
Building 6
Milwaukee, WI 53295

WYOMING
VA Medical and Regional Office
Center
2360 East Pershing Boulevard
Cheyenne, WY 82001
*Note: Loan guaranty consolidated
with Denver.*

APPENDIX C: AMORTIZATION FACTORS

To determine the monthly P and I (principal and interest)
payment:
1. Locate the factor for the desired interest rate and term.
2. Multiply this rate/term factor by the loan amount.

To determine the principal amount of the loan:
1. Locate the factor for the desired interest rate and term.
2. Divide the monthly P and I payment by this rate/term factor.

Term in Years	INTEREST RATE					
	4%	4¼%	4½%	4¾%	5%	5¼%
5	.0184165	.0185296	.0186430	.0187569	.0188712	.0189860
8	.0121893	.0123059	.0124232	.0125412	.0126599	.0127793
10	.0101245	.0102438	.0103638	.0104848	.0106066	.0107292
12	.0087553	.0088772	.0090001	.0091240	.0092489	.0093748
15	.0073969	.0075228	.0076499	.0077783	.0079079	.0080388
18	.0065020	.0066319	.0067632	.0068961	.0070303	.0071660
20	.0060598	.0061923	.0063265	.0064622	.0065996	.0067384
25	.0052784	.0054174	.0055583	.0057012	.0058459	.0059925
30	.0047742	.0049194	.0050669	.0052165	.0053682	.0055220
35	.0044277	.0045789	.0047326	.0048886	.0050469	.0052074
40	.0041794	.0043362	.0044956	.0046576	.0048220	.0049887

Term in Years	INTEREST RATE					
	5½%	5¾%	6%	6¼%	6½%	6¾%
5	.0191012	.0192168	.0193328	.0194490	.0195661	.0196835
8	.0128993	.0130200	.0131414	.0132640	.0133862	.0135096
10	.0108526	.0109769	.0111021	.0112280	.0113548	.0114824
12	.0095017	.0096296	.0097585	.0098880	.0100192	.0101510
15	.0081708	.0083041	.0084386	.0085740	.0087111	.0088491
18	.0073032	.0074417	.0075816	.0077230	.0078656	.0080096
20	.0068789	.0070208	.0071643	.0073093	.0074557	.0076036
25	.0061409	.0062911	.0064430	.0065970	.0067521	.0069091
30	.0056779	.0058357	.0059955	.0061570	.0063207	.0064860
35	.0053702	.0055350	.0057019	.0058710	.0060415	.0062142
40	.0051577	.0053289	.0055021	.0056770	.0058546	.0060336

Term in Years	INTEREST RATE					
	7%	7¼%	7½%	7¾%	8%	8¼%
5	.0198012	.0199193	.0200379	.0201570	.0202764	.0203963
8	.0136337	.0137585	.0138838	.0140099	.0141367	.0142640
10	.0116108	.0117401	.0118702	.0120010	.0121328	.0122653
12	.0102838	.0104176	.0105523	.0106879	.0108245	.0109620
15	.0089883	.0091286	.0092701	.0094128	.0095565	.0097014
18	.0081550	.0083017	.0084497	.0085990	.0087496	.0089015
20	.0077530	.0079038	.0080593	.0082095	.0083644	.0085207
25	.0070680	.0072281	.0073899	.0075533	.0077182	.0078845
30	.0066530	.0068218	.0069921	.0071641	.0073376	.0075127
35	.0063886	.0065647	.0067424	.0069218	.0071026	.0072849
40	.0062143	.0063967	.0065807	.0067662	.0069531	.0071414
50	.0060169	.0062089	.0064023	.0065970	.0067927	.0069896

Term in Years	INTEREST RATE					
	8½%	8¾%	9%	9¼%	9½%	9¾%
5	.0205165	.0206372	.0207584	.0208799	.0210019	.0211243
8	.0143921	.0145208	.0146502	.0147802	.0149109	.0150423
10	.0123986	.0125327	.0126676	.0128033	.0129398	.0130771
12	.0111006	.0112400	.0113803	.0115216	.0116637	.0118069
15	.0098479	.0099949	.0101427	.0102919	.0104422	.0105937
18	.0090546	.0092089	.0093644	.0095212	.0096791	.0098382
20	.0086782	.0088371	.0089972	.0091587	.0093213	.0094852
25	.0080523	.0082214	.0083920	.0085638	.0087370	.0089114
30	.0076891	.0078670	.0080462	.0082268	.0084085	.0085916
35	.0074686	.0076536	.0078399	.0080274	.0082161	.0084059
40	.0073309	.0075217	.0077136	.0079066	.0081006	.0082956
50	.0071874	.0073861	.0075857	.0077860	.0079871	.0081888

Term in Years	INTEREST RATE					
	10%	10¼%	10½%	10¾%	11%	11¼%
5	.0212471	.0213703	.0214940	.0216180	.0217425	.0218674
8	.0151742	.0153068	.0154401	.0155740	.0157085	.0158436
10	.0132151	.0133540	.0134935	.0136339	.0137751	.0139169
12	.0119508	.0120957	.0122415	.0123881	.0125356	.0126840
15	.0107461	.0108996	.0110540	.0112095	.0113660	.0115235
18	.0099984	.0101598	.0103223	.0104859	.0106505	.0108162
20	.0096503	.0098165	.0099838	.0101523	.0103219	.0104926
25	.0090871	.0092639	.0094419	.0096210	.0098012	.0099824
30	.0087758	.0089611	.0091474	.0093349	.0095233	.0097127
35	.0085967	.0087886	.0089813	.0091750	.0093696	.0095649
40	.0084916	.0086882	.0088857	.0090840	.0092829	.0094826
50	.0083911	.0085939	.0087972	.0090010	.0092052	.0094098

Term in Years	INTEREST RATE					
	11½%	11¾%	12%	12¼%	12½%	12¾%
5	.0219927	.0221184	.0222445	.0223710	.0224980	.0226254
8	.0159794	.0161158	.0162529	.0163906	.0165289	.0166678
10	.0140596	.0142030	.0143471	.0144920	.0146377	.0147840
12	.0128332	.0129833	.0131342	.0132860	.0134386	.0135921
15	.0116819	.0118414	.0120017	.0121630	.0123253	.0124884
18	.0109830	.0111507	.0113195	.0114892	.0116600	.0118317
20	.0106643	.0108371	.0110109	.0111857	.0113615	.0115382
25	.0101647	.0103480	.0105323	.0107175	.0109036	.0110906
30	.0099030	.0100941	.0102862	.0104790	.0106726	.0108670
35	.0097611	.0099579	.0101555	.0103537	.0105525	.0107519
40	.0096828	.0098836	.0100850	.0102869	.0104892	.0106919
50	.0096148	.0098200	.0100256	.0102314	.0104375	.0106438

Term in Years	INTEREST RATE					
	13%	13¼%	13½%	13¾%	14%	14¼%
5	.0227531	.0228813	.0230099	.0231389	.0232683	.0233981
8	.0168073	.0169475	.0170882	.0172296	.0173716	.0175141
10	.0149311	.0150789	.0152275	.0153767	.0155267	.0156774
12	.0137463	.0139014	.0140572	.0142139	.0143713	.0145295
15	.0126525	.0128174	.0129832	.0131499	.0133175	.0134858
18	.0120043	.0121779	.0123523	.0125276	.0127038	.0128809
20	.0117158	.0118944	.0120738	.0122541	.0124353	.0126172
25	.0112784	.0114671	.0116565	.0118467	.0120377	.0122293
30	.0110620	.0112578	.0114542	.0116512	.0118486	.0120469
35	.0109520	.0111524	.0113534	.0115548	.0117567	.0119590
40	.0108951	.0110987	.0113026	.0115069	.0117114	.0119162
50	.0108502	.0110569	.0112637	.0114707	.0116778	.0118850

Term in Years	INTEREST RATE					
	14½%	14¾%	15%	15¼%	15½%	15¾%
5	.0235283	.0236590	.0237900	.0239241	.0240532	.0241855
8	.0176573	.0178011	.0179455	.0180904	.0182360	.0183821
10	.0158287	.0159808	.0161335	.0162870	.0164411	.0165959
12	.0146885	.0148483	.0150088	.0151701	.0153321	.0154948
15	.0136551	.0138251	.0139959	.0141675	.0143400	.0145131
18	.0130587	.0132374	.0134169	.0135972	.0137782	.0139600
20	.0128000	.0129836	.0131679	.0133530	.0135389	.0137254
25	.0124217	.0126147	.0128084	.0130026	.0131975	.0133929
30	.0122456	.0124448	.0126445	.0128446	.0130452	.0132462
35	.0121617	.0123647	.0125681	.0127718	.0129758	.0131801
40	.0121213	.0123267	.0125322	.0127380	.0129440	.0131502
50	.0120930	.0122973	.0125072	.0127148	.0129225	.0131303

Term in Years	INTEREST RATE					
	16%	16¼%	16½%	16¾%	17%	17¼%
5	.0243181	.0244511	.0245846	.0247184	.0248526	.0249872
8	.0185288	.0186761	.0188240	.0189725	.0191215	.0192710
10	.0167514	.0169075	.0170643	.0172217	.0173798	.0175385
12	.0156583	.0158225	.0159874	.0161530	.0163193	.0164862
15	.0146871	.0148617	.0150371	.0152133	.0153901	.0155676
18	.0141425	.0143257	.0145096	.0146942	.0148795	.0150654
20	.0139126	.0141005	.0142891	.0144782	.0146681	.0148584
25	.0135889	.0137855	.0139825	.0141800	.0143780	.0145764
30	.0134476	.0136494	.0138515	.0140540	.0142568	.0144599
35	.0133847	.0135895	.0137945	.0139998	.0142053	.0144109
40	.0133565	.0135630	.0137696	.0139764	.0141832	.0143902
50	.0133381	.0135459	.0137538	.0139617	.0141697	.0143777

Term in Years	INTEREST RATE					
	17½%	17¾%	18%	18¼%	18½%	18¾%
5	.0251222	.0252576	.0253935	.0255296	.0256662	.0258032
8	.0194212	.0195719	.0197233	.0198751	.0200274	.0201804
10	.0176979	.0178579	.0180186	.0181798	.0183417	.0185041
12	.0166539	.0168222	.0169912	.0171608	.0173311	.0175021
15	.0157458	.0159247	.0161043	.0162844	.0164652	.0166467
18	.0152519	.0154391	.0156269	.0158153	.0160042	.0161938
20	.0150494	.0152410	.0154332	.0156258	.0158190	.0160127
25	.0147753	.0149746	.0151743	.0153744	.0155748	.0157757
30	.0146633	.0148669	.0150709	.0152750	.0154794	.0156841
35	.0146168	.0148228	.0150289	.0152352	.0154417	.0156483
40	.0145973	.0148045	.0150118	.0152192	.0154266	.0156342
50	.0145858	.0147939	.0150020	.0152101	.0154183	.0156264

GLOSSARY

acquisition cost Cost of acquiring a property, in addition to purchase price, such as title insurance and lenders' fees (e.g., with FHA, acquisition is a set amount based on the appraised value of the property).

addendum rider An addition to the standard contract (e.g., the lender attaches the due-on-sale clause to the loan via an addendum rider).

adjustable rate mortgage (ARM) A mortgage tied to an index that adjusts based on changes in the economy.

adjustment period The period during which an ARM adjusts (e.g., six months, one year or three years).

alienation clause (due-on-sale clause) A type of acceleration clause in a loan, calling for payment of the entire principal balance in full, triggered by the transfer or sale of a property.

amendatory language Language usually added to FHA and VA sales contracts when the contract is written prior to the completion of the appraisal. (This specifies what the options are if the appraisal amount varies from the offering price.)

amortization Retiring a debt through predetermined periodic payments, including principal and interest.

appraisal An estimate of value.

ARM Adjustable rate mortgage.

assignment The transfer of rights to pay an obligation from one party to another, with the original party remaining secondarily liable for the debt, should the second party default.

assumption To take over one's obligation under an existing agreement. (Note: This can be done with varying degrees of release—see *assignment, novation* and *subject-to*).

automatic approval The processing of a VA loan, which is done solely by the lender, without prior submission of the documents to the regional office.

balloon payment A principal sum coming due at a predetermined period of time (may also contain payment of accrued interest).

biweekly mortgage A mortgage under which one-half of the regular amortized monthly payment is payable every two weeks, giving the benefit of 13 full payments per year; this allows a 30-year loan to retire in approximately 18 years.

blended rate The melding together of two rates to create a lower overall rate of interest. For example, blending the rate of an 8 percent first mortgage, and a 10 percent second mortgage, allows the buyer to more readily qualify.

buydown Permanent: Prepaid interest that brings the note rate on the loan down to a lower, permanent rate. Temporary: prepaid interest that lowers the note rate temporarily on the loan, allowing the buyer to more readily qualify and to increase payments as income grows. (A common example of a temporary buydown is the 3-2-1 plan—3 percent lower interest the first year, 2 percent the second, and 1 percent the third.)

cap A ceiling, usually found on ARM loans; can be expressed as "per period," for example, annual, or lifetime, meaning for the entire loan term.

carryover An interest rate that is too great to add to the ARM adjustments because of the predetermined caps, so the interest amount is carried over until it can be applied. Note, however, that this amount is *not* added onto the principal balance, such as in negative amortization. (Because of the 2 percent annual cap on a loan, an additional 1 percent interest adjustment cannot be applied—so it is held until the annual adjustments fall short of their cap, and then applied.)

cash reserves The amount of buyer's liquid cash remaining after making the down payment and paying all closing costs.

Certificate of Commitment The lender's approval of a VA loan, which is usually good for up to six months.

Certificate of Eligibility VA certification, showing the amount of entitlement used and the remaining guaranty available.

Certificate of Reasonable Value (CRV) The formal name for a VA appraisal.

chattel Personal property.

collateral/collateral agreement Means "additional," but is generally termed to mean security for a debt.

commitment period The period during which a loan approval is valid.

contract for deed (installment sales and land sales contract) A document used to secure real property when it is seller-financed; contains the full agreement between the parties, including purchase price, terms of payment and any additional agreements.

convertible ARM An adjustable rate mortgage containing a clause allowing for the rate to become fixed during a certain time period (e.g., between months 13 and 60 of the loan term).

convertibility option The clause that allows the ARM loan to convert to a fixed rate during a certain period.

CRV Certificate of Reasonable Value.

debt assumption letter/assignment of debt The formal transfer of debt from one person to another, backed by a formal contract of assumption, signed by the parties. This is done to reduce the amount of a person's long-term debt.

debt ratios The comparison of a buyer's housing costs to his or her gross or net effective income (based on the loan program); and the comparison of a buyer's total long-term debt to his or her gross or net effective income (based on the loan program used). The first ratio is termed *housing ratio;* the second ratio is *total debt ratio.* (See particular programs for applicable ratios.)

deed of trust (trust deed) A document used to secure the collateral in financing the property; title is transferred to the trustee, with payments made to the beneficiary by the trustor (grantor in some states).

direct endorsement lender Lenders approved by FHA to make loans without having loans first approved by the regional FHA office.

direct loan, VA A loan made to the veteran borrower by the VA, without using a lender (done infrequently, and then only in remote outlying areas).

discount points (points) A point is equal to 1 percent of the amount financed. Points are used to increase the lender's yield on the loan, so as to bridge the gap between what the lender could get with conventional monies, and the lower rates of VA and FHA.

discounting, seller Reducing the sales price in lieu of paying points or other fees from the seller's gross price.

distributive share MIP The FHA mortgage insurance plan in effect prior to 1983.

dual contracts Double contracts on the same property by the same buyer. Usually refers to an illegal second contract requesting a higher loan amount from a lender, even though the first contract bears the agreed-upon price between the seller and buyer.

due-on-sale clause (alienation clause) See *alienation clause.*

entitlement Also known as VA guaranty; the amount of the veteran's eligibility in qualifying for a VA loan.

equity The difference between what is owed and what the property could be sold for.

equity loans Tapping into an owner's equity, with the property used as the collateral.

escrow An impartial holding of documents pertinent to the sale and transfer of real estate; also the term used to describe the long-term holding of documents, such as with seller financing. Called a long-term escrow or escrow collection.

escrow holder An impartial third party who holds the documents pertinent to the transfer and sale of real estate.

Federal Home Loan Mortgage Corporation (FHLMC) Called "Freddie Mac"; a part of the secondary market, particularly used to purchase loans from savings and loan lenders within the Federal Home Loan Bank Board.

Federal Housing Administration (FHA) The FHA is part of the federal government's Department of Housing and Urban Development. It exists to underwrite insured loans made by lenders to provide economical housing for moderate-income persons.

Federal National Mortgage Association (FNMA) "Fannie Mae," a privately owned part of the secondary mortgage market used to recycle mortgages made in the primary market, purchases conventional, FHA and VA loans.

FHLMC Federal Home Loan Mortgage Corporation ("Freddie Mac").

fixed-rate mortgage (FRM) A fixed-rate mortgage is a conventional loan with a single interest rate for the life of the loan.

FNMA Federal National Mortgage Association ("Fannie Mae").

foreclosure A proceeding, in or out of court, to extinguish one's rights in a property, and pay off all outstanding debts via a sale of the property.

FRM Fixed-rate mortgage.

fully indexed rate The maximum interest rate on an ARM that can be reached at the first adjustment.

funding fee An origination fee on VA loans, usually equal to 1 percent of the amount financed.

Garn–St. Germain Act Legislation in 1981 that allowed savings and loans to diversify out of their investments into more risky ventures; this also predicated strict enforcement of the alienation (due-on-sale) clause in mortgages.

GEM Growing equity mortgage.

gift letter A letter from a relative (or party with whom a strong relationship has been established—for some loans) stating that an amount will be gifted to the buyer, and that said amount is not to be repaid.

GNMA Government National Mortgage Association ("Ginnie Mae").

Government National Mortgage Association (GNMA) "Ginnie Mae" is a governmental part of the secondary market that deals primarily in recycling VA and FHA mortgages, particularly those which are highly leveraged (e.g., no or low down payment).

graduated payment mortgage (GPM) A type of conventional loan containing a fixed rate for the life of the loan, but graduates, or increases the payment during a certain period of the loan. (Example: 7.5 percent payment increase for the first seven years of the loan, then the payment remains fixed at that level.)

growing equity mortgage (GEM) The GEM has a fixed interest rate for the life of the loan; but payments increase 3 percent, 5 percent, or 7.5 percent (depending on the program) for a period during the loan (usually not to exceed ten years), with all payment increases applied directly to reduce the principal. Thirty-year amortized GEM loans typically pay off between 13 and 15 years.

guaranty, VA The amount which the Veterans Administration will indemnify the lender against loss on a VA loan.

housing expense ratio The amount of either gross income or net effective income (depending on the loan program) that can be allocated for borrower's housing expense. This percent will also vary based on the loan-to-value ratio of the loan.

income qualifications The amount of either gross income or net effective income (depending on the loan program) required by the lender for loan qualifying.

index An indicator used to measure inflation, which is a basis for the ARM loan. There are various sources of indexes, including treasury securities, treasury bills, 11th district cost of funds and the index of the Federal Home Loan Bank Board. The index, plus the margin, becomes the interest rate in the ARM.

inflation An increase in value; most often used as an indicator of the economy. When inflation is high, real estate performs well, since it appreciates in times of inflation.

initial interest rate The introductory interest rate on a loan; signals that there may be rate adjustments later in the loan.

in-service eligibility Qualifying a veteran buyer for a VA loan while still in active duty.

installment sales contract (contract for deed) See *contract for deed.*

"interest only" Payments received are only applied to accrued interest on the loan; therefore, there is no principal reduction.

interest rate The note rate charged on the loan.

interest rate cap The maximum amount of interest that can be charged on an ARM loan. Can be expressed in terms of annual or lifetime figures.

jumbo loans Mortgage loans that exceed the loan amounts acceptable for sale in the secondary market; these jumbos must be packaged and sold differently to investors and therefore have separate underwriting guidelines.

kickback The illegal payment of a fee or other compensation for the privilege of securing business referrals from a source. (Example: a lender illegally receives $50 per referral sent to the title company.)

lease option A lease with an option to buy; said option can either be exercised to culminate in a purchase or forfeited by the optionee.

lease purchase A type of delayed closing. A lease purchase is drafted on a purchase and sales contract, stating the terms of the purchase, as well as a date for closing the sale. Should the buyer default, the seller has all of the remedies available under the sales contract.

leverage Using a small asset to purchase a larger asset; using "OPM"—other people's money! Leverage allows a buyer's down payment to go further. (Example: Instead of using

$50,000 down on a $100,000 property, the buyer could use $10,000 down on five properties of $100,000.)

liability, release of The type of liability release for the original borrower, found under a novation.

LID (local improvement district) A legal entity (district) established under state law to benefit a certain geographic area. Districts issue bonds to finance real property improvements such as water distribution systems, sidewalks and sewer systems. To repay funds, districts then levy assessments on real estate located in the geographic area affected.

lifetime cap The maximum amount of interest an ARM loan can reach during the life of the loan.

loan qualifying Meeting the criteria for a loan as required by a mortgage lender; varies greatly from program to program.

loan-to-value ratio The amount of the loan as compared to the appraised value of the property.

lock-in The fixing of an interest rate or points at a certain level, usually during the loan application process. It is usually done for a certain period of time, such as 60 days, and may require a fee or premium in the form of a higher interest rate.

long-term debt For qualifying purposes, debts that cannot be paid off within a certain amount of time, which varies depending on the loan type. (Example: conventional long-term debts are considered to be those in excess of ten months, six months for FHA and 12 months for VA. Note, however, that individual lenders could choose to be more restrictive than these national guidelines.)

margin An amount added by the lender to an ARM index in order to compute the interest rate. The margin is set by the lender at the time of loan inception and remains constant for the life of the loan. The margin is considered to be the lender's cost of doing business plus profit.

maximum entitlement The maximum amount of VA guaranty available to a veteran.

mortgage insurance premium (MIP) The mortgage insurance required on FHA loans for the life of said loans; MIP can either be paid in cash at closing or financed in its entirety in the loan. The premium varies depending on the method of payment.

negative amortization An interest payment shortfall which is added back *onto* the principal balance.

nonsupervised lender An FHA lender that operates outside of strict governmental control (such as mortgage companies), and is able to be an automatic approval lender upon application to the FHA regional office.

note rate The rate of interest shown on the face of the promissory note, or in the contract of sale language; the rate of interest charged on an obligation.

notice of separation The VA form received when the veteran is discharged from the service.

novation From the root word *nova,* meaning new. A novation is a total release of liability to the first borrower under a loan, and the substitution of a subsequent borrower; usually not automatic, requiring a lender's approval (see *assignment, assumption* and *subject-to*).

on-the-job benefits Noncash compensation to an employee, such as car or day care provided or extra guaranteed per diem. Lenders may consider this for loan qualification if a trackable history can be shown.

owner occupancy Occupied by the buyer of the property; a requirement in VA loans; many times a requirement in conventional and FHA programs as well.

package mortgage A mortgage loan that includes the financing of personal property.

PAM Pledged account mortgage.

payment cap The maximum amount the payment can adjust in any one time frame (e.g., 7.5 percent per period).

payment shock The shock of the payment change affecting the buyer's ability to repay the loan.

PITI Principal, interest, taxes (property) and insurance.

pledged account mortgage (PAM) Instead of using all of the down payment at closing, part of the funds are placed in an interest-bearing account, and drawn from over time to help pay the mortgage payment. These impounded funds are said to be "pledged" to the lender.

PMI Private mortgage insurance.

portfolio lending Instead of selling the mortgage into the secondary market, the lender keeps it "in portfolio" (in his or her in-house file) for the life of the loan.

power of attorney Also termed "attorney in fact." A legal power given to a person to act on behalf of another. This right can either be specific (for special circumstances), or general (in all activities).

prepaids Property expenses that are paid in advance and will usually be prorated at the time of closing (e.g., insurance).

prepayment privilege The right of the borrower to prepay the entire principal sum remaining on the loan without penalty.

private mortgage insurance (PMI) Insurance that indemnifies the lender from the borrower's default, usually on the top 20 percent of the loan. Premiums are paid as an initial fee at time of closing, and as a recurring annual fee based on the principal balance, but paid monthly with the PITI payment. Both the initial and recurring fees are customarily paid by the buyer.

prohibited costs Certain costs that cannot be paid by a particular party to the transaction, as determined by a certain type of loan. (Example: buyers cannot pay discount fees under VA loan guidelines.)

PUD (planned unit development) A type of housing development based on high density (cluster buildings) and maximum use of open space generally resulting in lower-cost housing requiring less maintenance.

The common areas of ground are owned by a nonprofit community association, not by individuals. Developers will often mix residential with light commercial zoning to maximize land use. PUDs can also be used for resort housing and shopping center projects.

qualifying ratio Percentages used by lenders to compare the amount of housing expense and total debt to that of the buyers' gross income or net effective income (depending on the loan program).

RAM Reverse annuity mortgage.

rate cap The maximum amount of interest that can be charged on an ARM loan; expressed as either per period or lifetime, or both.

rate ceiling The maximum to which the rate can go in an ARM loan, specified in an interest amount, e.g., 14 percent.

rate gap The difference between where the rate is now and where it could adjust to on an ARM. Also used to compare the difference between a current conventional rate and that of an ARM.

ratio A percentage; used as a qualifying guideline in mortgage lending.

Regulation Z A federal regulation requiring disclosure of the overall cost of borrowing (truth in lending); states that if you disclose one piece of financial information, you must disclose in its entirety (including the total of all payments and the number of payments). The only exception to this rule is the use of the annual percentage rate. If this is used, no other piece of financial information is necessary.

release clause A clause allowing a portion of the real estate to be released as security from the loan; usually occurs upon a payment of a substantial portion of the principal.

renegotiable rate mortgage (RRM) The forerunner of today's ARM; RRMs got a black eye in the late 1970s in that lenders required the borrower to renegotiate and requalify at specified intervals during the loan.

reservist A person who has served in a reserve branch of the armed forces.

residual income Monthly leftover income after deducting housing costs and fixed obligations from the net effective income in qualifying for a VA loan.

RESPA The Real Estate Settlement Procedures Act is the up-front view of the costs of borrowing in a mortgage loan, including the APR (annual percentage rate), which is the note rate plus the up-front costs of borrowing.

restoration of eligibility/entitlement When a VA loan is paid in full or otherwise satisfied, or when a veteran assumes another veteran's VA loan, reinstating the first veteran's eligibility.

reverse annuity mortgage (RAM) A loan developed for senior citizens to unlock a portion of their equity in their home without selling the property.

RRM Renegotiable rate mortgage.

sales concession A cost paid by the seller or other third party, even though the cost is customarily paid by the buyer. Some loan programs have limits as to the amount of sales concessions that can occur before overage would decrease the amount of loan available.

SAM Shared appreciation mortgage.

secondary market Comprised of FNMA, GNMA and FHLMC, which recycle lent funds from the primary market.

Section 203 FHA programs, divided as follows:

203(b): the standard single-family FHA program

203(h): disaster-victim financing

203(i): loans to outlying areas

203(k): rehabilitation loan program

203(n): co-op financing

203(v): (FHA/VA) for veteran borrowers

220: urban renewal

220(h): urban renewal repair

221: low-cost housing

222: in-service military FHA plan

245: graduated payment mortgage

251: adjustable rate mortgage

security document A legal document that creates a lien against a property as security for repayment of a debt (such as mortgages or deeds of trust).

seller financing The seller allows the borrower to finance the property, using a portion of the seller's equity in the property.

SEM Shared equity mortgage.

shared appreciation mortgage (SAM) A mortgage under which a co-borrower investor gives; facetiously called the "CYD" (call your dad) loan.

shared equity mortgage (SEM) A co-borrower mortgage wherein the equity of the property is shared when the property is sold.

simple assumption A type of loan assumption that is actually a no-qualifying assignment with the lender. The original obligor remains secondarily liable should the assumptor default.

subject-to The transfer of rights to pay an obligation from one party to another, with the first party remaining secondarily liable should the second party default. In addition, the first obligor could be responsible for any deficiency judgment caused by the second borrower. (See *assignment, assumption* and *novation.*)

supervised lender An FHA lender that is generally supervised by a governmental regulating body, such as a commercial bank that is a member of FDIC.

surviving spouse The widow or widower of a deceased veteran.

sweat equity Materials or labor used by a buyer in addition to, or in lieu of, cash.

teaser rate An unusually low introductory rate for an ARM, used to entice borrowers into a loan and allow them to more readily qualify.

transfer charge The cost of transferring or assuming an existing mortgage.

Veterans Affairs, Department of (VA) A branch of the federal government that guarantees lenders against borrowers' default in order to assist veterans in the purchase of single-family dwellings.

WDAGO A veteran's notice of separation.

wraparound An original loan obligation remains stationary, while a new amortizing obligation wraps around the other loan. One payment is made (many times to an escrow holder), out of which the underlying payment is made, with the remainder going to the seller.

yield Return on investment.

zero-net When the seller is receiving little or no net proceeds from selling the property.

INDEX

http://www.inkrest.com